Which? Way to Save and Invest

WHICH? WAY TO
SAVE AND INVEST

**Published by Consumers' Association
and Hodder & Stoughton**

Which? Books are commissioned and researched
by The Association for Consumer Research
and published by Consumers' Association,
2 Marylebone Road, London NW1 4DF
and Hodder & Stoughton, 47 Bedford Square,
London WC1B 3DP

First edition 1982
Second edition 1983
Third edition 1988
Fourth edition August 1989
Fifth edition January 1991
Sixth edition January 1993
Copyright © 1993 Consumers' Association Ltd

British Library Cataloguing in Publication Data:
A catalogue record for this book is available from the
British Library

ISBN 0-340-56654-X

Typographic design by Paul Saunders
Cover photograph by Patrick Doherty/The Image Bank
Cover design by Steve Ridgeway
Typeset by Litho Link Ltd, Welshpool, Powys, Wales
Printed in England by Clays Ltd, St Ives plc

Acknowledgements

Revisions Editor Jane Vass

With thanks to the following for their contributions:
Kathryn Deane, Evelyn Filmer, Joanna Hanks,
Graeme Jacobs, Amanda Jarvis, Joanna Langenhan,
Mark Shanahan, Roger Taylor, Sue Thomas

March 1993 Budget

A Budget update sheet will be prepared immediately after the March 1993 Budget. If you would like to receive a free copy, please write to *Which? Way to Save and Invest*, Publishing Department, Consumers' Association, 2 Marylebone Road, London NW1 4DF, enclosing a large stamped, self-addressed envelope.

CONTENTS

Section III   Other ways of investing

INTRODUCTION

Whether you're a newcomer to the investment world or a seasoned investor, whether you have a large lump sum to invest or a small amount you want to set aside from your regular salary or income, you will find out what options are available from *Which? Way to Save and Invest*, which draws on *Which?* magazine's many years of experience in this area.

Some things change . . .
Even if you don't have new money to invest, it makes sense to review your investments from time to time in the light of both your own changing circumstances and those of the world at large.

Over time some sorts of investment have their tax advantages removed or gradually whittled away – such as investing in housing using a mortgage. Others become more favourable for certain groups of people: an example is bank and building society accounts, which have become worth considering for non-taxpayers as well as taxpayers now that they pay interest before tax.

New types of investment have been introduced. We tell you about building society Permanent Interest-Bearing Shares on p. 165, and on pp. 184 and 185 we explain a new type of National Savings scheme.

Just before we went to press, in an unprecedented day of chaos on the foreign exchange markets, interest rates were raised five percentage points in one day as the Government struggled to keep the £ within the exchange rate limits of the European Exchange Rate Mechanism (ERM). The attempt failed: the Government withdrew the £ from the ERM, allowing its effective devaluation, and interest rates fell again by six percentage points. So if any of your money is invested abroad, you should be prepared for extra fluctuations in its value. The Government reaffirmed its commitment to keeping inflation low, but if you're pessimistic about the chances of their doing so you might want to consider investments which protect your money against rising prices.

... and some things stay the same

Whatever is happening in your life or in the wider world, the underlying principles of sensible investment don't change. The first section of this book, *Choosing a home for your money*, explains how to work out an investment strategy, the investment choices open to you, how tax can affect those choices, and what protection you have if things go wrong.

Getting the basics sorted out

Before embarking on riskier investments, you'll need to think about your home and your pension arrangements. The second section of the book, *Where to put your money first*, looks at these first ports of call for your money. It also looks at low-risk deposit accounts available from banks, building societies and National Savings. These provide a secure home for some of your money, and allow you easy access to it, should you need it in a hurry.

Going for more risk and more reward

Once you've worked out your own investment strategy and sorted out the basics, you may feel prepared to take a greater risk with your money in the hope of a better return. The third section of the book, *Other ways of investing*, looks at individual types of investment – including shares, unit trusts, British Government stocks, life insurance and annuities.

It also takes a look at the pros and cons of investments you may not have considered – investments abroad, commodities or 'alternative' investments like diamonds and vintage wine.

Making the right choices

No one investment can be all things to all people. Where you choose to put your money will depend on your personal circumstances and investment aims. Our aim in this book is to guide you through the complexities of the savings and investment world so that you can make the decisions which are right for *you*.

Choosing a Home for Your Money

1

INVESTMENT STRATEGY

Whether you're a small-scale investor, or looking for a home for many thousands of £££, your problem will not be lack of choice. The difficulty arises in making sensible choices from all the investments available, and, in some cases, finding out all the details needed to come to these decisions. Your aim should be to end up with a number of different investments, covering your differing needs. So before getting down to the nitty gritty of the various investments, we've set out a plan for working out your overall investment strategy.

In the next chapter we give examples of different people putting their individual strategies into effect. The two chapters after that look in detail at the particular questions to be answered when investing for retirement and for children. We then look at where to go for advice and what to do if things go wrong. Chapter 7 explains how tax affects your investments. And in Chapter 8 we give a bird's-eye view of the different investments open to you – you'll find more details on each in the rest of the book.

Of course, deciding now on a particular set of investments isn't the end of the story. It's important to keep a close eye on your investments and to review them periodically – see p. 26 for things to bear in mind.

Investment priorities checklist

Your personal circumstances are bound to affect your choice of investments. But no matter what your situation is, some things are worth considering *before* you start thinking about investments in detail.

Are your dependants protected?
What would happen if you died tomorrow? Would your mortgage be paid off? Would your wife have to go back to

work earlier than planned? Would your husband have a big enough income to pay someone to look after the children?

For most people, the solution to this protection problem is life insurance, not saving and investing. A cheap type of life insurance is *term insurance* – see p. 313.

Have you put some money aside for emergencies?

Could you cope with an unexpected disaster (major car repairs or damage to your home, say)? If not, concentrate on building up an emergency fund in some place from where you'll be able to withdraw it at short notice (within a week, say). See p. 19 and Chapter 2 for investments to consider.

Are you buying your own home?

Although buying a home has proved a good long-term investment in the past, the current slump in the housing market and the gradual reduction in tax relief on mortgage interest in recent years mean that housing as an investment faces an uncertain future. Even so, before you go for any long-term investment, think about your home and mortgage – and read Chapter 9. If you've got money to invest, you might be better off using it to repay part of your mortgage, depending on how big your mortgage is, how interest rates on borrowing and investing compare, and how much access you might need to a loan in future.

Are you planning for your retirement?

Don't assume that the state pension on its own will safeguard your standard of living. In Chapter 12, we give details of pension schemes, both from the state and from employers. Try to work how how well off the state pension together with any employer's pension and income from your savings will leave you – see Chapter 3. If you're self-employed, or not in an employer's pension scheme, consider taking out a personal pension plan – see Chapter 13 for details.

Investment strategy checklist

Once you have covered the priorities set out above, your next step is to choose the investments which are best for you, taking your own personal circumstances and aims into account.

Some investments make sense only for people of a certain age (annuities for the over-70s, say); others (e.g. school fees policies) are obviously only suited to those with children to educate. These are extreme cases of the ways in which your personal circumstances can shape your investment strategy, but there may also be less dramatic repercussions. Most people will be saving and investing for a number of purposes. Are you saving for something in particular – a trip to the Bahamas, for example – or just to accumulate cash?

Different investments may be suitable for each purpose, so most people ought to end up putting their money into a variety of investments. It's worth thinking about the points below, and reading the sections on keeping up with inflation (see p. 17) and on risk (see p. 18), before you decide on a particular investment. And when comparing interest rates on different investments, see p. 27.

Your age
If you are 50, for example, you are more likely to be concerned with saving up for retirement and thinking about how to invest any lump sum you get, than with building up a deposit for your first home. Your children are likely to be off your hands too, and you have more spare cash to save than you had in your 30s.

Your health
If you have a weak heart, for example, you may find it difficult (or expensive) to get the right kind or amount of life insurance. You may want to supplement your life cover with additional savings. Investing through a life insurance policy is likely to be less worthwhile for you than for someone in good health.

Your family
You may want to save up (or invest a lump sum) for your children's education. And you need to think about how your assets will be passed on when you die. You may want to build up a capital sum for your heirs to inherit.

Your expectations
If you expect your income to drop at some point (when you start a family, perhaps, or when you retire), you may want to build up savings to draw on when you're hard up. On the other hand, if you expect a big rise in salary (when you get an additional qualification, say, or finish training) you may feel you can run down your savings a bit since you expect to be better off later. Or you may be coming into a large inheritance and need to find a suitable home for it.

Your tax position
Some investments are particularly suitable for non-taxpayers, while others may be particularly good for higher-rate taxpayers. We cover tax in Chapter 7. People aged over 64 should look out for the effect of losing age-related allowances – see p. 52.

What you want from your investments
If you want to build up a fund for next year's holiday, you probably need to consider a different range of investments from those of someone saving up for retirement or to pass on a capital sum to his or her heirs. Similarly, if you are looking for a fixed income from your investments, the investments you select will differ from those chosen by someone prepared to accept an income that varies with general interest rates. For more details, see Chapter 2.

How much you can invest
How much money can you afford to invest? Some investments are open to you only if you have a sufficiently large lump sum. And other investments are open only to those who can save a regular sum each month. Others are more flexible and can take your savings as and when they arise.

How long you can invest for
Think carefully before you commit yourself to saving a definite amount each month for a long time (25 years, say), or locking up a lump sum for a lengthy period. All sorts of changes could happen over the period of the investment that might make it hard to continue, and most long-term savings plans penalise you if you cash in early.

The range of investments you're prepared to consider
When you save or invest your money, it will be put to work – for example, a unit trust company may well use your money to buy shares in a company which the unit trust managers think will provide them with a good return. You may want to restrict the uses to which your money might be put, if you don't want it to be invested in companies making weapons, say. Or you might want to see your money going to help causes you support. These days, there is a range of *ethical investments* designed to make this easier – see p. 25.

Keeping up with inflation

With some investments the value of the capital you invest stays the same; but, of course, this doesn't allow for the effects of inflation. If you invest £1,000 now, spend the income from the investment and get your £1,000 back in five years' time, it will be worth only £784 or so in terms of today's buying power if inflation averages five per cent a year. And (with the same rate of inflation) if you got your money back in 20 years' time, it would be worth only £377 in terms of today's buying power.

Looked at another way, an inflation rate of five per cent means that you have to see the value of your investments (after allowing for tax) rise by at least five per cent a year on average just for them to be worth the same to you in the future as they are now. That's before you draw an income from your investment.

The diagram below shows the devastating effect of inflation, even at the current low levels. Bear this in mind when considering how much your investments (or the income from them) will be worth in the future.

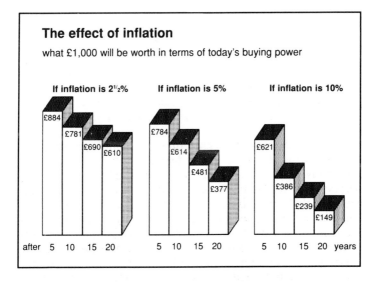

The effect of inflation

what £1,000 will be worth in terms of today's buying power

One strategy you could consider for long-term investing is to go for index-linked investments which guarantee to keep pace with inflation (and perhaps give a little extra interest too). Alternatively, you could go for riskier investments like unit trusts, shares or alternative investments which might do a lot better than keep up with inflation (but could do a lot worse, or even end up worth less than at the start).

In the diagram on pp. 20 to 21, we compare the rates of return you might have got over different periods of time for various lump sum investments. You can see that over the longer period some of the riskier investments such as shares and antique furniture have made a better job of keeping up with inflation than safer ones such as building societies. On the other hand, looking at the shorter period, the gap in performance between shares and some of the most conservative homes for your money, such as building society ordinary shares, has been much narrower. (Note that over different periods the results could have been very different, so don't use this diagram to draw conclusions about where to invest your money.)

Of course, you may be prepared to put up with a drop in purchasing power because, for example, you're looking for a particularly 'safe' investment, or you want to be able to withdraw your money at short notice (e.g. for your emergency fund).

Risk

One of the major risks you face is seeing the purchasing power of your investments drop over time as a result of inflation. This applies to practically any investment or savings scheme. But there are two additional risks you face:

■ **risk to capital** – the value of what you've invested in shares, unit trusts, property and so on is likely to fluctuate. You may find that when you need to cash in your investment, the value of, say, your shares or unit trusts is particularly low. Alternative investments (e.g. antiques, jewellery, Persian carpets) are at risk in this way too – when you want to sell, you may not be able to find a buyer at a price which gives you a reasonable return. Also, a dealer's mark-up may be particularly high.

■ **risk to income** – the size of the interest (or dividend) you get may vary considerably, depending on the performance of the company, fund, investment or whatever. At worst, you might get no income from the investments at all.

To minimise the impact of these risks on your investments, the golden rule is to spread your money around.

Decide first what proportion of your capital (if any) you are prepared to put into risky investments, and what proportion you want in safe ones. Accepting a degree of risk is, in the main, a price you may have to pay to stand at least some chance of increasing the buying power of your investments.

Aim to spread your money among different types of investments, e.g. a pension, unit trusts, building societies. With riskier investments in particular, try to put your money with a number of different companies issuing each type of investment. Also, try to stagger investing over a long period (at least a year, preferably longer). By spreading your investments in these ways you'll reduce the risk of doing very badly. Bear in mind though that you'll also reduce your chances of doing extraordinarily well.

If you decide to go for a relatively high-risk investment (like shares or alternative investments), don't be tempted to withdraw your emergency fund from its safe home and invest it in the same way. This should cut down the risk of having to sell your investments (to pay for a new roof, say) when prices are low. And steer clear of direct investment in shares unless you've got a substantial amount to invest – see p. 244.

If you know you'll need your money on a particular future date, be prepared to cash in investments beforehand (a few years in advance, if need be) ideally at a time when their value is high. If you wait until you need the money, you may find you have to cash your investments when prices are low.

Investing your emergency fund

When deciding on a home for this part of your capital, you want to look for three things:
■ safety – no risk that when you cash in you'll get fewer £££ back than you put in
■ instant accessibility – you don't usually get even two weeks' notice of an emergency, so you want to be able to get the money back on the spot, or in a couple of days at most
■ highest possible return – but you'll have to be prepared to take less than you'd get for an investment that ties your money up for longer.

See the route maps on pp. 34 to 37 for some suggestions. Remember to update regularly the amount of money you keep in reserve for emergencies. Inflation will erode its buying power.

Investments compared: What you'd get back in the first quarter of 1992 on £1,000 invested 5, 10, 15 and 20 years before in various investments

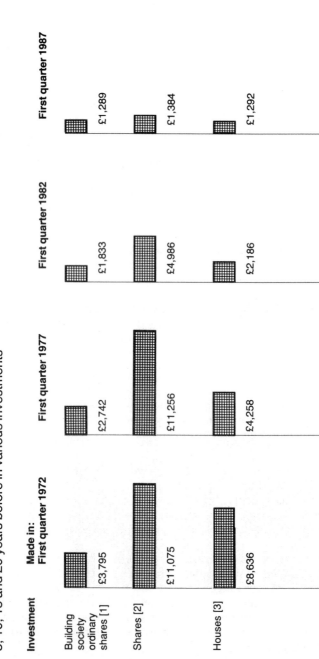

Investment	Made in: First quarter 1972	First quarter 1977	First quarter 1982	First quarter 1987
Building society ordinary shares [1]	£3,795	£2,742	£1,833	£1,289
Shares [2]	£11,075	£11,256	£4,986	£1,384
Houses [3]	£8,636	£4,258	£2,186	£1,292

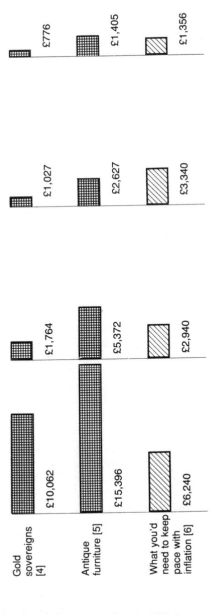

Gold sovereigns [4]
£10,062
£1,764
£1,027
£776

Antique furniture [5]
£15,396
£5,372
£2,627
£1,405

What you'd need to keep pace with inflation [6]
£6,240
£2,940
£3,340
£1,356

[1] Figures supplied by Nationwide Building Society. Assumes income reinvested
[2] Based on the FT Actuaries All-Share Index, assuming income reinvested on an offer to bid basis (but no allowance for Capital Gains Tax); source Micropal
[3] Based on Nationwide Index of Average House Prices
[4] Source: Mocatta & Goldsmid with allowances for VAT and differences between buying and selling price
[5] Based on Antique Collectors' Club Antique Furniture Price Index, with allowances for costs of buying and selling at auction
[6] Based on Retail Prices Index

Your aims in investing

Many people want their investments to produce an income now. Others will invest for capital growth, either to provide an income later (on retirement, say) or to pass on to their heirs, or to build up a fund to buy something (a house or car, for example). Below, we outline some factors to consider in each of these cases.

You might in fact want a combination of income and growth, although, to some extent, the line between income and capital growth is an artificial one. You can always cash in some investments from time to time to give you income. And if you reinvest income from your investments, the value of your capital should go up over time. There are tax considerations, though (see the box on p. 24).

Investing for income now

You need to consider how long you're likely to go on needing the income for your investments. If it's for more than a couple of years, you can't afford to ignore the effect of inflation on the purchasing power of any income your investments produce. You'll need a rising income. To achieve this, you are likely to have to put some of your capital at risk, or buy an index-linked investment. It may be sensible to invest some of your money for capital growth, with a view to cashing part of it in on a regular basis to provide income.

You have to make your own choice about how much of your capital to risk. Put the remainder in a place where the income from it will be safe – see the route maps on pp. 34 to 37 for suggestions.

If you don't anticipate having to rely on your extra investment income for longer than a year or two, you may well decide there is no point taking risks to get an income that will keep up with inflation.

If you don't pay tax, some investments may be particularly attractive if the interest is paid without deduction of tax. These investments are marked with ● in the route maps on pp. 34 to 37. On the other hand, some investments, where the return is tax-free, look more attractive the higher your rate of tax. These investments are marked with ★ in the route maps. Check in the route maps (and with current rates of return) that your investments are giving you as good a return as possible.

Investing to provide income later

If you're going to need your capital to give you an income later, you can't afford to risk all of it. But you do need to try to make up for the effects of inflation on its buying-power over the years between now and the time you plan to draw the income.

You could consider investing part of your money in Index-Linked National Savings Certificates. With this investment, the value of what you've invested is adjusted each month in line with inflation (provided you've held the certificate for at least a year). You can invest up to £5,000 per person, or jointly as a married couple (from November 1992). You could also consider index-linked British Government stocks – see Chapter 17.

If you have capital left over, it makes sense to put some of your money into investments which may give a return high enough to make up for inflation. To minimise the chances of all your risky investments doing a nose-dive at once, follow the advice on p. 18.

Investing to pass on more for your heirs

You may feel you can take risks with more of your capital for longer if the main aim is to pass money on to your heirs.

What you need to be particularly aware of is the impact of inheritance tax on what your heirs will get when you die, though it won't strike unless what you leave (together with taxable gifts made in the seven years before your death) tops £150,000 (in the 1992–3 tax year). To minimise the effect of inheritance tax, consider:
- giving away each year as much as is allowed without incurring any liability to inheritance tax
- taking out life insurance with the proceeds going straight to your children
- leaving your possessions directly to the youngest generation (your grandchildren rather than your children) if you want the possessions to go to them eventually.

For more details on inheritance tax, see p. 116.

Investing to build up a fund to buy something

If you are investing in order to buy something in the future, bear in mind that the value of some investments (e.g. shares, property or alternative investments) tends to fluctuate, so you may find that when you want to cash in your investments the return is not very good. It makes sense to steer clear of these investments if the time when you are going to want to use the money is very close at hand.

If, on the other hand, you'll need the money in, say 10 years' time, you could still go for investments which fluctuate in value, but be prepared to cash the investments *before* you need the money (preferably when they're doing well). Don't be forced into cashing your investment when its value is depressed – by a slump in the share or property markets, for example.

And before you decide to take extra risks with your capital in the hope of getting a greater gain, consider borrowing money to buy now rather than waiting until you have built a larger fund.

Cashing in investments to give income

With certain lump sum investments (e.g. single-premium bonds), it's possible to cash in part of the investment each year to give yourself an income. But note that with, for example, single-premium bonds or unit trusts which run a withdrawal scheme, because the value of your investment fluctuates, you may have to cash in a higher proportion of your investment frm time to time, or else face a drop in income. And if you cash in more than the growth of your bond, you'll be eating into your capital.

With other investments (e.g. shares, alternative investments and so on) there are no special schemes. And you may get a poor price at the time you want to cash part of the investment to provide income.

Building capital by reinvesting income

As the tax system stands, if you invest for income with a view to reinvesting it to build up capital, you may pay more tax than if you had got an equivalent rise in value through a straight capital gain. Investment income is taxed at either 20 per cent, 25 per cent or 40 per cent for the 1992–3 tax year, depending on your taxable income. Capital gains are taxed at the same rate, but the first £5,800 of capital gains you make by disposing of assets in the 1992–3 tax year is tax-free. If you haven't used up all of this tax-free allowance it may be sensible to invest for capital gains rather than income.

Ethical investment

The investment policies of institutions such as banks may be shrouded in secrecy for legitimate commercial reasons. So finding out how the money in your savings account is being used is difficult. And it can be equally difficult to be sure that the company you're investing in is using your money in a way you would approve of. But there are positive steps you can take to screen for companies you would be happy to invest in or save your money with. And for several years there have been companies offering off-the-peg ethical investments.

Ethical investment means that money is invested either by you or on your behalf so that certain areas are either avoided or promoted: for example, you might want to avoid investing in companies involved with tobacco, or promote environmental causes by helping companies developing alternative sources of energy. There are now ethical unit trusts, investment trusts, life insurance funds, personal pension plans and even a building society – the Ecology Building Society – while the Co-operative Bank has publicly stated what sort of businesses it will and won't do business with and also offers an Ethical Savings Account.

Most ethical investment goes on through unit trusts. With these, your money goes into a pool or fund that is invested in a range of investments, mainly company shares. The fund is managed on a day to day basis by a fund manager but the assets are held by trustees (usually a bank). It is the trustees who have to authorise the issuing and reclaiming of units and make sure that the management of the fund is in accordance with the trust deed. In the case of ethical unit trusts there may also be a research committee and/or a vetting committee involved in the decisions over which shares to buy and sell.

However, it's difficult to be entirely sure that your money is being used as you would wish. There is no agreed definition of what constitutes an ethical investment and this is reflected in the diveristy of areas that different funds seek to avoid. Some keep it very simple, such as one scheme which only avoids companies materially involved in the tobacco industry. Others have policies on everything from advertising complaints to repressive regimes. The ethical criteria used may be inexact and open to interpretation: advisory boards might be presented with too little information to make a proper judgement; you can't assume that the fund managers have the same perception of a company as you do. Investors should look out for the following:

- whether there is an advisory committee and who it is made up of
- the way in which any advisory committee is consulted – either before or after shares are purchased and whether they are given sufficient information in sufficient time to make informed decisions
- how investors are involved – whether they are invited to regular unitholder meetings
- whether investors are kept in touch with how the fund is managed beyond the six-monthly reports required by regulation.

If the off-the-peg options of ethical investment are not to your taste, it's possible to have a portfolio tailored to your own individual requirements. But there are possible problems:

- you need a lot of money – to get the same spread of risk that a unit trust provides you need to invest in a wide range of shares
- you need access to information – what may be an ethical investment one day might not be the next, and vice versa.

A natural starting place when looking for a home for your money is company reports and accounts. Keeping an eye on the financial press will also be useful. If you want research done on your behalf, the *Ethical Investment Research Service (EIRIS)* will screen shares according to your own ethical concerns and also produces a quarterly newsletter. EIRIS is at 504 Bondway Business Centre, 71 Bondway, London SW8 1SQ (tel: 071-735 1351).

Finally, remember that it may prove impossible to meet all of your aims in investment. You may have to compromise if, for example, the sort of investment which would really suit your financial needs doesn't tie in with your ethical aims.

Review your investments regularly

You can't assume that the best investments for you today will still be the best in a few months' time. For example, the rates of return offered by different investments will change. New types of investment may come on the market. Tax laws may change too. Inflation will mean that your investments need topping up. And changes in your circumstances, not to mention the effect of external factors (like political pressures throughout the world), could make a nonsense of your original choice. So it's vital to keep an eye on what's happening and alter your investments when necessary.

Keep an eye on interest rates

One difficulty in comparing the return you can get with different types of investment is that the rates of interest quoted with some investments aren't strictly comparable. This is because they don't make any allowance for how frequently interest is paid out. To make comparison easier, banks, building societies and finance companies should follow a Code of Practice which lays down rules about how rates of interest should be advertised. The only problem with this is that the Code allows them to quote *several* different rates in an advertisement, and sorting out which rate to use for comparison can be a bit difficult. See the box on p. 29.

Interest rates aren't always what they seem

When interest is paid out to you, you can spend it or reinvest it: if you reinvest it, you earn interest on the interest. The more frequently interest is paid to you, the sooner you can reinvest it and the higher will be the overall return.

Suppose, for example, that you invest £1,000 for a year at 10 per cent interest a year. If the interest is paid out just once a year, £100 is all you can get. But if the interest is paid out at six-monthly intervals and you reinvest it, you will end up with more. This is because after six months, £50 (5 per cent of £1,000) will be added to the £1,000, giving £1,050; in the second six months, another 5 per cent interest will be earned on this £1,050, i.e. £52.50. The £50 plus £52.50 gives interest of £102.50 for the year – the same as you'd get if you put your money in an investment paying 10.25 per cent just once a year.

If the interest is paid quarterly, the return is even higher at £1,103.81. Monthly interest would bring the return up to £1,104.67. And these differences would build up over the years, as Table 1 below shows. So the true rate of return depends not just on the amount of interest paid out, but also the frequency with which it is paid out.

Table 1   How £1,000 grows if interest at 10% is added

	yearly	half-yearly	quarterly	monthly
after 1 year	£1,100	£1,103	£1,104	£1,105
after 2 years	£1,210	£1,216	£1,218	£1,220
after 5 years	£1,611	£1,629	£1,639	£1,645
after 10 years	£2,594	£2,653	£2,685	£2,707
true return	10%	10.25%	10.38%	10.47%

Find the true rate of return

The rates quoted on investments where interest is added once a year are true rates of return – this applies to the National Savings Investment account, for example. The returns quoted on National Savings Certificates and the redemption yields on British Government stocks are also true returns which can be directly compared one with another.

But many other investments add interest more often than once a year: with most building society accounts (other than regular savings accounts), bank deposit and savings accounts and finance company deposits, interest is added twice a year (sometimes quarterly). National Savings Income Bonds pay out income monthly, and you can ask for monthly interest with some other savings accounts. In all these cases, you need to know the true rate of return to compare them with investments paying out interest less frequently.

Table 2, opposite, sets out the true rates of return for a variety of quoted rates, when the interest is paid out half-yearly, quarterly or monthly. Banks, building societies and finance companies should quote true rates in their advertising – they call them the *compounded annual rates*, or CAR.

Note that with the National Savings Ordinary account, interest is paid once a year, but only for complete calendar months. So if you pay in or withdraw money during a month, the true return may be *lower* than the quoted rate.

Table 2 True rates of return

quoted rate	true rate if interest is paid out or added		
	half-yearly	quarterly	monthly
5%	5.06%	5.10%	5.12%
6%	6.09%	6.14%	6.17%
7%	7.12%	7.19%	7.23%
8%	8.16%	8.24%	8.30%
9%	9.20%	9.31%	9.38%
10%	10.25%	10.38%	10.47%
11%	11.30%	11.46%	11.57%
12%	12.36%	12.55%	12.68%

Gross rates of return

Interest on most types of savings account is now usually paid after deduction of tax at the *basic rate*. There is no more basic-rate tax to be paid on the interest. If you expect to be a non-taxpayer, even after taking into account

---

The different rates – what they mean

Various different rates of return may be quoted in savings advertisements by banks, building societies and finance companies which follow the voluntary Code of Practice:

■ **tax-free** – if interest from the account is not liable to income tax

■ **net** – if you draw out the income and don't reinvest it, the rate you'll get with no more basic-rate tax to pay

■ **gross** – the rate you'd have to get before deduction of tax to end up with the net rate afer basic-rate tax had been deducted

■ **net compounded annual rate (CAR)** – if you reinvest the income, the rate you'll get with no more basic-rate tax to pay

■ **gross compounded annual rate (CAR)** – the rate you'd have to get before deduction of tax to end up with the net compounded annual rate after tax had been deducted at the basic rate.

If you're choosing between different investments, some paying interest after deduction of tax and some before tax, make sure you compare like with like to see which gives the better return. Suppose, for example, you want to compare the National Savings Investment account (interest paid before tax) with a building society account (interest paid after tax). The National Savings Investment account pays out interest once a year, so the quoted interest rate is the true rate of return. Compare this with the gross CAR for the building society.

interest from your savings, you may be able to have the interest paid out before tax by filling in form R85 (from your bank or building society).

Advertisements for such investments often quote a *gross* rate of return to compare with the return from investments which pay interest tax-free or without deduction of tax (mainly National Savings schemes). The gross interest rate is the rate which a basic-rate taxpayer would have to earn from an investment which pays interest before tax is deducted, to give the same after-tax return as from a bank or building society (for how to work out the gross rate from the after-tax rate, see p. 102).

Suppose, for example, that you get 9 per cent net interest from a building society account. With a basic rate of tax of 25 per cent, you'd have to earn a before-tax rate of interest of 12 per cent to have 9 per cent left after tax (12% less 25% of 12% = 12% less 3% = 9%). So the gross rate would be 12 per cent.

2

INVESTMENT CHOICES

Once you've worked out your investment strategy, you can start to think about the investments themselves. To help narrow down the choice of investments to those which would be most suitable for you, use the route maps on pp. 34 to 37. One is for lump sums, the other for savings (either on a regular basis or piecemeal).

Follow the route maps for each sum of money you want to invest, e.g. your emergency fund, money you're willing to see fluctuate in value and money you can invest for 10 years. You'll end up with a different shortlist for each sum.

For any investments you think might suit you, read the relevant chapter in the book. Then find out what is happening to that investment at the moment. In each chapter, we tell you where to get more information. Also, check in the newspapers for the up-to-date rates of return being offered by the investments you have in mind. There's a bird's-eye view of different types of investment in Chapter 8.

Armed with these facts, narrow down the investments on your shortlists to those which suit you best. Don't forget that work on your investments doesn't end there – you'll need to keep them under review to make sure that they continue to suit you.

To show you how this can be done, we look at the choices facing a number of investors. For example, Roger and Rose Steele want to find homes for both a lump sum and for their savings. Their strategy and decisions are followed through from start to finish. The other six examples look at only one of the problems each investor faces. Three investors have lump sums of varying sizes to invest; with the other three investors, it's savings of various amounts which are presenting difficulties.

Of course, your own final choice out of the shortlist each investor ends up with might – because of your particular preferences – be different from that in our examples.

Planning your investments

Roger and Rose Steele have one child, Alex. Roger earns around £18,000 a year as a teacher; Rose doesn't go out to work. They want to save for quite a few things: a holiday next year, and then a new car, furniture and so on. They don't want to lock their money away for too long. They've already got some money saved up in a building society instant access account and wonder whether that's the best place for it.

How Roger and Rose decide what to do with their money

First of all, they look at the investment priorities checklist on p. 13.

Both Roger and Rose have life insurance cover. They have policies which will pay out lump sums and a regular income if either partner dies. At present they have £3,000 put aside in a building society instant access account. But they feel that £1,000 is as much as they need in an emergency fund.

Roger and Rose are buying their own home and don't intend to move in the next few years; their £40,000 mortgage is quite low compared to the value of their house. Roger is in the teachers' pension scheme, which offers good benefits.

Roger and Rose would like to save something each month. So they've got to decide how to invest:
- their £1,000 emergency fund
- the additional £2,000 lump sum
- the money they manage to save in future.

They use the investment strategy checklist (see p. 14) to help sort out their investment plan:
- age – Roger is 34 and Rose 28. Rose is hoping to go back to work when Alex, their three-year-old, goes to school, but they're not going to rely on this
- health – both are in good health
- family – apart from Alex, there are no immediate dependants. But they feel that if any of their parents were widowed or became ill, they'd like to help out. At the moment, this prospect seems unlikely, but it means they don't feel like committing themselves to very long-term savings, which they might not be able to keep up if they do have to help out. They don't intend giving Alex a private

education. If they did, they would consider saving in a school-fees scheme

■ expectations – if Rose can't go back to her old job, she might need some sort of retraining. This could involve some expense – they don't really know. There are no large inheritances coming their way, though eventually they will share in the proceeds from the sale of their parents' houses

■ tax – Roger is a basic-rate taxpayer, and any investment income won't put him into the higher-rate tax bracket. However, Rose doesn't pay tax, and any investment income is unlikely to put her into the basic-rate bracket. It would make sense to put all their investments in her name only, so that she can make use of her personal allowance

■ what they want from their investments – their main aims are: to pay for a holiday next year and later for a new car; to pay for any retraining that Rose may need in a couple of years or so; and to be able to help out their parents, if necessary. They aren't looking for income from their investments

■ how much they can invest – apart from the £3,000 in the building society, they can save about £50 a month, but most of this is earmarked for their holiday next year

■ how long they can invest for – the Steeles have decided to keep £1,000 as an emergency fund. And they need £40 a month of their regular savings available for their planned holiday. The other lump sum of £2,000 and £10-a-month regular savings can be invested for somewhat longer. But long-term investment clearly doesn't suit their needs

■ the range of investment they're prepared to consider – although their main aim is to find a suitable type of investment, they're interested in ethical investments, particularly those which might benefit the environment.

Once Roger and Rose have chosen their investments they'll keep an eye on what's happening and may move their money around from time to time. But first they follow the route maps on pp. 34 to 37 to see what choices they have.

How Roger and Rose choose their investments

Lump sum

First of all they try to sort out what to do with the £3,000 they have. They intend keeping £1,000 of this as an emergency fund, and following the route map find three types of investment where they can put this money and get it out at short notice: a bank or finance company deposit

Route map for lump sums

Start here for each chunk
of your money

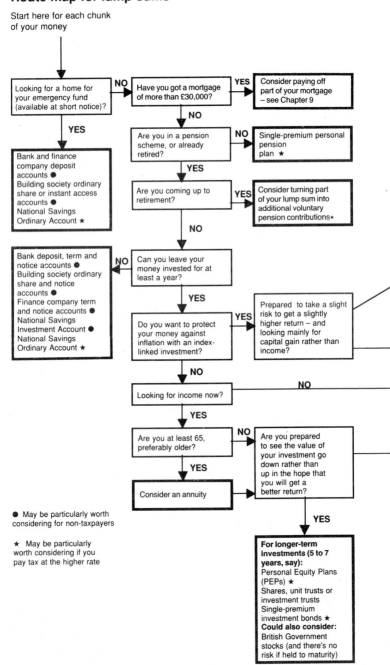

Looking for a home for your emergency fund (available at short notice)? **NO** → Have you got a mortgage of more than £30,000? **YES** → Consider paying off part of your mortgage – see Chapter 9

YES ↓

Bank and finance company deposit accounts ● Building society ordinary share or instant access accounts ● National Savings Ordinary Account ★

Have you got a mortgage of more than £30,000? **NO** ↓

Are you in a pension scheme, or already retired? **NO** → Single-premium personal pension plan ★

YES ↓

Are you coming up to retirement? **YES** → Consider turning part of your lump sum into additional voluntary pension contributions★

NO ↓

Bank deposit, term and notice accounts ● Building society ordinary share and notice accounts ● Finance company term and notice accounts ● National Savings Investment Account ● National Savings Ordinary Account ★ ← **NO** Can you leave your money invested for at least a year?

YES ↓

Do you want to protect your money against inflation with an index-linked investment? **YES** → Prepared to take a slight risk to get a slightly higher return – and looking mainly for capital gain rather than income?

NO ↓

Looking for income now?   **NO**

YES ↓

Are you at least 65, preferably older? **NO** → Are you prepared to see the value of your investment go down rather than up in the hope that you will get a better return?

YES ↓

Consider an annuity

YES ↓

For longer-term investments (5 to 7 years, say):
Personal Equity Plans (PEPs) ★
Shares, unit trusts or investment trusts
Single-premium investment bonds ★
Could also consider:
British Government stocks (and there's no risk if held to maturity)

● May be particularly worth considering for non-taxpayers

★ May be particularly worth considering if you pay tax at the higher rate

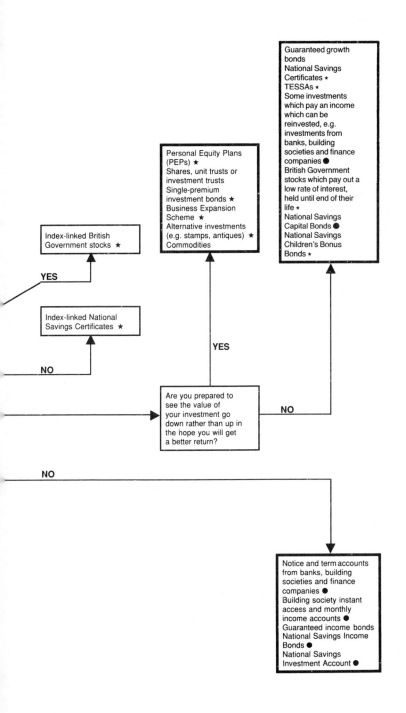

Route map for savings

Start here for each chunk
of your money

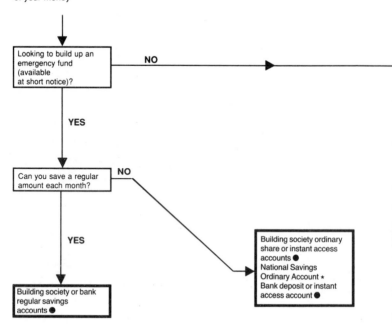

Looking to build up an emergency fund (available at short notice)?

NO →

YES ↓

Can you save a regular amount each month?

NO

YES ↓

Building society or bank regular savings accounts ●

Building society ordinary share or instant access accounts ●
National Savings Ordinary Account ★
Bank deposit or instant access account ●

● May be particularly worth
considering for
non-taxpayers

★ May be particularly worth
considering if
you pay tax at the
higher rate

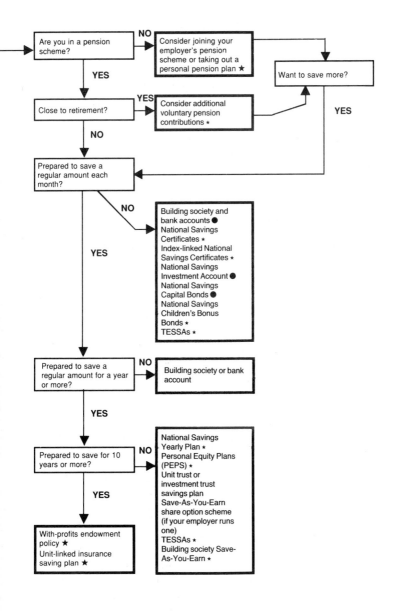

Are you in a pension scheme?

NO → Consider joining your employer's pension scheme or taking out a personal pension plan ★

YES ↓

Want to save more?

Close to retirement?

YES → Consider additional voluntary pension contributions ★

NO ↓

YES

Prepared to save a regular amount each month?

NO → Building society and bank accounts ●
National Savings Certificates ★
Index-linked National Savings Certificates ★
National Savings Investment Account ●
National Savings Capital Bonds ●
National Savings Children's Bonus Bonds ★
TESSAs ★

YES ↓

Prepared to save a regular amount for a year or more?

NO → Building society or bank account

YES ↓

Prepared to save for 10 years or more?

NO → National Savings Yearly Plan ★
Personal Equity Plans (PEPS) ★
Unit trust or investment trust savings plan
Save-As-You-Earn share option scheme (if your employer runs one)
TESSAs ★
Building society Save-As-You-Earn ★

YES ↓

With-profits endowment policy ★
Unit-linked insurance saving plan ★

account, building society instant access account or National Savings Ordinary account. They read about these and check on the rates of return currently offered. They choose a building society tiered interest account which pays a higher than normal rate of interest on £1,000 or more. They'll keep a close watch on rates of return in the future in case other investments offer a better return.

Now they follow the route map again to see what they could do with the £2,000. They skip the next few steps – they have a moderate mortgage compared to the value of their home, are in a pension scheme, not close to retirement and can leave their money invested for at least a year. At the next step they see they should consider an index-linked investment. They'd like to put about half the money somewhere it won't lose its buying power so it can pay for a new car. They plump for Index-linked National Savings Certificates.

They go through the route map again for the last part of their lump sum, which they are prepared to risk in the hope of a windfall. After answering *No* to the question *Looking for income now?* they come to investments they should consider if they're prepared to see the value of their investments go down rather than up in the hope of a better return. They see that these include Personal Equity Plans (PEPs), shares, unit trusts, investment trusts and single-premium investment bonds. Despite the uncertainties of the stock market, they look to the long term and pick a PEP with low charges; £1,000 can go into unit trusts within a PEP to spread the risk (see p. 262). Their PEP manager offers a range of funds, including an ethical fund which they choose.

Regular saving

They follow the route map on the next pages to see what to do with the £50 they reckon they'll be able to save each month. They come to the question *Prepared to save a regular amount for a year or more?* for the £40 a month they're saving for their next year's holiday. As the answer is *No*, they have a choice of building society and bank savings schemes. After checking on current interest rates, they decide that a building society account with a high interest rate will offer them the best overall return and the opportunity to withdraw their money at short notice without being penalised. For the remaining £10 a month they are prepared to consider saving for more than a year, but not as long as 10 years. At £20 a month, the minimum monthly investment for National Savings Yearly Plan is too high. They plump for a building society Tax Exempt Special Savings Account (TESSA).

Summary
They're going to invest £1,000 in a building society account, £1,000 in Index-linked National Savings Certificates and £1,000 in unit trusts through a PEP. They're going to save £40 a month in a building society high-interest account and £10 a month in a TESSA.

Saving for something special

Anne Stevens is a basic-rate taxpayer. She wants to go to Australia to see her daughter and her grandchildren, and needs about £1,000 for the return air fare. She can afford to save around £25 a month, so will need an investment lasting four or five years to save up the fare (which is likely to rise further through inflation).

She follows the route map until she gets to the question, *Prepared to save a regular amount each month?* Answering Yes, she moves on to consider just how long she can commit herself – over one but but not as long as 10 years. That presents various options: share option schemes (not an option for Anne as her employer isn't offering one); unit trust or investment trust savings plans or a PEP, which are a mite too risky for her liking; building society SAYE and National Savings Yearly Plan and TESSA accounts.

Yearly Plan doesn't quite fit her needs: each year's savings have to be left for a further four years to get the maximum rate of return, so her second year's savings wouldn't earn the full rate unless left until year six, the third year's until year seven and so on. She is likely to want all the money back at the end of five years and so would lose out on the full rate of return.

She considers a building society SAYE, which does pay the top rate of return on every £ paid in over five years (and a bonus if the money is left for another two years). Anne could get a slightly higher rate of interest in some types of building society account, but since interest rates look set to fall she decides to plump for the fixed interest offered by SAYE. To help build up the sum for her trip Anne decides that whenever she has spare money she'll try to put it in another building society account – a suitable home for small, irregular sums of money. She also decides to approach her bank manager to see whether, once she's saved for some time, she could get a loan.

Investing with an eye on tax

Paul is in his late-40s, and finds himself with £50,000 from a life insurance pay-out following the death of his wife Sheila. He lives in his own home with a £75,000 repayment mortgage, has an adequate emergency fund, a TESSA account and enough life insurance to take care of his children's needs should he die. Paul belongs to an excellent company pension scheme (though he won't quite qualify for a full pension when he reaches 65 as he only joined the scheme in his 30s).

Despite Paul's high salary, private school fees make a big dent in his income, and will continue to do so for some time. So he'd like to invest about £20,000 of his lump sum to increase his income while these fees continue, but is worried about extra income tax he might have to pay (he pays tax at the higher rate of 40 per cent). He also wants to invest £5,000 with as little risk as possible (he's hoping to buy a boat in five years' time when the children are older).

Following the route map, he sees that it suggests paying off part of the mortgage if it's more than £30,000 (above which you get no tax relief on the mortgage interest). This makes a lot of sense for Paul – his mortgage is his second biggest outgoing after the school fees, and higher rate taxpayers no longer get higher rate tax relief even on interest below the £30,000 limit. Each £10,000 of his mortgage above the £30,000 limit that he repays will save him around £1,000 a year in interest and capital repayments, while if he were to invest the £10,000 instead he'd be lucky to get that much in income from his investment unless he were to choose a risky investment. So he decides to repay £24,000 of his mortgage, which will give his income an immediate boost. He doesn't want to pay off more because having some money in investments he can cash in gives him some flexibility.

He goes on through the route map for the safe investment. He checks investments with a * next to them carefully (these are particularly worth considering if you pay tax at the higher rate). Early on he comes to Index-linked National Savings Certificates which guarantee to maintain the buying power of his money. After a year, he can withdraw some money (tax-free) if he needs it and still get index-linking. He sees he should also consider index-linked British Government stocks if he's prepared to take a slight risk. He checks on the current prices for the stocks and finds that, for his rate of tax, the return should just beat inflation. He decides to put £2,500 into each of these index-linked investments.

Next he follows the route map for his longer-term investment until he comes to the question about whether he is looking for income now. Yes, he is. He passes over the next question about age and is then asked if he is prepared to see the value of his money go down rather than up in the hope of a better return. Once again the answer is *Yes*. He sees he can choose between Personal Equity Plans (PEPs), shares, unit trusts, investment trusts and single-premium investment bonds plus even riskier investments like antiques and commodities. Deciding to give the riskier options a miss he decides to invest the maximum £6,000 in a Personal Equity Plan to benefit from the tax advantages. The remaining £15,000 is invested in unit trusts – ones that aim for capital growth rather than income. He plans to cash in some of his units each year to help with the school fees, but will make sure that he doesn't make net capital gains of more than the £5,800 limit free of capital gains tax. As he approaches retirement and the school fees come to an end, he'll consider making additional voluntary contributions to his pension scheme to make up for the missing years.

Saving for a rainy day

Mike and Sue English are in their late-20s, with one baby and another due soon. Mike pays some tax at the basic rate, Sue pays no tax at all. They've got little cash left over at the end of each month, what with food, rent and so on. They are worried because they have no savings or life insurance.

For people in their position, with dependants, life insurance should come before any attempt to save money. If Mike died, Sue would have to rely on social security to make ends meet. And if Sue were to die, Mike would have a hard time looking after the baby *and* going to work. They realise that investment-type life insurance is not really for them. With this firmly sorted out in their minds, they decide to go to an insurance adviser to arrange protection-type life insurance, to cover them should one or other partner die.

Next they think about their emergency fund, follow the route map on p. 34 and see that they are recommended to consider building society instant access accounts, a bank deposit account or National Savings Ordinary account. They go for a building society instant access account which seems to have the edge over the others. A bonus is that they'll get a cash card giving them access to their money round the clock from the machines outside hundreds of building society branches – useful in a real emergency.

Once they've built up a large enough emergency fund, they'll go through the route map again and look for a somewhat longer-term investment for their additional savings. They will probably transfer money to a savings account which pays a higher rate for higher minimum levels of investment, even if they have to give notice before withdrawing money. This account will be opened in Sue's name only as she doesn't pay tax. (They decide to open the instant access account in joint names so that both can have access to it in an emergency.)

Investing a windfall

Marianne Fortune, 21, has just inherited £6,000 from her grandmother. She's single, lives with her parents, has a large enough emergency fund and is a basic-rate taxpayer. She reckons that some time in the future she'll want to buy a home, and decides to put £5,000 towards this. She decides to try to turn the remaining £1,000 into something bigger; she's prepared to take risks with it.

Marianne follows the route map for lump sums and sees that investing the £5,000 earmarked for a future home might not be easy if the housing market recovers and house prices start to rise faster than prices in general, so Marianne wants an investment which offers the chance of outstripping inflation in the future. Index-linked investments do that, but only just, so she rules them out. Accepting that she is going to have to take some risk, Marianne plumps for a couple of unit trusts – both growth funds with any income reinvested.

She goes back to the route map, to see how she should invest the £1,000 with which she's going to gamble. She looks up the shortlisted investments in the table and in the chapters later in the book. She toys with investing her money in shares but could really only afford to invest in one company – a very risky idea. She decides instead to put the £1,000 towards improving the eighteenth-century glass collection she started a couple of years ago; even if the bottom drops out of antique glass, she'll get a bit of pleasure out of the collecting.

Investing for extra income

Miss Simmons is aged 80, and lives alone. She lives on her state pension and a small pension from her ex-employer and wonders what to do with the £5,000 she has to invest, which is at present in a bank deposit account. She's alarmed at the way inflation has made inroads into the buying-power of the interest she receives. She'd like to get a bit of extra income to allow herself a few more treats.

She realises that she can leave some of her money in the bank deposit account to act as an emergency fund, but she reckons she won't need more than £300 for this. Thinking about it, though, she decides to leave twice this amount in her account – so that she can draw on it if she wants extra income.

Miss Simmons already owns her home, so doesn't need to worry about getting a mortgage. She hasn't got any index-linked investments, and reckons that Index-linked National Savings Certificates will suit her very well. Although this investment doesn't pay out a regular income, she sees she could cash certificates to get an income. She realises that the value of what she invests will go up in line with the Retail Prices Index (though not if she cashes the certificates before a year is up). This index-linking seems to offer a big advantage to Miss Simmons, so she decides to put £2,000 into these certificates, and, after the first year, to cash bits of her investment if she feels particularly hard-pressed.

She decides not to put any money into index-linked British Government stocks – she wants to take no risks, and besides they don't provide a worthwhile income (nor can they be cashed cheaply in bits and pieces).

As Miss Simmons is over 70, she could consider an annuity or cashing in on her home through a home income scheme. She's not really tempted by a home income scheme as she may want to move home later, so she decides to put the remaining £2,400 into an annuity. She realises that the income from this won't be protected against inflation and decides to give more thought to moving to a smaller house, and investing any money from the sale to give her more income. She realises also that there are heavy expenses involved in buying and selling property and that she'll have to allow for these before going ahead.

Saving for retirement

Bob Mason, self-employed, earning around £20,000 a year, and his wife, Cathy, are in their late-40s. Their three children have all left home and Cathy thinks it's time they started saving for their retirement. They don't want to rely on their business for their retirement funds.

The Masons already have an adequate emergency fund, permanent health insurance in case either of them is too ill to work and are buying their home with a mortgage. They follow the route map for savings to the question *Are you in a pension scheme?* Bob is self-employed, and already contributes £50 a month (£600 a year) towards a personal pension plan. He asks the insurance company which runs the pension plan what he might get in the way of a pension at 65 if he kept up this level of saving. They say about £750 a month, but this could look rather feeble by the time Bob retires if inflation eats into it. So Bob and Cathy decide to step up the amount they save.

Bob can get tax relief on up to 25 per cent of his £20,000 a year, i.e. £5,000 a year or around £417 a month. The Masons reckon that they can afford another £50 a month without too much trouble, so take out a second personal pension plan for this amount (having plans with two companies means that they haven't got all their eggs in one company basket).

Like many self-employed people Bob has earnings which fluctuate from month to month, and even with these higher pension contributions Bob and his wife would have something extra to save in good months. So the Masons decide to add occasional savings to their emergency fund in a building society instant access account. Their emergency fund is over £500, so they switch it to a tiered interest rate account where they get a higher than normal rate of interest. If the account drops below £500, they won't lose out: the interest rate falls back to the lower rate. Once their emergency fund is up to £1,000, Bob and Cathy plan to look again at their pension provision. They'll need to put away much more than £100 a month if they're not to suffer a hefty drop in income on retirement and the tax relief on any increased contributions eases the burden.

3

INVESTING FOR RETIREMENT

For many people, ensuring an adequate income in retirement is a major motive behind saving and investing. This chapter will help you formulate a strategy to achieve this, whether you're still working, close to retirement, or have already retired.

The first step in sorting out your retirement finances is to look at how your income measures up to your expenditure when you retire. Chapters 12 and 13 of this book look in detail at the various types of pension schemes – use these to work out how much you can expect from pensions. If the answer is not enough, then you will need to consider the option for boosting your income in retirement.

Of course, inflation makes budgeting for your retirement difficult if you're looking a good many years ahead. Currently, though, the state retirement pension is increased regularly in line with rising prices. And the amount you can expect from an employer's pension should go up too, at least in the period up to retirement. But the buying-power of the income you can expect from any savings could be drastically reduced by inflation, even at the current low level. The best you can probably do is to work out what you'll get (and what you'll need) in terms of today's prices and pensions. Then make regular checks – once a year, say – that you aren't going too far off course.

What you'll get

Your chief sources of income are likely to be some or all of:
- your state retirement pension
- a pension from your job (and from any earlier jobs)
- pensions from personal pension plans
- income from working after retirement
- income from any savings.

Your state retirement pension

Everyone who has worked for long enough (and paid enough National Insurance) is entitled to a *basic* pension – £54.15 a week for a single person, £86.70 for a married man – new rates will apply from April 1993. Anyone who worked for an employer after April 1979 and who was not contracted-out of the state scheme will be entitled to an *additional* pension under the State Earnings Related Pension Scheme (SERPS) as well. People who were employed between April 1961 and April 1975 may also get a *graduated* pension. See Chapter 12.

A pension from your job

What you will get from an employer's pension scheme depends on how the scheme is set up. With *final pay* schemes you get a proportion (one-sixtieth or one-eightieth, say) of your final pay (as defined by your scheme) for each year you've been in the scheme. With *money purchase* schemes, your pension is the income that your and your employer's contributions can buy at the time you retire. See Chapter 12 for more details, and check with your employer how your scheme works, and approximately how much you could hope to get when you retire.

The problem with a pension from a job is that though it may seem handsome when you first retire, it's likely to look less appealing after 10 years or so if it hasn't increased in line with inflation. The table on p. 17 shows the effect of inflation on the buying-power of your money.

Many schemes have some pension increases built in. Some employers have, in the past, given special increases to help cope with inflation. And in future, final pay pensions from employers will have to be increased by five per cent (or the actual price inflation rate if lower) once they start being paid. But this will apply only to pension rights built up after a certain date (still to be fixed as we went to press). Unless you belong to a scheme where the pension is fully index-linked (e.g. the Civil Service and other public sector schemes), you should allow for inflation in working out how well off you'll be after you retire.

If your scheme provides a lump sum in addition to your pension (or in place of part of your pension if you choose) deciding which to take isn't easy – see p. 203 for what to take into account.

It's unlikely that you'll stay in one job all your working life, and changing jobs may mean you end up with less pension than if you'd stayed with one employer.

You will have several options to consider:
- a *deferred pension* from the job you leave (based on the number of years you were in the scheme)
- a *transfer payment* from your old pension scheme into the new one you're joining, to increase the benefits you'll get from it
- a *transfer payment* into a personal pension scheme (see below).

For employees leaving a final salary scheme, taking a preserved pension has become a more attractive option. By law, if you leave a final salary scheme on or after 1 January 1991 your pension rights must be increased in line with the Retail Prices Index up to a maximum of five per cent a year. If you left before then, any pension built up *since* 1 January 1985 must be revalued in the same way. Some schemes increase preserved pensions by more than the legal minimum.

With a transfer payment into another employer's pension scheme based on final pay, you may be credited with years of membership in the new scheme; this would ensure that your whole pension was linked to your final pay.

Personal pensions

If you're self-employed, or in a job but not in a pension scheme at work, you can contribute to personal pension plans (see Chapter 13). These are marketed by insurance companies, building societies, banks and other investment managers, and what you will get depends on the amount of contributions you have paid. Check up with the pension provider (if they haven't told you already) how much pension your payments have so far earned you, and how much you'll get if you keep paying a certain amount into a plan each year. You'll have to adjust the figure you're given to allow for inflation between now and retirement. To build up an adequate pension, you should aim to pay up to the maximum allowed for tax relief – see p. 235. (Even if you're in an employer's scheme, a personal pension plan can also be used for contracting out of the State Earnings Related Pension Scheme – see p. 198).

Working after retirement

Be wary of setting too much store by this. The economic situation may make jobs for people over retirement age hard to come by, your health may have deteriorated, or you may find yourself less and less inclined to go on working. So don't rely on this source of income to carry you through a major part of your retirement. Note that if you do work after pension age, you may be advised to put off drawing your state pension, and thereby build up more – see p. 192.

Income from savings

If you have money saved already, or plan to save in the future, you can add on to what pensions you receive any income you'll get from investments. But bear in mind:
■ if you invest your money for maximum safety, its value (except for a few investments – see p. 50) may not keep pace with inflation; its buying-power, and that of the income you get from it, will fall over the years
■ if you've accepted some degree of risk in the attempt to safeguard the buying-power of your money, you stand the chance of losing at least some of it. So it's sensible to make a pessimistic estimate of the income your investments will provide in, say, 20 years' time.

Widows, widowers and other dependants

While planning your retirement finances, it's vital to check that your family wouldn't be left short should you die. Many employers' pension schemes provide a pension for widows (and some even for widowers) on the death of the employee, whether before or after retirement. If your family couldn't manage on this (together with any income from their jobs, your savings and state benefits) you need life insurance. This book doesn't cover this aspect of your family finances – for how to work out how much life insurance you need, see *Paying Less For Life Insurance*, in *Which?* November 1991, p. 639.

What you'll need

Around the time you retire, a shift in your spending pattern is very probable. You may be able to predict some of this change fairly easily, especially the part that relates to simply stopping work. You won't have to pay for fares to and from work, for example, or for lunches at work. And you may also know that you'll be spending more on particular hobbies – golf, gardening or painting, say – when you have the time to give to them. You may also know that some of your current financial commitments – the mortgage or school fees, for example – will have ended by the time you retire.

It's less easy to take into account the effects of simply growing older. As you get older, you may well want to spend more than you do now on, for example, staying warm, transport, labour-saving appliances and holidays (you may not want to rough it any more).

Giving realistic weight to this kind of age-related spending change is very hard, particularly if you're trying to look 20 or 30 years into the future. But it's still worth trying to allow for it when you work out your future spending needs: that way you stand a better chance of coming closer to the truth than you do if you assume you'll spend your money the same way in your retirement as in your 30s or 40s.

Taking the long-term view

If you are looking ahead some time to retirement, you need to be thinking of ways of protecting your long-term savings against inflation, until the time comes when you'll actually need them.

The first two chapters of this book will help you in making your choices. If you're employed and there's a pension scheme at work, this is likely to be a worthwhile way of saving; and you could consider making additional voluntary contributions (see p. 202), especially in the last few years before retirement. Both your own and your employer's pension contributions are normally free from income tax. And they go into a special fund which doesn't have to pay income tax or capital gains tax. In addition, a pension in a final pay scheme is linked to your pay when you leave your job, giving you some protection against inflation until you retire.

If you don't belong to an employer's pension scheme, or if you're self-employed, you should consider taking out a personal pension. This is, in effect, a pension scheme run by an investment manager (e.g. insurance company or unit trust manager) for individuals rather than groups of employees. Like an employer's scheme, you get tax relief on your contributions, up to a certain limit. The fund your payments go into pays no income tax or capital gains tax, so you should get a good return on your money; but you won't be able to get it out before the age of 50 at the earliest.

If you've got the choice of an employer's scheme but feel its benefits are poor, check whether you'd do better by choosing a personal pension, though you're unlikely to get any help through employers' contributions.

Consider putting most of your other long-term savings into investments where your money at least stands a chance of maintaining its buying power. Index-linked National Savings Certificates guarantee inflation-proofing and offer the chance of earning a bit more. Index-linked British Government stocks can also protect savings against inflation, depending on when you buy and sell them. Investments in shares, property, commodities and alternative investments such as antique furniture or gold coins may keep pace with inflation over longer periods, but this will not be guaranteed. Be prepared to move your money around to take advantage of the investment opportunities of the day. Bear in mind the rate of tax you pay. Make sure your investments give you the best return, taking both income tax and capital gains tax into account – see Chapter 7.

Making ends meet in retirement

Your major sources of income in retirement are likely to be your pensions (from the state, and from any other schemes you were in) and the income from your savings. If you've already retired, there's likely to be little scope for building up extra savings to increase your income. And you may find that, because of inflation, an income which seemed adequate at the start of retirement is looking on the low side now. The table on p. 17 shows how inflation can whittle away your buying-power – bear this in mind when considering how much income you'll need over your retirement years.

Before checking on ways in which you could boost your income, consider ways of cutting your expenses. For example, check that you are claiming all the help that's available from social security (income support, and other benefits) or from your local authority (housing benefit, community charge benefit, meals on wheels, home helps and so on). Check at your local social security office and town hall. Also, make sure you're not paying more tax than you need – the current *Which? Tax-Saving Guide* should help. Look carefully at how you're spending your money *now* to see if there are any areas where you could cut back relatively painlessly.

You could also think about moving to a house which is cheaper to run – one with lower fuel bills, or a smaller garden, perhaps – or to an area where amenities, such as shops, are closer. But don't put off this decision for too long as it may be easier to make the move and establish new friends and social activities earlier in retirement.

If you've managed to cut down your expenses, you could either invest the money, or use some or all of it in ways which will cut costs later on, e.g. insulating or making repairs to your home. This sort of investment may not give you the best return on your money, but knowing that there'll be fewer large bills to meet later in retirement may be worth it for peace of mind.

Boosting the income from your investments

Check that your investments are working as well as they can for you (taking into account the way you are taxed – see p. 52). You should be looking for investments that stand a chance of maintaining their buying-power, either through an increasing income as time passes, or through capital growth with the possibility of withdrawing regular amounts to use as income. No one investment can fully match these needs, so keep an eye on your investments overall to see how they're doing and are likely to do. For general advice on planning your savings, see the first two chapters of this book.

Chapter 8 gives you a bird's-eye view of a wide range of investments. But some investments are particularly worth considering in retirement. Index-linked National Savings Certificates, for example, can protect at least part of your capital against inflation. The limit on the amount you can invest is £5,000 – see p. 174 for details. To protect more of your savings against inflation, consider Index-linked British Government stocks – see Chapter 17. Whether you get a return greater or less than inflation depends on the price you buy at, whether you can hang on until redemption, or, if not, the price at which you sell.

An annuity is an investment designed especially for the elderly. You hand over your capital to an insurance company in return for a guaranteed income for the rest of your life – see Chapter 22.

Getting an income from your home

You may be able to use your home to raise extra income in retirement. One way of doing this is to sell it and move to a cheaper one, chosen with an eye to lower running costs. This should leave you with a lump sum to invest.

If your home is of a convenient size and easy to run, you may feel there is no need for you to move. You could instead consider getting extra income through a home income scheme, which is specially designed for older people (the over-70s, say) – see p. 355.

An alternative way to use your home to raise money, without moving out, is to let part of it, or to take in a lodger. Before you decide to try this, however, get up-to-date information on your rights (and duties) as a landlord – in particular, what your rights are about getting your lodger or tenant out at some later date. The Department of the Environment publishes a series of leaflets which give the current rules – you can get them from your local Citizens Advice Bureau. And remember that when you take a lodger or tenant you are going into business on a small scale: you should keep careful records of income and expenses, and keep an eye on changes in the law which may affect you. It would be prudent to get advice from a solicitor before becoming a landlord.

Tax after retirement

Like everybody else, the over-65s are liable for tax. But they can claim higher allowances than younger people, so more of their income can be tax-free.

Age-related allowances

If you reach the age of 65 or over during the tax year, you can claim a higher personal allowance, and it's higher still if you reach 75 or over: you can claim up to £4,200 (£4,370 if you're over 75) in 1992–3. Likewise, you can claim a higher married couple's allowance if either you or your husband or wife is 65 or over during the tax year, and it's higher still if either of you is 75 or over during the tax year. The figures for 1992–3 are £2,465 and £2,505 if either of you is 75.

But age-related allowances are reduced by half the amount by which your 'total income' (see p. 96) exceeds a certain limit – £14,200 for the 1992–3 tax year. The allowance is never reduced below the level of the basic personal and married couple's allowance. Note that even if a married man gets a higher married couple's allowance based on his wife's age, it is *his* total income figure which determines the amount of allowance he can get.

If your 'total income' is within the range where your age-related allowances are being reduced, bear in mind that each extra £ of taxable income you get will effectively be taxed at a fairly high rate – 37½ per cent in the 1992–3 tax year. This might make investments where the return is not taxable (e.g. National Savings Certificates) worth considering.

See below for a complication which can arise if you cash in part of a life insurance policy.

Gains on life insurance policies

If you've invested in a single-premium life insurance policy (see p. 328) and would like to cash part of it in, be careful. If you're getting age-related allowances there could be snags. Although any taxable gain you make when you cash in this type of life insurance policy is free of basic-rate tax, it is counted as part of your investment income for the year. And increasing your income can mean you get less age-related allowance (see above), so pay more tax.

If you cash in part of a life insurance policy, for each year that you've held the policy, you're allowed to cash in five per cent of the premiums you've paid so far without it affecting your tax position at the time. If you cash in more than this, the excess is counted as a 'gain' in the year you make it, regardless of how much of it (if any) is in fact gain and how much is return of premiums. This would be added to your 'total income' and could reduce your age-related allowances dramatically. So it's wise not to cash in more than the allowances you've built up, unless you cash in the whole of the policy (in which case only the actual gain is added to your income).

See p. 329 for more on the taxation of single-premium life insurance policies.

4

INVESTING FOR CHILDREN

Choosing an investment for a child under 18 involves much the same principles as for an adult: you have to take account of how much there is to invest, how long you want to invest it for, what rate of tax will be paid on the income and so on. But the range of investments to choose from is not quite the same as for adults:

- there are age limits for some investments (7 or 16 are common ages), while some are not open at all to children under 18
- there are investments open only to children, usually offering perks and free gifts to win the custom of the next generation of money magnates. In general, these are variations on the standard accounts open to adults, but they may offer different rates of return to younger customers.

When investing for a child, follow the guidance in Chapters 1 and 2 on sorting out an investment strategy and finding a shortlist of likely investments. Then use the table on pp. 56 to 57 to eliminate any investments which are barred to children or which require too high a minimum investment. You can find more details of particular investments in Chapters 9 to 25.

How tax affects your choices

Which investment to choose will depend very much on the child's (or, in some cases, the parents') tax position.

The first point to note is that income of more than £100 a year which comes from investing money given by a child's parents is taxed as the parent's income. Note that a child under 18 ceases to be taxed as a child if married.

Any other income the child gets is taxed as the child's, whether from investments handed on by doting grand-parents, earnings from a paper round or appearance fees

Which investment suits your child

type of investment	age child can buy the investment [1]	minimum investment
Bank deposit accounts	from birth, but normally no withdrawals until 7	£1
British Government stocks bought through Post Office	from birth	none [2]
National Savings Certificates	from birth	£100
National Savings Ordinary Account	from birth	£5
National Savings Investment Account	from birth	£5
National Savings Income Bonds	from birth	£2,000
National Savings Capital Bonds	from birth	£100
National Savings Yearly Plan	from birth	£20 a month
National Savings Children's Bonus Bonds	16: bonds for a child aged under 16 must be bought by a person aged 16 or over	£25

Building society ordinary shares/instant access account	varies – often 7	often £1
Building society regular savings accounts	varies – often 7	normally £1 a month
Building society notice or term shares	varies – often 7	£500 upwards
Premium Bonds	can be held from birth, but only bought by child at 16	£10 for children under 16 (until February 1993); otherwise £100
Building society Save-As-You-Earn	16	£1 a month
Finance company deposits	varies – often 18	often £100 to £1,000
Life insurance policies	varies widely – often 16 to 18, can be younger	often £15 to £20 a month; lump sum usually £250 to £1,000
Shares	18	none – but £1,000 a sensible minimum [2]
Unit trusts	varies – often 18	often £250 to £500
British Government stocks bought through stockbroker	18	none – but £1,000 a sensible minimum [2]

[1] See p. 58 for ways of investing on behalf of a child, if the child is too young to invest in his or her own name

[2] You have to pay commission each time you buy or sell so investing or withdrawing small amounts may not be worthwhile

from advertisements. And it won't be taxed at all unless it exceeds the personal allowance (£3,445 for the 1992–3 tax year). For more details about children and tax, see p. 67.

Special children's investments

Banks and building societies know that today's young savers are the next generation of investors, and aim to catch them young. Some offer higher rates of interest to young savers; others tempt the nation's youth with perks such as books, badges, magazines, school gear and the like. A few offer both, though, not surprisingly, the higher the rate of interest, the fewer the goodies.

Some of the gifts are designed to help children learn about money and draw up budgets – you might find them worthwhile even if the rate of interest isn't top of the league. And if money boxes, torches, tee-shirts or real china piggy banks help children to learn thrift, you mightn't be too concerned at the loss of a £ or two in interest. But if it's interest you want, don't let the goodies distract your attention from the best rates going.

Example

Samantha (who is 16) is saving up for a portable stereo radio/cassette recorder costing £120. She has a £12 birthday present from her parents to start her off and reckons on saving £2 a week out of her pocket money. She earns the occasional few £££ from baby-sitting and any cash gifts at Christmas could also be added. She doesn't pay tax, and the interest from her savings isn't going to add up to enough for her parents to worry about paying tax on her interest.

Using the route map on p. 36, she whittles her choice down to a National Savings Investment account or some sort of bank or building society account. She think she'll find a suitable deposit account from a bank or building society in her local high street, and doesn't mind going for an account where she has to give one month's notice. But she'll also find out how a National Savings Investment account compares.

Trusts

If you're planning on giving substantial amounts of money to a child, you may be worried that he or she might squander it. You could, of course, keep the money in your own name and hand it over when the child reaches 18, say. But doing this has disadvantages. For example, *you* may be tempted to squander the money, or it might mean more inheritance tax to pay if you were to die within seven years of making the gift, and so on.

A way out of this problem is to set up a trust for the child. A trust is managed by *trustees* for the benefit of those for whom it was set up (the *beneficiaries* of the trust). The people setting up the trust (the parents, say) can act as trustees; or they can appoint friends or relatives; or a professional adviser (such as a solicitor or accountant) can be appointed as one of the trustees. Below we give brief details of how a trust is set up, and on p. 60 look at some short-cuts you can take.

A trust can have more than one beneficiary, so you can, for example, set up a trust for the benefit of all your 10 grandchildren (plus any more that come along). In this chapter we normally assume a trust has only one beneficiary, but what we say holds equally well for more than one.

When a trust is set up, the trustees may be given the power to invest in specified investments, or to invest *as they think fit*. If they aren't given these powers, there are special rules about how they can invest the money.

Putting money into a trust could mean an inheritance tax bill, though – see p. 69.

Setting up a trust

The rules about trusts are extremely complicated, so we recommend you ask a solicitor with experience of setting up trusts to draw up a *trust deed* for you. This will specify who the trustees are, who is entitled to benefits from the trust, when income and capital are to be paid out, ways in which the trustees can invest the money, and so on.

Even a fairly straightforward trust might cost between £100 and £300 to set up, and there could be a charge each year from the trustees for running the trust (as much as £100 or more, say). So it's probably not worth setting up a trust unless you plan to give a lot of money to your children (at least £5,000; possibly as much as £20,000, say) and feel the cost of setting up and running the trust is worthwhile, or would be outweighed by tax savings.

There are two basic types of trust:
■ **fixed trusts** (often called *interest in possession* trusts) where a particular person (or people) has the right to the income from the trust (or the equivalent of income, e.g. the right to live in a rent-free home). The trustees have no

choice but to hand over the income to the beneficiaries at the times stated in the trust

■ **discretionary trusts** where it is left to the discretion of the trustees which of the possible beneficiaries should be paid income. They may also be free to decide which beneficiary should get capital. If the trustees have the power to accumulate income, i.e. not to pay it out at all (until the trust ends), the trust is called an *accumulation* trust. An *accumulation and maintenance* trust is a type of accumulation trust from which income can be paid out only for the maintenance, education or benefit of the beneficiaries (until the beneficiaries get an interest in possession, that is).

The trust deed may say that beneficiaries shouldn't get any payments (or other benefits) from the trust unless some event happens, e.g. they get married, or reach the age of 25. This type of trust may be fixed or discretionary.

The distinction between fixed and discretionary trusts is important because there are special tax rules for the different types of trust – see pp. 67 to 69.

Broadly speaking, the current tax rules mean that:

■ setting up a fixed trust for your own child won't normally save you income tax – the income from the trust will be taxed as yours

■ setting up an accumulation trust means that income which is accumulated will be taxed at 35 per cent (in the 1992–3 tax year) and there'll be no further income tax to pay as long as it isn't paid out before your child reaches 18. So this could be worthwhile if you pay tax at more than 35 per cent (i.e. 40 per cent).

Note that once you've set up a trust, you can't normally change your mind and take the money back. And, while you can indicate your preferences to the trustees about how they should manage the trust's affairs, the trustees do not have to follow them.

If you think you or your family could benefit from a trust, you should discuss it with a solicitor or other professional adviser.

Short-cut trusts

There are ways of making sure that money you invest for your children is held in trust for them without going to the expense of setting up a tailor-made trust.

Life insurance policies

You can take out a life insurance policy (on your, or your

husband's or wife's life) with the proceeds made payable to your child. Perhaps the simplest way of doing this is to get a policy worded according to the *Married Woman's Property Act*. In this case, the policy (and any money it pays out) is held in trust for the child until he or she reaches an age you specify when taking out the policy.

The policy can be a single-premium one (e.g. a managed bond) or a regular-premium one (e.g. a unit-linked savings plan or an endowment policy).

The premiums you pay count as gifts for tax purposes (but will probably come into one of the tax-free categories – see p. 117). There's no inheritance tax to pay on money paid out by the policy. And if the policy is handed over to the child after the age of 18, any taxable gain on the policy is taxed as the child's, not the parents'. But if the policy ends before it is handed over, the gain is taxed as the parents', though the trust pays the tax.

Unit trusts

A few unit trust management companies run schemes which set up accumulation and maintenance trusts if people want to invest for children.

The minimum investment ranges from £100 to £500, and there's sometimes a small fee for setting up the scheme. But before going ahead with one of these schemes, check whether the unit trusts available would be suitable for your child – see Chapter 15 for what to look for.

Example

Leslie and Lucretia Lime both pay tax on the top slice of their income at 40 per cent. They've got £5,000 from a with-profits endowment policy, and want to invest it for their 10-year-old daughter, Sally. They don't want her to have the money until she's 18.

They consider whether to set up an *accumulation and maintenance* trust (which could save them income tax), but they decide that the amount they're investing doesn't justify the expense of setting up a tailor-made trust. So they put £3,000 into a single-premium managed bond, taken out on Leslie's life, but with the proceeds payable to Sally and the policy being handed over to her when she is 18, so that any gain on it will count as hers for tax purposes. They invest the remaining £2,000 in unit trusts on behalf of Sally – the income from this will count as the Limes' for tax purposes (though any gains will be taxed as Sally's).

The £5,000 will count as a gift for inheritance tax

purposes. But Mr and Mrs Lime have not used their tax-free quota of £3,000 each for this year (i.e. they have £6,000 tax-free in hand). So they can invest the money for Sally without fear of inheritance tax. And there'll be no inheritance tax to pay when the investments are handed over to Sally.

Planning for school fees

If you've decided to send your child (or children) to a private school, you're going to be faced with substantial bills. School fees range from £1,800 a year for the cheapest day preparatory school to over £11,000 for the most expensive senior boarding school.

You may well find paying fees out of your current income hard going. So if there's time in hand, it's worth looking into ways of saving now for school fees in the future. When working out how much you might need, don't forget that school fees (along with prices in general, and your earnings) are likely to rise over the years. In recent years, school fee increases have outstripped the rise in the cost of living.

Various insurance companies and investment advisers specialise in arranging schemes to provide the money that's needed for fees at the time it's needed. In the main, these schemes are based on investment-type life insurance policies and annuities.

Below, we give details of the main types of school fees schemes. Broadly speaking, they fall into two groups:
- **capital** schemes where you invest a lump sum now to provide fees in the future
- **income** schemes where you save on a regular basis to build up the money needed to pay school fees.

Depending on your circumstances, a mixture of the different types may suit you best.

Note that these schemes do not *guarantee* to pay a child's school fees, whatever they are – they simply pay out sums of money at various intervals (which may turn out to be less than, or more than, enough to pay the fees).

It's worth bearing in mind that there's nothing magical about school fees schemes. They are simply a way of investing money in order to make a set of payments some time in the future, and they use the sorts of investment which you might well choose to invest in yourself if you were arranging to save up for school fees independently.

However, there has to be careful timing of the investments to make sure there's money around when the fees are due, and there are tax complications which have to be taken into account. So although you can go it alone, you may decide it's best to make your investments through a special school fees scheme.

Where to go for school fees schemes

A reputable independent financial adviser should be able to help you, or put you in touch with an insurance company or broker specialising in school fees schemes. Or you could try the *Independent Schools Information Service (ISIS)* for help – write to 56 Buckingham Gate, London SW1E 6AG (tel: 071-630 8793) for help. But get quotes from more than one source – different schemes suit different people, and you could save money by shopping around.

How capital schemes work

Educational trusts

You pay a lump sum to an educational trust either directly or via an insurance company or broker. Your lump sum is invested to provide guaranteed amounts each term for an agreed number of years, at a level decided by you at the outset. Your money can be used only for paying school fees (the trust will make out cheques for the fees only to the school) though you aren't tied to a particular school. If the fees have risen above the amounts guaranteed to be paid out, you'll have to meet the shortfall.

If, when the time comes, you don't need to pay school fees, you may be able to transfer the plan to a different child. Alternatively, you may be able to get back the amount of your original investment (though it may then be worth much less because of inflation).

Investment bonds

If you don't want your lump sum to be tied to paying school fees, you can buy a single-premium investment bond from an insurance company (for more about these, see p. 328). The money buys units in a fund of investments (e.g. shares and British Government stocks). Your lump sum grows if the value of the units goes up, but falls if the value goes down. Fees are paid by cashing in your units; and there's a risk that their value may be low when you need to sell them to pay the fees, although some companies now offer bonds guaranteed to match stock market rises.

Cutting the cost

Many schools offer scholarships to academically, musically or artistically gifted children, subject to entrance exam results. These can help pay part or all of the fees. A leaflet on grants and scholarships is available from the Independent Schools Information Service (ISIS) – for address, see p. 63. If you've already chosen a school, ask the bursar.

You may be able to get help with school fees through the Government's Assisted Places Scheme. For details in England, write to the Department for Education, Schools Branch 4D, Government Assisted Places Scheme, c/o Mowden Hall, Staindrop Road, Darlington, County Durham DL3 9BG; in Wales, the Welsh Office Education Department, Schools Administration Division, Phase II Government Building, Ty-Glaf Road, Llanishen, Cardiff CF4 5WE; in Scotland, write to the Scottish Education Department, Room 4/08, New St Andrews House, St James Centre, Edinburgh EH1 3SY; the scheme does not apply in Northern Ireland.

Some employers may help with fees, especially for staff posted overseas (there are schemes, for example, for parents working for the Diplomatic Service or serving in the armed forces). Financial help from an employer can count as a taxable fringe benefit in some cases – check with the Inland Revenue.

How much do you need to invest?

With most schemes there's a minimum investment, usually £1,000. Beyond this, the amount you need to invest will depend on how long there is until the fees start and what the fees are expected to be. If you have a newly born child, you should think about investing a lump sum of at least £60,000 to pay for private boarding education (assuming fees went up from current levels by 10 per cent a year).

Tax

An educational trust has charitable status and doesn't have to pay tax on its investments, as long as the money is used for educational purposes. And you don't have to pay tax on the money which goes to pay fees. A future government might choose to remove an educational trusts' charitable status; you would then have to meet the shortfall in fees created by losing the tax benefits.

With investment bonds, there may be some income tax to pay on money drawn by cashing in the units, but normally only at the higher rate. No tax is due if the parents (or the child if the scheme was set up by anyone other than the parents) pay tax at the basic rate only. For more details about the taxation of income drawn from investment bonds, see p. 104.

How much inheritance tax has to be paid and when depends on who gives the money:

■ **if the parents give the money** Payments made by the parents solely for the *maintenance, education or training* of their children are free of inheritance tax. So there's no inheritance tax to pay when the money is first invested, nor when the fees are paid. But if the money is not held in trust, or if it is held in trust and the parents keep the right to cash in the scheme, there may be inheritance tax to pay if the parent who gives the money dies. The cash-in value of the investment will form part of his or her estate, and will be taxed in the normal way. If the parent gives up the right to cash in a trust scheme, the money will remain in trust for the child and will be used for his or her maintenance, education or training – the money won't form part of the parent's estate

■ **if someone else (e.g. grandparents) gives the money** If the grandparents (or whoever) don't set up a trust scheme, the money they eventually pay over for school fees may count as gifts for inheritance tax.

If they do set up a trust scheme – and they give away the right to cash in the scheme – the money they invest in the first place may count as a gift for inheritance tax purposes. If they keep the right to cash in the scheme, what counts as a gift is the cash-in value of the scheme when fees start being paid (which will almost certainly be higher than the value of the original investment).

Note that even if there is a potential liability to inheritance tax, gifts of money can still be tax-free. For example, gifts made out of normal income are free of inheritance tax, as are gifts totalling up to £3,000 a year – for more details see p. 117.

Composition fees

You can, with many private schools, pay school fees in advance by what's known as a *composition fee*. In this case, the school then invests the money, often in an annuity which starts paying out when the child goes to school. The amounts you have to invest will vary from school to school but are broadly similar to those involved in capital schemes.

How income schemes work

There are a number of different ways in which these schemes can be set up, but most involve saving regularly by taking out a series of investment-type life insurance policies, which mature year by year as the fees become due.

For example, suppose you plan to send your child to private school in 10 years' time for five years. You could take out five with-profits endowment policies which end after 10, 11, 12, 13 and 14 years respectively. For the first 10 years you'd pay a flat amount (the premiums for all the policies). From the eleventh year onwards, the premiums would start to tail off, as each policy ended.

If you expect your income to go up over the years you might prefer to pay premiums which increase rather than decrease. In this case, it may be best to take out five 10-year policies in successive years. Your premiums will increase each year up to the fifth year, stay level for the next five years, then tail off as policies end.

Some companies use unit-linked policies (see Chapter 20) to provide part or all of the fees. And PEPS may be increasingly used now that new rules allow bigger investments (see p. 262). With either, there's the risk that when you want to cash in your investment what you get back will depend on how well the units, shares or whatever have performed. If their value was low, you might get less than you'd hoped for.

If you change your mind about sending your child to private school, what happens depends on whether or not the policies are being held in trust for the child. If they *are* being held in trust (which gives a possible inheritance tax advantage – see opposite) the money from the policies must be used for the benefit of the child. If they are not being held in trust you can either cash in the policies or keep them as a form of saving.

How much do you need to invest
As with capital schemes, the amount you need to invest will depend on how much time there is before your child goes to private school and what the fees are expected to be. If you were hoping to provide private boarding education for a child who's a baby now, you would have to think about investing around £8,000 a year (assuming fees went up from current levels at 10 per cent a year).

Tax
There's normally no income tax to pay on the money paid out by these schemes (except, in certain circumstances, when a life insurance policy has to be cashed in early).

If it's the parents who pay for the scheme there's no inheritance tax to pay on the premiums or on the money paid out by the policies. If people other than the parents pay for the scheme, there's no inheritance tax to pay as long as the premiums are paid out of their normal income or count as tax-free for some other reason – see p. 117. If the policies are being held in trust for the child, there's no inheritance tax to pay if the person who set up the scheme dies. But if the policies are not being held in trust, the proceeds on death count as part of the person's estate.

Failed to plan?

If you've left it too late, or the fees are more than you anticipated, you may be able to borrow the money for the fees. But first compare the monthly cost of any loan with the outlay if you pay as you go, to see whether you couldn't meet the cost out of your income. The occasional overdraft may be cheaper and you won't be committed to paying off loans for years to come.

Banks and insurance companies offer special loan packages for school fees, which usually involve a second mortgage on your home (and some sort of arrangement fee). The money is lent to you as the fees fall due, and you repay it after 25 years (or when you retire) with the proceeds of an investment-type insurance policy. The monthly cost (insurance premiums plus interest) rises as you draw more of the money to pay the fees.

If you manage most of the cost out of day to day income but need to top it up with more than an overdraft, you could ask your bank or building society for a straightforward loan. If you've got an investment-type life insurance policy, you may be able to borrow from the insurance company on the strength of it – see p. 317.

Children and tax

Tax-saving tips

We give details about tax as far as children are concerned on p. 55. And there's yet more on tax in Chapter 7. Here we point out the main things to bear in mind, and some ways you can take advantage of the income tax, inheritance tax and capital gains tax rules to keep tax bills when investing for children to a minimum.

■ **There's a limit to the tax you can save by giving money to your own children** Income of more than £100 a year which comes from gifts parents make to their own children counts as the parents' income for tax purposes; and, if it's taxable, it's taxed at their highest rate of tax.

■ **Giving money to your grandchildren (or any other children who aren't your own) could mean less tax to pay on the income it produces** Income which comes from gifts made to a child by anyone other than his or her parents counts as the child's own income for tax purposes. A child can have income of at least as much as the personal allowance (£3,445 a year in the 1992–3 tax year) before starting to pay tax.

■ **Giving money to your children during your lifetime could save inheritance tax** In general, you have to pay inheritance tax on anything over a set amount (£150,000 in the 1992–3 tax year) that you give away during the seven years before you die or on your death. But some types of gift are tax-free and don't count towards the £150,000 limit. It makes sense to take advantage of these tax-free ways of handing money to your children during your lifetime. For a list of the main tax-free gifts you can make, see p. 117.

And, in general, gifts which are taxable are taxed at a lower rate if you live for at least three years after making them, rather than leaving them in yor will. If you live more than seven years after making a gift, there will be no inheritance tax to be paid on it at all.

■ **You can, if you want, invest money for your children without their being able to get their hands on it for the time being** You can do this by taking out an insurance policy where the proceeds are made payable to your children – see *Short-cut trusts* on p. 60.

■ **Consider setting up an accumulation trust** if you pay income tax at 40 per cent, want to give your children large amounts of money and don't want to put the money into investment-type life insurance. Income which is accumulated is taxed at a flat rate – 35 per cent for 1992–3.

Tax on income from fixed trusts

A fixed trust pays tax at the basic rate on its income. Any income paid out of the trust comes with a tax credit of the amount of tax deducted (25 per cent of the before-tax income for the 1992–3 tax year).

If the trust was set up by the parents, the income counts as theirs (see page 67), and they get the 25 per cent tax credit. If the trust was set up by anyone other than the parents, the income counts as the child's and the child gets the tax credit.

If the parents (or child, as the case may be) don't pay tax, or pay less than the tax deducted, they can claim tax back. If the highest rate of tax the parents (or the child) pay is 25 per cent, the tax liability on income from the trust is automatically met by the tax credit. If the parents (or child) pay tax at a rate of more than 25 per cent, they will have to pay extra tax, calculated on the income paid out plus the tax credit.

Tax on income from discretionary trusts

These pay tax on their income at a special rate – 35 per cent for the 1992–3 tax year.

As with a fixed trust, any income paid out is taxed as either the parents' income (if the trust was set up by the parents) or the child's income (in any other case). But with a discretionary trust, the income comes with a tax credit of 35 per cent of the before-tax amount of income. Whether or not there's more tax to pay (or whether a rebate can be claimed) depends on whether the parents' (or child's) top rate of tax is more or less than 35 per cent. If the top rate is *less* than 35 per cent, it would be worth asking the trustees to pay as much income out as possible, as tax could then be claimed back from the Revenue. With an accumulation trust, if the income is accumulated and not paid out until your children are 18 or over, there'll be no further income tax to pay; but neither you nor your children will be able to claim tax back.

Inheritance tax

For brief details of how inheritance tax works, see pp. 116 to 119 in Chapter 7.

If you make a gift to your child (or set up a trust under which he or she benefits) it normally counts as a gift for inheritance tax purposes. But some gifts you make are free of inheritance tax – we summarise the main ones to bear in mind on p. 117.

Over the page, we tell you some of the special inheritance tax rules which apply to trusts. But the taxation of trust funds and settlements can be very complicated – one reason for getting professional advice if you're setting up a tailor-made trust.

Gifts to trusts

In general, the value of the money, property (or whatever) you put into the trust counts as a gift. With gifts to the following types of trust, there may be an inheritance tax bill if you die within seven years of making the gift (in the same way as for any other gift):

■ an accumulation and maintenance trust
■ a trust for disabled people
■ a fixed trust – provided the gift was made on or after 17 March 1987.

With gifts to all other trusts, you may have to pay inheritance tax at the time you make the gift, even though you live for more than seven years after the gift is made. The gift is added to the value of other such gifts made within the previous seven years; if the total comes to more than £150,000 then inheritance tax is charged on the excess at 20 per cent (which is half the rate payable for gifts on death). If you survive for seven years after the gift, no further inheritance tax will be due on it, but if you die within seven years, then the gift is included in the reckoning for inheritance tax on your death (with credit for the tax already paid).

Note that gifts to trusts count as tax-free if they would be tax-free when made to an individual (e.g. if made out of normal spending).

Inheritance tax on trusts

With a *fixed trust*, anyone with the right to income or the equivalent of income (e.g. the right to live in a rent-free home) from the trust is considered to own the trust's capital, or part of the trust's capital, if the rights to the benefits are shared among several people. When a person's right to the trust's benefit goes to someone else, this is considered to be making a gift, e.g. your son may have the right to income from a trust once he reaches 18. If this right passes to his younger sister when he reaches 21, he is considered to make a gift at that time. The gift is valued as the share of the trust's capital which he's considered to own, at the time the right to the income is transferred. Inheritance tax will be due if the son dies within seven years of the gift; but this tax is paid by the trust.

When the trust finally comes to an end, and the capital is handed over to beneficiaries who until that time had the right to the income, there's no more inheritance tax to pay.

Discretionary trusts (other than accumulation and maintenance trusts – see opposite) may be charged inheritance tax even if payments aren't made out of the trust. Inheritance tax is automatically charged on everything in the trust every 10 years – the *periodic charge*. The rules for calculating the periodic charge are complex, but the overall aim is to collect the same amount of tax as would be paid if the trust's property was owned by an individual and passed on at death every 33 years.

When payments are actually made from a discretionary trust's capital (or if fixed interests are created) the trust is also charged inheritance tax. The value of what's paid out (or turned into a fixed interest) is charged at the rate of tax which applied at the last periodic charge; but this rate is scaled down in proportion to the time since the last 10-yearly charge, e.g. if it's one year since the 10-yearly charge the rate is one-tenth of the rate at the last 10-yearly charge. If the payment from the trust is made within three months after a 10-yearly charge, there's no tax to be paid.

There are special rules for discretionary trusts set up before 27 March 1974.

Payments of capital from certain *accumulation and maintenance* trusts are free of inheritance tax. And these trusts are also free of the 10-yearly tax bills. To qualify, a trust must be for the benefit of one or more people under the age of 25, who must get the capital of the trust (or at least the right to the income, or use of the trust property) on or before their twenty-fifth birthday. If any income is paid out from the trust before this, it must be used only for the maintenance, education or training of the beneficiaries.

If the accumulation and maintenance trust was set up after 14 April 1976, it will be free of inheritance tax only if the children who benefit have a grandparent in common or the trust is less than 25 years old.

Capital gains tax

If you hand over assets (such as shares or your second home) to your children, or put them into a trust, you *dispose* of what you've given, and there may be some capital gains tax to pay (as well as inheritance tax). The asset is valued at its market value at the time you make the gift. For the rules about capital gains tax, see p. 107 onwards in Chapter 7.

Bear in mind that the first £5,800 (for the 1992–3 tax year) of net capital gains you make from disposing of assets during a tax year is tax-free.

Once a gift has been made, how much capital gains tax has to be paid on any further gains depends on whether the child controls the investment, or whether it's in trust.

Gains made by a child

Capital gains made by a child are taxed as the child's own gains, not as those of the parents. The normal rules for working out capital gains tax apply; so, for example, the child can make £5,800 of gains in the 1992–3 tax year without paying tax.

Gains made by a trust

Trusts set up after 6 June 1978 pay capital gains tax at a flat rate of 25 per cent for a fixed trust, 35 per cent for a discretionary trust (including an accumulation and maintenance trust). But the first £2,900 (for the 1992–3 tax year) of net capital gains is free of capital gains tax. This lower tax-free limit for trusts means that trusts are often liable for more capital gains tax than an individual.

If a beneficiary becomes entitled to some or all of the assets of the trust, e.g. on reaching 18, this counts as the trust disposing of the assets. If there are gains, capital gains tax may have to be paid by the trust.

5

SAFETY
FIRST

Investment can be both profitable and interesting, but it's not without its risks, e.g. investing in shares that do badly. There's no law to protect you against such risks, but there are some risks against which you can guard. The world of investment has its share of rogues who will not think twice before disappearing with your hard-earned cash. In this chapter we look at what legal protection there is to stop things going wrong, and to try and compensate *you* if they do. We also take a look at some actions you can take to protect yourself from the rogues.

The past

Regulation of investment businesses used to consist of a piecemeal collection of acts of Parliament plus the self-regulation of such bodies as the Stock Exchange. For example, bank deposits were, and still are, protected by the Banking Act (which, among other things, guarantees 75 per cent of the first £20,000 of your deposit if the bank goes bust) and life insurance policyholders by the Policyholders' Protection Act (which guarantees 90 per cent of your entitlement in a long-term policy).

But there were many loopholes and areas where there was no protection at all for the investor. For example, anybody could set themselves up as an 'investment consultant'. Someone doing this might have belonged to a trade association or have had professional indemnity insurance which might have paid out if he or she lost your money through fraud or negligence, but if this was not the case, you had no protection if you entrusted your money to such a person and things went wrong.

The Financial Services Act

In 1986, Parliament passed the Financial Services Act (FSA), a mammoth piece of legislation designed both to fill the gaps in investor protection and to boost confidence in financial services. Below are the main points of the protection you get under the Act.

But however sensible the rules are, they won't work unless they're enforced – see *How to complain* on p. 78 for what you can do if you suspect the FSA isn't being complied with. It's worth noting that the FSA does not apply to general insurance (e.g. for your home or car) or to tangible investments, such as gold coins or antiques, which you can inspect before buying. Existing criminal and civil laws dealing with fraud and breach of contract help protect you when buying *tangible* investments.

Under the FSA, statutory powers to authorise and regulate investment businesses have been delegated by the Department of Trade and Industry to the *Securities and Investments Board (SIB)*. SIB in turn recognises four *Self-Regulating Organisations (SROs)* and a number of *Recognised Professional Bodies (RPBs)*. However, at the time of going to press in October 1992 there were proposals to merge two of the existing SROs into a 'Personal Investment Authority' for most investment businesses dealing mainly with private individuals. See the end of this chapter for a list of the current SROs and RPBs. Between them, the SROs cover investment business ranging from commodity and financial futures trading through to the selling of life insurance and unit trusts. RPBs cover the investment professionals such as solicitors and accountants where the bulk of their income *doesn't* come from investment business.

Authorisation

All businesses dealing in or giving advice on investments, with certain very limited exceptions, must now be *authorised* to carry out their business. To become authorised, businesses have to show they are properly run, have sound financial backing and keep adequate records. Their staff should be adequately trained and competent (and systems are currently being set up to ensure that competence is tested and demonstrated). Anyone who conducts an investment business without such authorisation is committing a criminal offence, so any contracts you make with them will be void. Authorisation is given either by SIB or, more commonly, by an SRO or RPB. You can telephone SIB on 071-929 3652 to find out whether a firm is authorised or not, or consult the SIB Central Register on Prestel (available in some public libraries).

'Fit and proper' businesses

Once authorised, investment firms which fail to abide by the rules of their regulating organisation can be disciplined or, at worst, have their authorisation removed and be banned from the industry. SIB has overall responsibility for ensuring that the rules of each regulating organisation are adequate for investor protection and has issued 10 principles outlining the standards expected of investment businesses. The main points of the rules are:

■ investment businesses have to take into account *your* best interests when giving you advice

■ in most cases an adviser has to *know the customer*, i.e. be fully aware of your personal and financial situation

■ independent advisers must take into account the range of products on the market and your particular needs, and must not sell you a particular product if they're aware of another one which would meet your needs better – known as *best advice* under the current rules. Company representatives (or *tied agents*) have the same responsibilities as far as the range of products and services the company they're tied to provides. In either case, if nothing they can offer suits your needs, they must tell you so

■ at the start of the selling process, both independent advisers and company representatives must give you a leaflet making their status clear. Independent advisers must make it clear if they are paid on a commission basis (though they don't have to tell you how much they'll get unless you specifically ask them for this information). You'll be be told by a life company the amount of commission paid to an independent adviser when they send you product particulars (after you have made your investment but while you can still cancel it)

■ you should get all the information you need about what you are buying and what you are being charged. In the case of life insurance policies, the company will send you details of the effects of charges or expenses as part of product particulars sent to you after the sale, but normally while you can still cancel the policy. These charges or expenses will be expressed as a reduction in the yield you might otherwise have got. In future, companies will have to give you this information (plus a table of surrender values) before you buy, but there will be a two-year transitional period before this becomes compulsory

■ in most cases (but not when just buying life insurance or unit trusts), written *customer agreements* are required, which give details of the services being provided and their cost, set out your investment objectives and the responsibilities of your adviser and warn of the risks of certain investments

■ *best execution* rules apply for most transactions. This means that the firm must carry out the deal on the best terms available

■ advertisements and illustrations of benefits have to comply with rules about comparisons, references to past performance and give risk warnings if necessary

■ proper arrangements must be made for keeping your money (e.g. money awaiting investment) separate from an adviser's money. A really determined fraudster could still run off with your money, but at least the FSA should make it easier to get compensation – see opposite

■ some of this protection isn't available to you if you're classed as a professional or business investor, or if you're classed as an *experienced* investor in your customer agreement (i.e. one with plenty of recent experience in a particular field of investment). Watch out if this applies to you – read your customer agreement carefully and query it if you think your investor status should be different.

Independence

Advisers selling life insurance and unit trusts must either give completely independent advice on all the products of that type on the market, or act as representatives selling and advising on just one company's or group's products. (While you can ask a company representative to sell you another company's product, the rep can't actually give you advice on it.) This has become known as *polarisation* and has meant that banks and building societies, in particular, have had to change the way in which they operate.

In the past you could get general investment advice from your bank manager, say, yet he or she would also be able to sell you the bank's own products. Polarisation means that it should be made clear to you whether the company you're dealing with gives independent advice or advice on just one company's products. However, banks and building societies which have opted to be representatives can direct you to a subsidiary company for independent advice.

Cold-calling

Financial sales representatives used to be banned from *cold-calling*, i.e. visiting or telephoning you without your previous invitation, unless they were selling unit trusts, life insurance or pension plans. The rules have since been relaxed, though some riskier investments (e.g. *BES* schemes) are still not allowed to be sold in this way.

If you buy life insurance, a pension or unit trusts as a result of a cold-call, you get a cooling-off period, i.e. you can cancel within 14 days of getting a notice telling you of your rights (or before the first payment, if later). But this doesn't apply to unit trusts or single-premium life insurance bonds if you received no advice, or bought either through an advertisement or in line with your customer agreement.

Compensation

A compensation scheme is available if you lose money because your adviser goes bust or turns out to be a fraud (but see p. 154 for the protection you get with deposit accounts at banks and building societies). The scheme is financed by a levy on all investment businesses. You should be covered if your investments were made after 28 August 1988, when the scheme started. If you invested before then you might still be covered in some circumstances.

If you find yourself in the unfortunate position of having lost money in a bankrupt investment company, you should be contacted by the Investors' Compensation Scheme. If you're not contacted, contact them (see p. 81 for the address) with any proof you have of the amounts involved. The scheme can pay up to £48,000 – full protection for the first £30,000 invested, then protection for 90 per cent of the next £20,000. So, it's worth bearing in mind that, in most cases, you'll only be assured of getting all your money back if you've invested £30,000 or less. If you've invested through a member of a Recognised Professional Body you should also get compensation, but from a different scheme.

Suing a company

You also have the right to sue a company for damages if you believe that:

- the company has broken the rules of its regulating organisation, and
- as a result of this you have lost money.

How to complain

Under the FSA there are three stages which you can go through if you have a complaint about an authorised investment business. First, all authorised businesses must have a complaints procedure set up to deal with problems. You should approach the company in writing, providing evidence of your complaint.

Secondly, if your complaint isn't resolved satisfactorily, you can approach the appropriate regulating body – the stationery of all authorised businesses should tell you which this is. The regulating body involved will have a system set up to deal with investor complaints (in some cases, one of the Ombudsman schemes). If they think that the rules may have been broken, they will investigate. Complaints procedures vary between SIB, the SROs and the RPBs, but all have a number of ways of dealing with a justified complaint, such as giving a private or public reprimand or withdrawing authorisation (so that the firm will have to stop business). You may receive payment to compensate for any loss or suffering caused to you.

Finally, if you're unhappy about the way the SRO or RPB has handled your complaint, you can go to SIB. SIB will be able to look at any *procedural* problems you've had with the complaints system of the SRO or RPB (e.g they're taking too long to deal with the complaint). They won't be able to give an opinion on the actual outcome of your complaint. If you're not happy with the outcome, you can go to the regulating body's independent complaints investigator.

The complaints procedure under the FSA applies only if you are dealing with an authorised firm – unauthorised firms are illegal anyway, and if you come across one you should get in touch with SIB.

As well as SIB, the SROs and the RPBs there are other organisations and associations that deal with complaints against investment businesses. If you have a complaint about an investment adviser, see Chapter 6 for further information; if your complaint is about a particular type of investment, see also the chapter dealing with that investment.

Self-protection

Even though the FSA gives you a safety net, it's still a good idea to take precautions before deciding where and with whom to put your money. You should weigh up both the potential risks and benefits of your planned investments. Chapter 6 outlines a number of points to consider when choosing someone to advise you on what to do with your money. Other things to watch out for are:

- particularly good deals – don't allow greed to overcome your common sense. Investing money is a business like any other and a competitive one at that. If you come across an adviser who promises you returns way beyond the norm, the chances are that he or she's either not planning to return your money or there's a lot of risk involved, in which case you could also end up with nothing
- 'guaranteed' returns – if the sales pitch refers to a 'guaranteed return', find out exactly who or what is giving this guarantee. Words alone are not enough (especially if the company is based abroad)
- writing cheques – make cheques out to the company you're going to invest in rather than to the adviser you're dealing with, wherever possible
- high pressure selling – no deal is so urgent that you have to decide immediately whether to invest; it's your money, so don't allow yourself to be pushed into deciding what to do. Give yourself time to find out more
- commission – commission rates do vary, making some investments more attractive for advisers to sell. Despite the *conduct of business rules* of the FSA, it's still a good idea to ask how much commission your adviser is getting on each proposed investment. If you don't get a clear answer, you should consider finding another adviser who is prepared to tell you
- unauthorised advisers – never deal with anyone who doesn't have authorisation; report them to SIB (you can check with SIB as to who is authorised). And, if you find out that an authorised business is breaking the rules of their regulating body, report them too
- being classed as an *experienced* investor (see p. 76) – if you are, some of the protection outlined earlier in this chapter will not apply, e.g. the duty for an adviser to find out your needs before giving advice.

One final warning: remember that the FSA is there to protect you against rogues and the negligence of others, not the unavoidable perils of investment. Investment will never be totally risk-free.

Who are the regulators?

Securities and Investments Board (SIB)
Gavrelle House, 2–14 Bunhill Row, London EC1Y 8RA
Tel: 071-638 1240

Self-Regulating Organisations (SROs)

Financial Intermediaries, Managers and Brokers Regulatory Association (FIMBRA)
Made up of independent investment intermediaries who advise or manage portfolios for private individuals, e.g. life insurance and unit trust advisers.
Hertsmere House, Hertsmere Road, London E14 4AB
Tel: 071-538 8860

Investment Management Regulatory Organisation (IMRO)
Made up of corporate investment managers and advisers, e.g. pension fund managers, unit trust managers and some banks.
Broadwalk House, 5 Appold Street, London EC2A 2LL
Tel: 071-628 6022

Life Assurance and Unit Trust Regulatory Organisation (LAUTRO)
Made up of insurance companies, unit trusts and friendly societies, and mainly regulates the marketing of their investments.
Centre Point, 103 New Oxford Street, London WC1A 1QH
Tel: 071-379 0444

Securities and Futures Association (SFA)
Made up of members of the Stock Exchange, dealers in international stocks and bonds and money market investments, and advisers, managers and dealers in futures and options.
Stock Exchange Buildings, Old Broad Street,
London EC2N 1EQ
Tel: 071-256 9000

Recognised Professional Bodies (RPBs)

Chartered Association of Certified Accountants
29 Lincoln's Inn Fields, London WC2A 3EE
Tel: 071-242 6855

Institute of Actuaries
Staple Inn Hall, High Holborn, London WC1V 7QJ
Tel: 071-242 0106

Institute of Chartered Accountants in England and Wales
PO Box 433, Chartered Accountants' Hall, Moorgate Place,
London EC2P 2BJ
Tel: 071-628 7060

Institute of Chartered Accountants in Ireland
Chartered Accountants House, 87–9 Pembroke Road,
Dublin 4
Tel: 010 3531 680400

Institute of Chartered Accountants of Scotland
27 Queen Street, Edinburgh EH2 1LA
Tel: 031-225 5673

Insurance Brokers Registration Council (IBRC)
15 St Helen's Place, London EC3A 6DS
Tel: 071-588 4387

The Law Society
113 Chancery Lane, London WC2A 1PL
Tel: 071-242 1222

Law Society of Northern Ireland
Law Society House, 98 Victoria Street, Belfast BT1 3JZ
Tel: (0232) 231614

Law Society of Scotland
Law Society Hall, 26 Drumsheugh Gardens,
Edinburgh EH3 7YR
Tel: 031-226 7411

Compensation

Investors' Compensation Scheme, Gavrelle House,
2–14 Bunhill Row, London EC1Y 8RA
Tel: 071-628 8820

6

GETTING ADVICE

Lost of people offer investment advice. But how good will the advice be? In this chapter we look at the various sources of proessional advice, what they might offer, and what they might cost.

Who's offering advice?

Various groups of people give investment advice of one sort or another. For example:
- accountants
- banks
- building societies
- independent financial advisers
- insurance brokers
- insurance company representatives
- merchant banks
- solicitors
- stockbrokers.

As a result of the 1986 Financial Services Act, advisers have to be *authorised* and if they represent just one company, e.g. a particular insurance company, they will have to make this clear. This doesn't mean that their advice will always necessarily be good – you can only be completely sure of that with the benefit of hindsight. But you do have some comeback if things go wrong.

What types of advice can you get?

Investment advice falls broadly into two categories:
- general advice – such as how your money should be split between different types of investment
- specialist advice – such as which shares to invest in or which kind of investment-type life insurance to buy.

Ideally, someone who gives general advice should know a lot about all types of investment and about the tax rules affecting them. A specialist adviser should be an expert in one or two fields of investments, e.g. insurance or shares. Both types of adviser have a legal duty to be aware of your financial circumstances and of what you want from your investments, e.g. an income or capital growth. This rule doesn't apply when an adviser is acting for you on an *execution only* basis, e.g. buying or selling shares for you, under your instructions.

If your adviser manages all your investments for you (called *portfolio management*), you can often ask for the management to be *advisory*, where the adviser needs your prior approval to act, or *discretionary*, where he or she doesn't. Most advisers prefer discretionary management, so that they can act quickly when necessary. If you decide on discretionary management it's normal to agree broad limits to your adviser's discretion, e.g. not more than five per cent of your money to go into the shares of any one company.

Choosing an adviser

It's not hard to find an investment adviser – finding one that's right for you is the problem. Some general advisers, such as solicitors and accountants, normally give such advice as a sideline to their main business. Other advisers will not be interested in your business unless you've a lot of money to invest – £50,000 or even £100,000, say.

So it's best to do a bit of homework before you go out to look for an adviser. Opposite is a checklist of points which you should consider to help you decide what your investment needs and aims are. In going through this checklist you will have to put a bit of thought into exactly what you want from your investments: whether you are willing to risk losing money in hope of a capital gain, whether you want your money available at short notice and so on. See Chapters 1 and 2 for help in sorting out your priorities.

You should also expect to be asked about all these points by an adviser (unless your needs are very specific, e.g. you're just asking them to sell some shares). It's likely that your adviser will use a fact-finding questionnaire to establish what your circumstances and needs are. Advisers who don't ask the right questions won't be in a position to give you suitable advice and it's best to steer clear of them.

Checklist of points to consider

- your age
- your health
- whether you're married, single, separated or divorced
- number and ages of children and other dependants
- size and make-up of family income
- possible changes in your financial circumstances
- your regular financial commitments
- your tax position
- your investments
- your home and mortgage
- your pension
- existing insurance policies
- how long you want to invest for
- your reasons for investing, e.g. how important it is to you to get a high income or make a capital gain
- whether you want to be able to get your money back quickly
- what degree of risk you're prepared to take with your money
- whether there are any sorts of investments you're not prepared to consider – e.g. investing in weapons manufacturers.

Once you've decided on your investment aims, it should be a little easier to choose a suitable type of adviser – see our guide to the advisers for what each type offers. When you've found the adviser you want, check that it is authorised. You can do this either by contacting SIB or the appropriate regulating body – see pp. 80 to 81. Make sure you see more than one authorised adviser so that you can compare what they're offering.

It's not only the adviser who should ask questions – *you* should too. It's important you're clear about exactly what kind of adviser you're dealing with. You should find out:
- whether the adviser is independent or tied to selling the products of just one company
- which SRO or RPB it is regulated by
- what compensation scheme it is covered by
- whether it has professional indemnity insurance which will pay out if it loses your money through fraud or negligence.

Another important question you should ask is how the

adviser will be paid. Some advisers charge fees, usually a percentage of your investment. Others will get commission from the companies with which you invest money. Of this latter group, it's important to bear in mind that while the advice may seem free there *is* a cost involved. The commission will be deducted from the investors' funds. If you do pay a fee, the adviser may undertake to pass on to you any commission it receives. See the following pages for how each type of adviser is paid.

Don't make your final decision until you're satisfied on all these points. Steer clear of advisers who make fantastic claims for what they can do for your money. Investment that supposedly brings high returns may well be fraught with risk.

Once you've decided on your adviser, make sure you specify exactly what you want it to do and get it from them in writing. Under the Financial Services Act your adviser will, in most cases, have to draw up a *customer agreement* which sets out your investment objectives, the services to be provided, the responsibilities undertaken and the charges being made. Avoid making cheques out in your adviser's name if at all possible – make out your cheque to the company providing the investment. If a firm has *got* to handle your money, check that it's held in a separate client account. And, if an adviser is going to be looking after your money over a long period, make sure that it sticks to your customer agreement. Ask how it'll keep in touch, who'll be dealing with you and how often. Expect a report on your investments at least once a year.

Guide to advisers

Accountants

Generally, these aren't investment specialists, but they may offer independent advice to customers, or refer you to a specialist.
- **What they offer** – varies considerably, but includes general investment advice, tax planning, advice on wills and trusts, sometimes advisory or discretionary portfolio management, contact with specialist advisers, e.g. stockbrokers.
- **What they charge** – their normal fees, which depend on the time spent and can vary greatly, so shop around. They may get commission if you buy life insurance, unit trusts or shares through them. *Chartered accountants* are sup-

posed to tell you in writing about any commission they expect to receive as a result of your investment. *Certified accountants* are supposed to tell you about any commission and deduct it from their fee.

■ **What to watch out for** – some accountants may be well qualified to advise you about investments: others may not.

■ **Who to complain to** – the *recognised professional body* to which the accountant belongs – see p. 81. Check to see if your accountant has professional indemnity insurance; almost all should have this. If a large part of its business comes from advising on or managing investments, it may belong to *FIMBRA* or *IMRO* as well – see p. 80.

Verdict
Worth trying if you want advice on an overall investment strategy and can afford the fees.

Banks

All the high street banks offer investment advice. Most advise about their own investment products only, but a few advise about all products on the market – see p. 76. Banks that sell their own products at branch level generally also offer independent advice through a connected company, e.g. a trust company.

■ **What they offer** – varies from bank to bank and within banks themselves, but includes advice on the bank's own products (e.g. insurance and unit trusts), advice on buying and selling stocks and shares, advice on tax, advice on pensions, portfolio management.

■ **What they charge** – usually nothing if you buy life insurance or unit trusts, as the bank gets commission; normal stockbrokers' commission for buying and selling shares (maybe with an *administration fee* on top); for managing a portfolio, either a flat fee or half to one and a half per cent a year of the portfolio's value. There could be an extra fee for tax help.

■ **What to watch out for** – most banks' branches sell just their own products.

■ **Who to complain to** – if you can't get the head office of your bank to deal satisfactorily with your complaint, try the Office of the Banking Ombudsman, Citadel House, 5–11 Fetter Lane, London EC4A 1BR, tel: 071-583 1395. Depending on the part of the bank you've dealt with and the type of investment you've purchased, it may be better to approach *FIMBRA, IMRO, LAUTRO* or the *SFA* – see pp. 80 to 81 for addresses.

Verdict
Useful if you want advice on or management of smaller sums of money – under £10,000, say. For management of larger amounts you may have to approach a bank's trust company. Or you could go to a merchant bank, which can offer a more personalised service and usually advises only customers with large sums of money.

Building societies

Building societies can provide a wide range of financial services and products, e.g. share-dealing services in conjunction with stockbrokers.
■ **What they offer** – not all societies offer the full range of financial services the law allows them to provide, but you may be able to get share-dealing or unit trust services (through links with other financial bodies). Some also offer independent advice through a connected company.
■ **What they charge** – normally nothing, because the society gets commission from the company whose product you buy. If you are referred to another adviser, e.g. a stockbroker, you will pay that adviser's charges.
■ **What to watch out for** – many building societies offer advice only on the products of one company at branch level – see p. 76. They have a vested interest in selling insurance products, e.g. endowment mortgages, because of the commission.
■ **Who to complain to** – if you can't get the society's head office to deal satisfactorily with your complaint, try the Building Societies Ombudsman, Grosvenor Gardens House, 35–7 Grosvenor Gardens, London SW1X 7AW, tel: 071-931 0044. Under the Financial Services Act, building societies are generally authorised by *SIB* – see p. 80.

Verdict
An obvious (though rarely independent) choice for advice on ways of investing to pay off a mortgage. And worth contacting if you want advice on their own products, e.g. instant access accounts, or if you want to find out about any of the other services or products they may offer.

Independent financial advisers

This term covers a range of advisers, from those who mainly sell life and pensions products, through to those who deal in a wide variety of schemes, but, strictly speaking, they should all look at all types of investment when advising you. *IFA Promotions* (tel: 0483 461461) will send a list of six of their members in your area.

- **What they offer** – includes: general investment advice, advisory or discretionary portfolio management, advice on tax and pensions, advice on life insurance products, shares and unit trusts, advice on alternative types of investment.
- **What they charge** – usually nothing if they're just selling a life insurance policy or unit trust, as they get commission. For managing a lump sum, charges can range from half to one per cent a year of the value of your portfolio. Charges may be less for very large amounts. Instead, advisers may charge a flat fee, such as £100 a year or a slice of your profits, or even both. Services like tax help may cost extra. If you'd prefer to pay a fee for advice, rather than risk biased advice, *Money Management* magazine has a list of IFAs who charge fees. Write to them at Greystoke Place, Fetter Lane, London EC4 1ND.
- **What to watch out for** – charges for advice can vary widely. If your adviser charges a fee, ask if it will be reduced if commission is paid on any of the investments purchased.
- **Who to complain to** – if you have problems, get in touch with the appropriate regulating organisation, likely to be *FIMBRA* or *IMRO* – see p. 80 for addresses. Advisers should have professional indemnity insurance which will pay out if you can prove your money was lost through their negligence or fraud.

Verdict
Worth trying if you want general advice or someone to manage a lump sum for you (say, £10,000 plus).

Insurance brokers

Anyone can call himself or herself an independent insurance *adviser*, but to be a *broker* a person must meet set conditions and register with the Insurance Brokers' Registration Council (IBRC). Under the Financial Services Act, any advisers and brokers dealing with investment-type life insurance have to be authorised by an *SRO* or by the *IBRC*.

- **What they offer** – advice on life insurance and pensions, plus general insurance advice (for home, car, etc.) and sometimes tax advice and unit trust advice.
- **What they charge** – usually nothing, as they earn commission on what they sell.
- **What to watch out for** – commission rates can vary from product to product and and company to company. So ask

your adviser what commission they will get on each investment they recommend and then probe their recommendation. Research done for *Which?* in the past hasn't found registered brokers' advice to be any better than that of other independent insurance advisers.

- **Who to complain to** – if more than 49 per cent of a broker's business is involved with investments, they must be authorised by an SRO – probably *FIMBRA* (see p. 80). For other brokers contact the *IBRC*, 15 St Helen's Place, London EC3A 6DS, tel: 071-588 4387. This has a fund which may pay out if you lose money through a broker's negligence or fraud. Brokers must also have professional indemnity insurance.

Verdict
Worth trying, particularly if you've already decided that you want investment-type life insurance, pensions or unit trusts. Don't always expect general advice on all investments.

Insurance company representatives

Life insurance companies often employ representatives to deal with you in person. Some companies sell their products just through their representatives, press advertisments and direct mailing, others sell them just through independent advisers, while some use both methods. Some companies have a policy of passing direct enquiries on to independent financial advisers.

- **What they offer** – includes: advice on which of their products best suits your needs, advice on tax implications of their products, retirement planning advice, advice on their company's own unit trusts, general information on the financial markets (e.g. through talks and seminars).
- **What they charge** – nothing, since most representatives get commission from their company on the products that they sell.
- **What to watch out for** – in the past, it was not unknown for company representatives to pass themselves off as independent; this is no longer allowed. Don't be pressurised into buying their products if you're not convinced they're right for you. Also, get quotations from more than one company. You're unlikely to save any money dealing directly with a company (rather than through an adviser); commission costs are built into the price of an investment.
- **Who to complain to** – *LAUTRO* covers insurance companies, unit trust management groups and friendly

societies (see p. 80). If an insurance company head office won't deal satisfactorily with a complaint, see if the company belongs to the *Insurance Ombudsman Bureau*, City Gate One, 135 Park Street, London SE1 9EA (tel: 071-928 4488) or *Personal Insurance Arbitration Service*, 24 Angel Gate, 326 City Road, London EC1V 2RS (tel: 071-837 4483).

Verdict

Obviously, you will get advice on only one company's products. But if you know you want to invest with that particular company, and you're sure you can't get a better deal elsewhere, it's worth trying.

Merchant banks

These generally deal with companies and institutions rather than individuals, offering services such as international banking, corporate finance and investment management. Few merchant banks will consider advising individuals unless they have a large sum of money to invest – over £100,000, say. Some will not take on individuals at all. Contact The British Merchant Banking and Securities Houses Association, 6 Fredrick's Place, London EC2R 8BT, tel: 071-796 3606 for a list of members.

■ **What they offer** – services and products on offer will vary considerably, but include advisory and discretionary management of your investments (as long as you have a minimum amount to invest, commonly £100,000, but could be much more), advice on and purchase of stocks and shares, and tax advice.

■ **What they charge** – usually a yearly fee, between half and one per cent of your investments, say. If selling their own investment products or those of other companies, they could earn commission. Make sure you find out if this is the case.

■ **What to watch out for** – check whether the advice you're getting is independent or just about their own products. A bank has a duty to make this clear to you.

■ **Who to complain to** – the head office of the bank concerned, or the appropriate regulating body under the Financial Services Act (probably *IMRO*).

Verdict

Only for the rich. Merchant banks' main emphasis is on stocks and shares.

Solicitors

Solicitors aren't generally investment specialists, but nearly all will give existing clients advice; most will give it to anyone who comes to see them. All solicitors have to give independent advice.

- **What they offer** – varies considerably, but includes general advice, contacts with specialist advisers (such as stockbrokers), sometimes advisory or discretionary portfolio management, tax planning, advice on wills and trusts.
- **What they charge** – usually a fee based on the time spent (rates can vary so shop around). If commission is received it can only be kept with your permission. In practice, fees are sometimes reduced by the amount of the commission.
- **What to watch out for** – some may be well qualified to tell you where to put your money, others may not.
- **Who to complain to** – their *recognised professional body*, e.g. the Law Society (see p. 81). They all have professional indemnity insurance. They may also belong to *FIMBRA* if a large part of their business comes from advising on or managing investments.

Verdict
Worth considering for general discussion of investments.

Stockbrokers

These specialise in shares and British Government stocks, but many have widened their services in recent years.

- **What they offer** – mainly advice on buying and selling shares and British Government stocks, usually unit trusts too; also advisory and discretionary portfolio management (for sums starting at around £10,000, but often much more), unit trust portfolio management, their own unit trusts and Personal Equity Plans, investment research, general investment advice (sometimes through a subsidiary company).
- **What they charge** – commission for buying and selling shares on your behalf ranges from one to two per cent of the price of the shares, plus VAT. Most stockbrokers have minimum commissions of around £20 or £25. For portfolio management, there's an annual fee of, say, one per cent of the value of the portfolio. You may also be charged a small fee (around £5) to cover the cost of complying with FSA rules. Others may have increased commission rates to reflect this.

■ **What to watch out for** – charges both for buying and selling shares and for general management of a portfolio vary a lot, so it's worth shopping around. But don't expect a stockbroker to be able to choose shares that consistently do better than average; investing in shares is a risky business – see Chapter 14. Not all stockbrokers are prepared to deal with individuals.

■ **Who to complain to** – the *SFA* (see p. 80). Some may also belong to *FIMBRA* – see p. 80. If you're having problems with an individual unit trust company, you can go to the *Insurance Ombudsman Bureau* (if the trust company is a member), at City Gate One, 135 Park Street, London SE1 9EA (tel: 071-928 4488).

Verdict

If you want advice on shares, British Government stocks or unit trusts, a stockbroker may be your best bet. They are worth considering for management of a lump sum, say £10,000 plus, though some stockbrokers manage only very large sums.

7

TAX

Why bother about tax? Because tax can affect the return on your investments. Before you can judge the merits of an investment you need to gauge the effect of tax on it.

Let's take an extreme example. Dave Grabber pays income tax at the higher rate of 40 per cent – see p. 97. He has a choice between two investments:

■ investment A will pay him an income of 10 per cent a year

■ investment B won't pay any income, but will, he hopes, show a capital gain of 8 per cent a year.

Both these figures are before tax, and, at first sight, investment A looks more attractive. But let's assume that investment A pays an income of £10,000. The effect of income tax at 40 per cent will be to reduce this sum to £6,000. Investment B on the other hand, producing a gain of £8,000, is liable for capital gains tax. This tax is also at 40 per cent, but the first slice of total yearly gains (£5,800 in the 1992–3 tax year) is tax-free. So Dave would pay tax at 40 per cent on only £2,200, ending up with an overall return of £7,120 – higher than that from investment A.

Tax can also affect the cost of an investment, particularly where pensions and mortgages are concerned. With personal pension schemes, tax relief can save up to 40 per cent of the cost – see p. 235. And of course, most people qualify for basic rate tax relief on the interest they pay on the first £30,000 of their mortgages – see p. 147.

Which taxes?

The most common tax you'll have to pay is income tax on investment income. The other main tax to watch out for is capital gains tax. Inheritance tax doesn't directly affect the return you get on your investments, but we give the basic rules at the end of this chapter.

Which tax will hurt you most depends very much on your investment choice. You have an annual slice of tax-free capitals gains (see p. 107), and if your returns don't exceed this, you won't be hurt by tax at all if you go for investments which produce a capital gain rather than income. If, however, you've used all your tax-free slice for capital gains tax, you'll have to pay tax at the same rate as your top rate of income tax. So you should look for investments offering the highest rate of return *after* tax, either as income or as capital gain.

Income tax

There are three ways in which investment income can be treated. It can be:
- tax-free
- taxable, but not taxed before you get it
- paid with basic-rate tax deducted.

Income tax is charged on your income for a tax year. Tax years run from 6 April in one year to 5 April the following year. Your tax bill for 1992–3, say, may be based on your income from 6 April 1992 to 5 April 1993. But in some cases it's difficult to know in which year your investment income will be taxed. Your bill may be based on income you received in the tax year in question (*current year basis*), or it may be based on the investment income you received in the previous year (*preceding year basis*). In this chapter, we tell you which basis applies to which types of income, and how you can sometimes juggle figures to get a lower tax bill.

How much income tax?

All your income is added together, to arrive at your *gross income*   say £15,000
From this you deduct your *outgoings* (certain payments you make, e.g. expenses paid in connection with your work)
    say £2,000
This leaves what the Revenue calls your *total income*
    £13,000
From this you deduct your *allowances* (e.g. the personal allowance)   say £3,445
This leaves your *taxable income*   £9,555
Tax is charged on your *taxable income*.

Rates of income tax for the 1992–3 tax year
The first £2,000 of your taxable income is taxed at the new lower rate of 20 per cent: income between £2,001 and £23,700 is taxed at the basic rate of 25 per cent. Anything more is taxed at the higher rate of 40 per cent.

Independent taxation

In the past a married woman's investment income counted as her husband's for tax purposes, and so was added to his income to work out their joint bill. From 6 April 1990, all her income has been taxed as her own and she has been responsible for paying the tax on it: both husband and wife have their own personal allowance and they also get a married couple's allowance.

Married couples
If you are married and own investments in the joint names of you and your partner, income will automatically be treated as if it is paid to you both in equal shares, with each of you paying tax on half the income.

If you own the investment in unequal shares, the income can be taxed accordingly. You *both* have to make a joint declaration to one of your tax offices setting out how the capital and income are shared between you. To do this you need *Form 17* – you can use one form for more than one investment. The different tax treatment applies from the date that the declaration is made. You cannot *choose* the proportions in which the income from joint investments will be taxed. You can make a declaration only to be taxed according to your real shares in the capital and income.

As married women now have their own personal allowance and lower and basic-rate tax bands, it may be worth transferring some investments currently in the husband's name from husband to wife so that the income is counted as hers. Bear in mind that to be effective for tax purposes, such gifts have to be outright, i.e. without strings attached. Note that there is no capital gains tax on any disposals of assets between husband and wife.

From 6 April 1993 there's a further tax change which might help some married couples to reduce tax on their investments. Before that date, the married couple's allowance is given to the husband and can only be transferred to the wife if the husband's income is less than his total allowances – so they cannot use it to reduce their overall tax bill if he uses all his allowances but she pays tax at a higher rate than he does. From 6 April 1993, married couples will be able to choose how to split the married couple's allowance, by completing *Form 18* (from their tax office) and returning it before the start of the tax year. The effect will be that if a wife has a lot of income-producing investments in her name, say, and pays a higher rate of tax than her husband, she can claim half or all of the married couple's allowance to reduce her tax bill – and the couple's overall tax bill. Until that date, to achieve the same effect they would have to transfer ownership of some of her investments to the husband.

Tax-free investment income

■ proceeds from Save-As-You-Earn
■ proceeds from National Savings Certificates (and, in most cases, Ulster Savings Certificates if you live in Northern Ireland)
■ proceeds from a National Savings Yearly Plan
■ proceeds from National Savings Children's Bonus Bonds
■ some Friendly Society Savings plans
■ proceeds from a qualifying life insurance policy – see p. 104 for details
■ premium bond prizes
■ interest on tax rebates
■ first £70 interest each year from a National Savings Ordinary account
■ interest on Tax Exempt Special Savings Accounts (TESSAs) – see p. 163
■ interest received in connection with delayed settlement of damages for personal injury or death
■ part of the income from many annuities
■ income from a family income benefit life insurance policy
■ income from share dividends or unit trust distributions in a qualifying Personal Equity Plan (PEP).

Investment income taxable but not taxed before you get it

Interest from the investments listed below comes into this category:
■ National Savings accounts and National Savings Income and Capital Bonds
■ British Government stocks bought on the National Savings Stock Register, e.g. through a post office, and War Loan
■ interest on loans you make to private individuals

- deposits at non-UK branches of building societies and UK or overseas banks
- deposits made by people not ordinarily resident in the UK
- co-operative society deposits
- credit union dividends.

How it is taxed

The interest is paid gross, and you have to account to the Revenue separately for any tax you owe.

If you've been getting interest from one of these sources for a few years, it will normally be taxed on a preceding year basis, i.e. your tax bill for the 1992–3 tax year will be based on the interest paid (or credited) to you in the 1991–2 tax year. This bill must normally be paid by 1 January 1993, or within 30 days of the date on the Notice of Assessment you'll get, whichever is later. But if your interest doesn't vary much from year to year, and you pay tax under PAYE, the tax on your interest will probably be collected along with tax on your earnings.

Special rules

Special rules apply to the first three and last two years in which you get interest of this type – see the table on p. 101.

If you get interest of this type from more than one source, the Revenue will normally apply special rules to each source separately. But if there is a big change in the interest from a single source, e.g. if you greatly increase or decrease the size of your National Savings Investment account, the Revenue may treat such interest as coming from a new source, and apply the special rules.

You won't need to worry about these rules if your interest is much the same from year to year. But if it does vary, you may be able to reduce your tax bill.

If the amount of interest in year 3 is lower than in year 2, tell your tax office that you want your tax bill for year 3 to be based on the interest you actually got in year 3. You can make this choice at any time within six years of the end of year 3.

If the amount of interest in years 2 and 3 is high compared with the interest in year 4, consider closing your account (e.g. a National Savings Investment account) just before the end of year 4, and reopening it a week or so later (after the start of the next tax year). That way, your tax bill for year 4 will be based on the interest you actually receive in that year, rather than on the higher amount of interest you got in year 3.

If you have more than one account, you may need to close them all.

Investment income paid with basic-rate tax deducted

Examples of this type of income are:
- proceeds from National Savings FIRST Option Bond
- most interest from banks, building societies and other authorised institutions, e.g. finance companies
- interest from foreign currency deposits made at UK banks
- interest on most local authority loans issued after 18 November 1984
- share dividends from UK companies
- distributions from unit trusts
- interest on certain loans, e.g. loans to foreign governments
- interest on certain British Government stocks (normally all stocks bought through a stockbroker, except War Loan)
- interest on company fixed-income investments (loan stocks or debentures)
- part of the income from annuities
- income from certain income and growth bonds
- income from certain trusts and settlements
- income from a will, paid out to you during the administration period (i.e. while the details of who gets what under the will are being worked out).

How it is taxed

This type of income is taxed on a current year basis, i.e. your tax bill for the 1992–3 tax year is based on the income paid (or credited) to you in that tax year.

There's no basic-rate tax to pay on this type of income, because the basic-rate tax (or something equivalent to it) has been deducted before the income is handed over to you.

Until 6 April 1991 interest from most building society, bank and finance company accounts, and interest from most local authority loans, had *composite rate* tax deducted before it was paid out. This was equivalent to basic rate tax, except that the tax deducted couldn't be reclaimed even by non-taxpayers. From 6 April 1991, however, composite rate tax ended and this type of interest has had basic rate tax deducted instead. The effect is that non-taxpayers can now reclaim the tax, or (if they expect to be non-taxpayers during the next tax year) arrange to have the

Interest not taxed before you get it: what your tax bill is based on

	Tax is initially based on:	but for some years, there's a choice:
First tax year in which you get interest from this source (year 1)	interest you get in first tax year (current year basis)	no choice this year
Second tax year (year 2)	interest you get in second tax year (current year basis)	no choice this year, unless source of interest begins on 6 April in year 1. If it does, tax year 2 will normally be based on the interest you got in year 1 (*preceding year basis*), and you can choose to have tax for year 2 based on interest in year 2 instead (*current year basis*). Consider doing this if interest in year 2 is lower than interest in year 1. Note, in this case, you have no further choice in year 3
Third tax year (year 3)	interest you got in second tax year (preceding year basis)	**your choice:** you can choose to have tax based on interest you get in year 3 (current year basis). Do so if this is less than interest you got in year 2
Fourth and subsequent tax years. . .	interest you got in preceding tax year (preceding year basis)	no choice for these years
Until the last-but-one tax year in which you get interest from this source	interest you got in preceding tax year (preceding year basis)	**Revenue's choice:** when you tell the Revenue, at the end of the next tax year, that you've closed your account, it can revise your tax bill. The bill will be based on the interest you actually got in the last-but-one tax year (current year basis) if this comes to more than your original bill
Last tax year in which you get interest from this source	interest you get in this tax year (current year basis)	no choice this year

interest paid out before tax by completing Form R85, available from their bank or building society.

With dividends from UK companies and distributions from unit trusts, each dividend or distribution is accompanied by a tax credit. Your gross (before-tax) income is taken to be the dividend plus the tax credit. For the 1992–3 tax year, the tax credit is 25 per cent of the gross income. So if, say, the dividend is £75, the tax credit will be £25 and the gross income £100. You get a tax voucher from the company (or unit trust) showing the amount of the dividend (or distribution) and the amount of the tax credit.

With other types of income taxed before you get it, tax is deducted (usually at the 25 per cent basic rate) before the income is paid to you. Again, you normally get a tax voucher or a similar document from whoever pays you the money. This will tell you the gross (before-tax) amount of income, the tax deducted and the actual sum you get. Keep any tax vouchers as proof that tax has been credited or deducted.

The outcome of all this is:

■ if your income (including income of this type) is too low for you to pay tax, you can claim back all the tax that's been deducted or credited, or, with banks, building societies and a few other homes for your money, arrange to have it paid before tax – see above

■ if your income is high enough for you to pay some tax, but not as much as has already been deducted (for example you pay tax only at the lower rate of 20 per cent), you can claim back the difference

■ if you are liable for basic-rate tax (but no more) on the whole of your income of this type, your liability for tax on this income is automatically met by the tax deducted

■ if you pay tax at the higher rate, you will have to pay extra tax, calculated on the gross (before-tax) income. To calculate the grossed-up interest for the 1992–3 tax year, take the net interest and divide it by 0.75.

Any extra tax on income received between 6 April 1992 and 5 April 1993 has to be paid by 1 December 1993, or within 30 days of the date on your Notice of Assessment, if later.

Example

George Streatley is a higher-rate taxpayer. He got £450 in building society interest in the 1992–3 tax year. He divides £450 by 0.75 to find the grossed-up amount, £600. He's liable for tax at 40 per cent on £600, i.e. £240. However, he's treated as having already paid tax on this interest at the 25 per cent basic rate (i.e. £150 in tax). So he has to hand over only an extra £240–£150 = £90.

Points to watch

Annuities

If you've bought an annuity voluntarily with your own money (not, for example, as part of a personal pension), part of the income each year is treated as a return of capital, part as interest on the capital. Only the interest part is taxable; the insurance company will say how much this is. Non-taxpayers may be able to have the income paid out before tax; again, ask the insurance company.

Discretionary trusts

For the 1992–3 tax year, discretionary trusts pay tax at 35 per cent on most of their income. This applies whether the income is kept by the trust or paid out to you. If it is paid out to you, you get a credit of 35 per cent of the gross (before-tax) amount. If your income, including the income from the trust, is too low for you to pay tax, or you pay tax at a lower rate, you can claim back some or all of the tax deducted (but higher-rate taxpayers will have some more tax to pay).

Income and growth bonds

There are several different types of bond, which work (and are taxed) in different ways – see Chapter 21.

Unit trusts

With the first distribution you get from a unit trust, you're likely to get an *equalisation payment*. This is a return of part of the money you first invested, so doesn't count as income and isn't taxable. But see p. 115 for how it affects any capitals gains you make.

With an accumulation unit trust (where income is automatically reinvested for you) the amount reinvested, apart from any equalisation payment, counts as income and is taxable.

Personal Equity Plan

Cash may be deposited in a PEP for the purpose of buying investments. The interest is paid gross if it is reinvested in the plan or if the total amount withdrawn in any tax year is less than £180. But interest withdrawn of more than £180 a year is taxable and you will need to declare it on your tax return.

National Savings Capital Bond

Although interest is credited to your Capital Bond each year, you don't receive it until you have held the Bond for a full five years (or you cash in early). However, you still have to declare the interest and pay tax on it each year.

National Savings Ordinary accounts

You and your spouse are each allowed £70 interest free of tax from a National Savings Ordinary account. But you are taxed on anything more.

Any one person is allowed only £70 free of tax, however many accounts he or she has. So, if you have, say, £100 interest and your spouse has £20, *you* will have to pay tax on £30 of your interest, even though the combined interest isn't more than 2 × £70 = £140. If you have a joint account, however, you can have £140 interest between you free of tax.

British Government (and some other) stocks

If you sell British Government stocks before a date when you're due to receive an interest payment (normally twice yearly), part of the price you get is deemed to be the interest you would otherwise have received. It is calculated on a daily basis and taxed as income. This is known as the *accrued income scheme*, and also applies to building society Permanent Interest-Bearing Shares (PIBS) and to sales of local authority and company loan stocks. However, it won't apply if the *nominal* or face value of all the stocks covered by the scheme that you hold does not exceed £5,000 at any time in the tax year. See p. 297 for how to work out your accrued income.

Income tax and life insurance

There are two main types of life insurance policy for tax purposes. These are:
- qualifying policies – including most regular-premium policies, e.g. most endowment policies and low-cost endowment policies linked to mortgages
- non-qualifying policies – e.g. single premium policies.

The insurance companies' investment funds are taxed, but you don't have to pay basic-rate income tax on policy proceeds yourself (and as the proceeds always count as income, there's no capital gains tax to pay).

When you do have to pay tax

You have to pay tax only if you're a higher-rate taxpayer (or would be once the gain from the policy is added to your income) and:
- *either* the policy is a non-qualifying policy

- *or* the policy is a qualifying policy but you cashed it in or made it paid up in its first 10 years (or the first three-quarters of its term, if less).

So you may need to work out your *taxable gain*. This is the amount you get when a policy comes to an end (plus any amounts you've had from the policy in the past), less the total premiums paid (including any subsidy you got on the premiums).

If you cash in only part of a policy before it matures, you get an allowance for each 12-month period since you first took out the policy. If you've received more from the policy than the amount of your allowances, the excess counts as your gain. For the first 20 years of the policy, the allowance is five per cent of the total premiums paid so far. For each year after that, the allowance is five per cent of the total premiums paid in that year and in the previous 19 years.

This means that you can take a yearly income from non-qualifying policies up to the yearly allowance without paying any tax until you finally cash in the policy. Any income above the yearly allowance is free of basic-rate tax, but if you are a higher-rate taxpayer you will have to pay tax at the higher rate for the year in which you take the income. If you don't use the full five per cent allowed in any tax year, you can use it in future years.

Should a taxable gain arise because the person insured dies, you work out the gain by taking the cash-in value of the policy just before death, and deducting the total of premiums paid.

How the gain is taxed

Any gain is added to your income for the tax year in which the policy matures or is cashed in. There's no basic-rate tax to pay on the gain, only any higher-rate tax. So if you are liable to tax at the higher rate of 40 per cent, you'll pay tax at $40 - 25 = 15$ per cent.

If adding the gain to your income means that part of your income is pushed from the basic to the higher tax bracket, you should claim *top-slicing relief*. This spreads the gain over the years that the policy has run. Your tax bill is based on the average gain for each complete year that the policy has run, multiplied by the number of years. If the average gain added to your other taxable income doesn't take you into the higher tax bracket, there's no further tax to pay (but see p. 53 for a possible complication if you are aged 65 or over).

Example: how top-slicing relief can save tax

Arnold Archer bought a £20,000 single-premium bond in December 1987, and cashed it in for £30,000 in July 1992, making a gain of £10,000. He already has taxable income for 1992–3 (after deducting his allowances and outgoings) of £18,000. If his taxable income exceeds £23,700 (in the 1992–3 tax year) he would become liable to higher-rate tax.

Without top-slicing relief

rate of tax %	income on which you pay this rate £	tax on income £	gain on bond £	tax on gain £
20 (first £2,000)	2,000	400		
25 (£2,001 to £23,700)	16,000	4,000	5,700	1,425
40	nil	nil	4,300	1,720
total gain			10,000	
basic and higher-rate tax on gain				3,145
subtract tax at basic rate on gain (25% of £10,000)				2,500
higher-rate tax bill on gain				645

With top-slicing relief

rate of tax %	income on which you pay this rate £	tax on income £	average yearly gain on bond £	tax on gain £
20 (first £2,000)	2,000	400		
25 (£2,001 to £23,700)	16,000	4,000	2,500	625
40	nil	nil	nil	nil
subtract tax at basic rate on average yearly gain (25% of £2,500)				625
so tax bill on average yearly gain is				nil
higher-rate tax bill on gain (nil × 4)				nil

Arnold realises he can claim top-slicing relief. With this, the average yearly gain of £2,500 (the £10,000 total gain divided by the four complete years the bond ran for) is added to his other income for the year. His total tax bill on the gain is the tax on the average yearly gain multiplied by the number of complete years for which he held the bond.

Top-slicing relief means that Arnold doesn't have to pay any tax on the gain and so saves £645 – see the table opposite. The introduction of the lower rate tax band has no effect on the calculation.

Tax relief on your premiums
Premiums on qualifying policies taken out before 14 March 1984 get a subsidy of 12.5 per cent from the Revenue, irrespective of whether you pay tax or not.

You'll continue to get the subsidy unless you alter the policy in a way which increases the benefits payable. That could include taking up an option attached to the policy, e.g. to increase your premiums and therefore your amount of cover, to extend the term, or to convert the policy into another kind of policy. You won't lose the subsidy if the increased benefits are due to an increase that's built-in, e.g. if premiums and cover automatically increase by a fixed percentage. But there's a limit on premiums of £1,500 or one-sixth of your total income, whichever is greater, and if you pay premiums of more than this you won't get the subsidy on the excess.

Capital gains tax

You can make a capital gain (or loss) whenever you stop owning something, no matter how you came to own it. But you won't always be taxed on gains when you dispose of an asset. Anything you own (whether in the UK or not) counts as an asset, e.g. houses, jewellery and shares.

You dispose of an asset not only if you sell it, but also if you give it away, exchange it or lose it. You also dispose of an asset if it is destroyed or becomes worthless, if you sell rights to it (e.g. grant a lease), or if you get compensation for damage to it (e.g. insurance money) and don't spend it all on restoring the damage. But a transfer of an asset between a husband and wife doesn't count as a disposal (unless they are separated), nor does the transfer of an asset you leave when you die. Some types of gain are tax-free altogether (see p. 109) and the first slice of total chargeable gains made in the tax year is also tax-free. In the 1992–3 tax year, your tax-free slice is £5,800.

Working out the gain

To work out the gain (or loss) you make when you dispose of an asset, you have to:
■ take the *final value* of the asset when you dispose of it – its sale price (or market value at the time, if you gave it away or sold it for less than its full worth)
■ deduct its *initial value* when you got it – the price paid (or the market value at the time if you were given or inherited it). For assets acquired before 31 March 1982, you have a choice of initial value – see p. 114
■ deduct any *allowable expenses* you incurred in acquiring, improving or disposing of the asset, such as the costs of advertising, commission, legal fees and stamp duty.

If the answer is a plus figure you have made a *gain*, and if the answer is a negative figure you've made a *loss*. You can subtract losses from gains to reduce the amount liable to capital gains tax.

A capital gains tax bill can be reduced or eliminated by *indexation*. This increases the amount of your initial value and allowable expenses in line with the Retail Prices Index (RPI) and prevents you being taxed on gains caused purely by inflation. See p. 110 for how to calculate the allowance.

Gains after indexation are called *chargeable gains*, any losses after indexation are called *allowable losses*. You can deduct your losses from your gains, and any losses left over can be carried forward to future tax years and used to reduce your chargeable gains to the level of the tax-free slice.

Your chargeable gains *less* any allowable losses *less* your tax-free slice leave your *net taxable gains*. In our route map on pp. 112 to 113 we take you through the sums involved, with an example of how the figures could work out.

Capital gains tax applies only to gains made after 31 march 1982. See p. 114 for how to work out your taxable gain for assets acquired before that date.

How much tax?

Capital gains tax is charged at the same rate you'd pay if your gain was your top slice of income. So if you pay only lower-rate tax you'll pay capital gains tax at 20 per cent, if you pay basic-rate tax you'll pay capital gains tax at 25 per cent, and if you pay higher-rate tax you'll pay tax at 40 per cent (1992–3 tax rates). If you're in the 20 or 25 per cent tax bands, but your net taxable capital gains plus your taxable income (see p. 96) come to more than the amount of that tax band, you pay tax on the excess at 25 or 40 per cent, whichever is the next rate up. Suppose you had net taxable gains of £10,000 and taxable income of £15,000, i.e. £25,000. You would pay higher-rate tax on £25,000 minus the amount of the basic-rate tax band (£23,700 in 1992–3), i.e. on £1,300, and basic-rate tax on the rest.

You must tell the Revenue about any chargeable gains you have made in the 1992–3 tax year by 1 October 1993. Any tax due has to be paid either on 1 December after the end of the tax year in which the gains were made, or 30 days after the date on your assessment, whichever is later. If you disagree with an assessment, take it up with your tax office in writing within 30 days.

Tax-free gains

The gains you make on some assets are tax-free, but any losses you make on them can't be used to offset chargeable gains. The main tax-free gains are those on:

- your own home – see p. 148
- private cars
- British money (including post-1837 gold sovereigns and Britannia gold coins)
- foreign currency for personal and family expenditure (e.g. for a holiday abroad)
- British Government stocks
- National Savings Certificates, Save-As-You-Earn, National Savings Yearly Plan, Premium Bonds, Capital Bonds, Children's Bonus Bonds and FIRST Option Bonds
- personal belongings with a predictable life of less than 50 years when you got them (e.g. electronic equipment)
- personal belongings expected to last more than 50 years (e.g. antiques, jewellery and other moveable items) provided their value when you dispose of them is £6,000, or less. If their value is higher, your gain is taken to be the lower of *either* the actual gain *or* the final value, minus £6,000 multiplied by $5/3$. But if you dispose of something for less than £6,000 and make a loss, your loss is worked out as if you had actually got £6,000 for the item
- gifts to charities
- gifts to some *natural heritage bodies* (e.g. some museums and the National Trust)
- proceeds from life insurance policies, unless you bought the policy from a previous holder
- *qualifying* corporate bonds – those quoted on the Stock Exchange or traded in the Unlisted Securities Market, and acquired after 13 March 1984 (including building society Permanent Interest-Bearing Shares)

■ shares issued after 18 March 1986 under the Business Expansion Scheme (on their first disposal only)
■ disposals made after 1 July 1986 of futures and options in British Government stocks and qualifying corporate bonds. This doesn't apply to disposals of commodity futures, financial futures and traded options
■ shares, unit trusts and investment trusts held in a Personal Equity Plan
■ betting winnings.

Route map: how much capital gains tax?

The route map overleaf takes you through the steps involved in working out your capital gains tax. It's illustrated with an example, showing how much tax Matthew Parsons had to pay when he sold his holiday cottage (Matthew's main home is exempt from capital gains tax, so there'll be no tax to pay when he sells that).

He bought his cottage in April 1982 for £20,000, and sold it at the end of August 1992 for £50,000. He had buying costs of £700, spent £2,000 installing central heating in June 1983, and had selling costs of £1,200 – costs of £3,900 in all.

Matthew has made no other disposals for capital gains tax purposes, except for an unlucky share investment in 1983, when he made an allowable loss of £2,000. His taxable income is £25,000 so he is a higher-rate taxpayer.

Indexation

Indexation allows for inflation by linking the values of your assets and expenses to changes in the Retail Prices Index (RPI). It is worked out from the date you acquired the asset or incurred the expense until the date you dispose of it (but see p. 114 for assets owned on or before 31 March 1982). So if you incurred an expense in a different month from acquiring the asset, you need to work out the indexation allowance for that expense separately.

To work out your indexation allowance you first need to find out the RPI for:
■ A – the month of disposal
■ B – the month in which you acquired the asset, or incurred the expense (or March 1982 if later).

The RPI is announced every month by the Department of Employment and published in the Department's *Employment Gazette* (try your local library). See the box opposite for a list of RPI figures since March 1982: the latest published RPI figure is also available as a recorded message by phoning 0923 815281.

The calculation is as follows: take the RPI for the month of the disposal and subtract the RPI for the month when indexation begins. You then divide the result by the RPI for the month when indexation begins, and work out this figure (called the *indexation factor*) and round to the nearest third decimal place. Or, for the mathematically minded:

$$\frac{A - B}{B} = \text{indexation factor}$$

The indexation factor, multiplied by the initial value of the asset, or your allowable expense, gives you your indexation allowance.

So before Matthew starts the route map he gathers together the RPI figures he needs:

■ A – RPI for month of disposal; for August 1992 this figure was 138.9
■ B – RPI for month of indexation; April 1982 for the house and costs of buying it (81.04), June 1983 for the cost of installing central heading (84.84).

Retail Prices Index

Use these figures for working out your capital gains tax bill. The RPI was rebased (i.e. went back to 100) in January 1987. We've reworked the figures for previous months so that they are comparable with the rebased figures

	1982	1983	1984	1985	1986	1987	1988	1989	1990	1991	1992
Jan	[1]	82.61	86.84	91.20	96.25	100.0	103.0	111.0	119.5	130.2	135.6
Feb	[1]	82.97	87.20	91.94	96.60	100.4	103.7	111.8	120.2	130.9	136.3
Mar	79.44	83.12	87.48	92.80	96.73	100.6	104.1	112.3	121.4	131.4	136.7
Apr	81.04	84.28	88.64	94.78	97.67	101.8	105.8	114.3	125.1	133.1	138.8
May	81.62	84.64	88.97	95.21	97.85	101.9	106.2	115.0	126.2	133.5	139.3
June	81.85	84.84	89.20	95.41	97.79	101.9	106.6	115.4	126.7	134.1	139.3
July	81.88	85.30	89.10	95.23	97.52	101.8	106.7	115.5	126.8	133.8	138.8
Aug	81.90	85.68	89.94	95.49	97.82	102.1	107.9	115.8	128.1	134.1	138.9
Sept	81.85	86.06	90.11	95.44	98.30	102.4	108.4	116.6	129.3	134.6	139.4
Oct	82.26	86.36	90.67	95.59	98.45	102.9	109.5	117.5	130.3	135.1	–
Nov	82.66	86.67	90.95	95.92	99.29	103.4	110.0	118.5	130.0	135.6	–
Dec	82.51	86.69	90.87	96.05	99.62	103.3	110.3	118.8	129.9	135.7	–

[1] Indexation allowance only runs from March 1982

Will you have to pay capital gains tax?

Have you made a gain?   **Matthew's calculations**

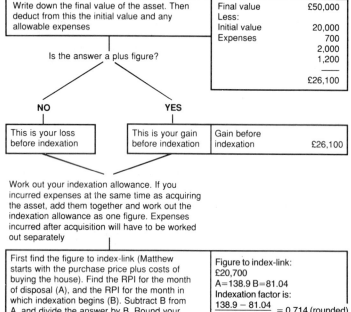

Write down the final value of the asset. Then deduct from this the initial value and any allowable expenses	Final value	£50,000
	Less:	
	Initial value	20,000
	Expenses	700
		2,000
Is the answer a plus figure?		1,200
		———
		£26,100

NO   **YES**

This is your loss before indexation	This is your gain before indexation	Gain before indexation	£26,100

Work out your indexation allowance. If you incurred expenses at the same time as acquiring the asset, add them together and work out the indexation allowance as one figure. Expenses incurred after acquisition will have to be worked out separately

First find the figure to index-link (Matthew starts with the purchase price plus costs of buying the house). Find the RPI for the month of disposal (A), and the RPI for the month in which indexation begins (B). Subtract B from A, and divide the answer by B. Round your answer to three decimal places. This gives your indexation factor. Multiply the initial value by the indexation factor	Figure to index-link: £20,700 A=138.9 B=81.04 Indexation factor is: $\frac{138.9 - 81.04}{81.04} = 0.714$ (rounded) Indexation allowance is: £20,700 × 0.714 = £14,779.8

Did you incur any expenses in a different month from the acquisition?

NO   **YES**

Work out indexation allowance for each expense (Matthew does this for his central heating installation costs)	Figure to index-link: £2,000 A=138.9 B=84.84 Indexation factor is: $\frac{138.9 - 84.84}{84.84} = 0.637$ (rounded) Indexation allowance is: £2,000 × 0.637 = £1,274

Work out your gain or loss after indexation

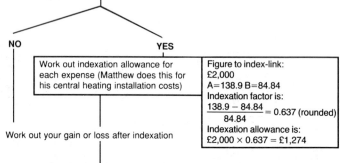

Write down your gain or loss before indexation. Subtract your total indexation allowances		£26,100.00
	Less:	£14,779.80
		£1,274.00
		———
	Gain after indexation	£10,046.20

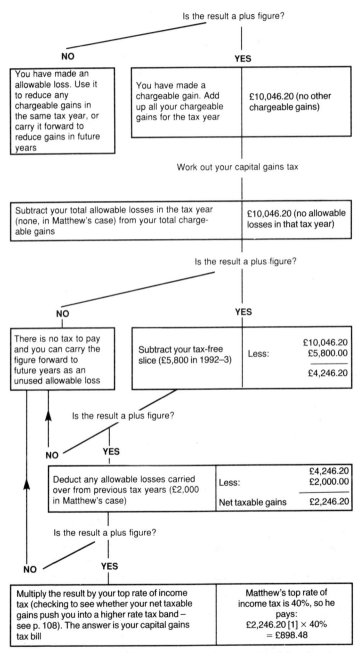

Is the result a plus figure?

NO — You have made an allowable loss. Use it to reduce any chargeable gains in the same tax year, or carry it forward to reduce gains in future years

YES —
| You have made a chargeable gain. Add up all your chargeable gains for the tax year | £10,046.20 (no other chargeable gains) |

Work out your capital gains tax

| Subtract your total allowable losses in the tax year (none, in Matthew's case) from your total chargeable gains | £10,046.20 (no allowable losses in that tax year) |

Is the result a plus figure?

NO — There is no tax to pay and you can carry the figure forward to future years as an unused allowable loss

YES —
| Subtract your tax-free slice (£5,800 in 1992–3) | Less: | £10,046.20 £5,800.00 |
| | | £4,246.20 |

Is the result a plus figure?

NO **YES**

| Deduct any allowable losses carried over from previous tax years (£2,000 in Matthew's case) | Less: | £4,246.20 £2,000.00 |
| | Net taxable gains | £2,246.20 |

Is the result a plus figure?

NO **YES**

| Multiply the result by your top rate of income tax (checking to see whether your net taxable gains push you into a higher rate tax band – see p. 108). The answer is your capital gains tax bill | Matthew's top rate of income tax is 40%, so he pays: £2,246.20 [1] × 40% = £898.48 |

[1] You are taxed on whole pounds only – Matthew would be taxed on the 20p only if another 'whole pound' were made when the gain is added to his taxable income.

Points to watch

Assets owned on 31 March 1982
Capital gains tax first came into force in 1965, but from 6 April 1988 the law was changed so that only gains made after 31 March 1982 are now taxable. This means that if you dispose of an asset you already owned on 31 March 1982, you can choose whether you want to be taxed under:

- the new rules: you use the market value in March 1982 as the initial value, ignoring the asset's value when you got it. But you can't deduct expenses incurred before 31 March 1982
- the old rules: you generally use the market value of the asset when you got it as the initial value and you can deduct expenses incurred before 31 March 1982. However, the indexation allowance for both initial value and pre-March 1982 expenses still runs only from 31 March 1982, so you always use the March 1982 RPI figure when working out the indexation factor.

You can elect for all your assets to come under the new rules – i.e. all your assets will be treated as though you acquired them on or after 31 March 1982, even if you acquired some or all of them before then. This election can't be revoked. You'll be no worse off making the election if all or most of your assets were worth more on 31 March 1982 than they were when you acquired them.

If you don't make the election, whichever rules produce the smaller gain or loss will be used. And if you make a gain under one set of rules, but a loss under the other, it will be treated as though you made neither a gain nor a loss. There'll be no tax to pay, but you won't be able to use the losses to reduce other gains.

Gifts
If you give an asset away, or part with it for less than its true worth, your gain is worked out as though you had sold it for its full market value. But there's a special form of relief available when you make certain types of gifts on which the tax is due, called *hold-over relief*. The effect of this relief is to avoid a capital gains tax bill at the time of the gift. Tax is put off until the recipient parts with the gift, although it could mean a higher tax bill then.

Gifts on which you can claim hold-over relief are:
- gifts of business assets including certain unquoted shares
- gifts of heritage property
- gifts to heritage maintenance funds

- gifts to political parties
- lifetime gifts on which you'd have to pay inheritance tax
  – see p. 116.

As the recipient, you will be counted as acquiring the asset at its market value when the giver first acquired it. You can count as your own the giver's allowable expenses, and benefit from the indexation rules up to the time of the gift, as well as any indexation allowance due from the time you receive the gift.

Both you and the giver must apply jointly for hold-over relief by contacting the Revenue.

There's no point in claiming this relief if the giver's gains for the year (including the gain on the gift) won't exceed £5,800. The giver won't save tax, and the recipient might pay more.

Shares and unit trusts

If you own one lot of the same type of shares in the same company (or units in a unit trust), and you acquired them all at the same time, they are treated in the same way for capital gains tax purposes as any other asset. However, if you bought shares or units of the same type, in the same company, at different times, the Revenue has special rules for deciding which ones you've sold when you come to sell them. These special rules decide which shares you've disposed of, how much they cost you, and what your indexation allowance is – see Inland Revenue leaflet *CGT13*, available from local tax offices and Tax Enquiry Centres. But the rules are very complicated and you may need to get professional advice to sort matters out.

You may get an *equalisation payment* from a unit trust – see p. 103. The payment itself is not taxable, but it must be subtracted from the purchase price of the units when working out your capital gain or loss. So if you bought some unit trusts for £1,000, and received an equalisation payment of £5, the purchase price of the units for tax purposes is £1,000 − £5 = £995.

With an *accumulation* unit trust, the income for your units is automatically reinvested for you. This affects the purchase price of your units for capital gains tax purposes. Working out the purchase price is complicated, and depends on exactly how the income is reinvested. Check with the unit trust company.

How to reduce your capital gains tax bill

- Be sure to deduct from a gain, or add to a loss, all your allowable expenses.

- If you have things which have increased in value and on which you will have to pay capital gains tax when you sell them, you'll avoid tax if you can keep the gains you make each year below £5,800. It's worth making use of this £5,800 allowance each year if you can – it can't be carried forward to the next year.
- If your losses for the year add up to more than your gains, you can carry forward the balance of the losses to set against gains you would have to pay tax on in later years. So keep a careful record of your losses.
- Husband and wife now each have their own tax-free band (£5,800 in 1992–3). You may be able to save tax by giving assets to your spouse to dispose of, so that they use their tax-free slice or previous losses – but it must be a real gift, with no strings attached.

Inheritance tax

Roughly speaking, inheritance tax is a tax on the value of what you leave when you die, and on some gifts you make during your lifetime. So it's not a tax that affects investments very much. Here we give a brief outline of the rules, and then look at life insurance policies, where a little care can keep inheritance tax at bay.

When does inheritance tax have to be paid?

There may be inheritance tax to pay:
- if you die within seven years of making certain gifts, known as *potentially exempt transfers (PETs)*. These include gifts to people other than your spouse (e.g. gifts from parents to children), and some gifts to trusts
- if you make a *chargeable* transfer. These are any gifts which are neither tax-free nor counted as PETs, and include gifts to companies and gifts to discretionary trusts
- if you die, and the value of all your possessions plus any PETs and chargeable transfers you've made in the seven years before death is more than a set amount – £150,000 in the 1992–3 tax year.

However, some gifts are tax-free (see opposite) and ignored by the Revenue. For example, gifts between a husband and wife are normally tax-free, no matter when they're made. So if you die worth £200,000, and leave the lot to your spouse, the value of your estate, for inheritance tax purposes, is nil. Of course, when your husband or wife dies, there may be tax to pay on his or her estate.

Most other gifts made by individuals will count as PETs and so will be taxable only if you die within seven years of making them. Chargeable transfers are the only type of gift on which you might have to pay tax during your lifetime.

Any gifts which aren't tax-free start to clock up on a running total. When your running total of chargeable transfers goes above a certain level – £150,000 in the 1992–3 tax year – tax is payable at half the rate of tax due on death. At present the tax rate on death is 40 per cent, so the rate would be 20 per cent. The tax-free level will be increased in line with inflation in the Budget each year unless Parliament decides otherwise.

Any gifts made more than seven years ago are knocked off your running total, so it can fall as well as rise.

Note that inheritance tax replaced capital transfer tax in March 1986, but gifts on your running total before then still count now.

Tax-free gifts

Some gifts are tax-free only if made during your lifetime. Others are tax-free whenever they are made. Gifts that are tax-free during your lifetime include:

■ gifts which are part of your normal expenditure out of income. These must be regular, e.g. covenant payments, and not reduce your standard of living
■ gifts to people getting married, with a maximum of £5,000 from each parent of the couple, £2,500 from a grandparent and £1,000 from anybody else
■ maintenance payments to ex-husbands or wives
■ gifts of reasonable amounts needed to support a dependent relative
■ gifts for the education, maintenance or training of your children if they are still in full-time education or training, or not more than 18 years of age
■ small gifts of up to £250 to each recipient each year
■ your annual exemption – gifts of up to £3,000 a year. This exemption is in addition to all the tax-free gifts above except that you can't give £3,000 plus £250 (the 'small gifts' exemption) to the same person. If you don't use the full £3,000 in one year you can carry what's left forward for up to one year (i.e. up to £6,000 in the second year), but you must use up the current year's exemption first.

Gifts which are tax-free whenever they are made include:

- gifts between husband and wife (provided the recipient is domiciled in the UK)
- gifts to UK-established charities
- gifts to political parties
- gifts to most museums and art galleries, to universities, the National Trust, local authorities and similar bodies
- gifts of property and possessions of outstanding national interest made to various non-profit-making bodies
- broadly speaking, gifts of shares to a trust which will hold more than half of a company's ordinary shares and which was set up for the employees' benefit, provided the trustees have voting control.

Inheritance tax on life insurance

Regular premium life insurance policies are an excellent way of giving chunks of tax-free capital to your dependants, or indeed to anyone.

The premiums will count as a gift, but there shouldn't be any inheritance tax to pay on them, since they'll normally be in one of the tax-free categories above.

What to avoid

Try to make sure that the proceeds of your policies don't count as part of your estate. If they do, they'll be added on the rest of what you leave, and your inheritance tax bill could rise.

You can avoid this by getting the policy written in trust so that the proceeds go to someone else. If a policy on your life is for the benefit of your wife (or husband) or children, the *Married Women's Property Act* provides a simple way of doing this. Otherwise, you'll need to get a declaration of trust written on the policy. Ask the insurance company what to do. Alternatively, you could give away the policy after taking it out; but this could count as a gift for inheritance tax purposes.

Types of policy

- **endowment policy** – see p. 309
what it is: a policy which pays out a lump sum on a fixed date or when you die, if this is earlier.
useful for: people who want to give tax-free capital away in their lifetime.
- **whole life insurance** – see p. 321
what it is: a policy which pays out on your death.
useful for: paying the inheritance tax bill when you die. A husband and wife who are going to leave everything to each

other could take out a last survivor or joint life and last survivor policy, which pays out on the second death (i.e. when the inheritance tax bill will arrive). The premiums are lower than for a policy on a single life. A joint life first death policy is useful for paying any tax bill on the first death.

■ **term insurance** – see p. 313

what it is: a policy which pays out only if you die before the policy ends (within three years, or ten years, say). If you survive, it pays nothing.

useful for: someone who will be faced with a large inheritance tax bill only if death occurs within a certain time. For example, someone who has received a PET may be caught by a tax bill if the giver dies within seven years.

8

A BIRD'S-EYE VIEW

Before you can put your investment strategy into effect you'll have to get to grips with the nitty-gritty of what different investments offer and what their particular advantages and disadvantages are.

In this chapter we give you a summary of the main types of investment open to you, starting on p. 124. The most important points about each investment are picked out in the table (see below for why each row is important).

In the later chapters of the book you'll find much fuller details of each type of investment.

The rows in the table

Regular saving or lump sum?
Some investments are very flexible. The minimum amount you can invest is fairly low, so they can be used as homes for lump sums, regular savings and odd bits of spare cash.

But some investments are open only to people who have a fair-sized lump sum of money to invest, and others only to people who want to save a regular amount each month or year, say. Of course, if you've a lump sum, you can invest it bit by bit on a regular basis, if you like.

Minimum investment
This row tells you the minimum sensible amount you can invest. This isn't necessarily the same thing as the minimum amount you're *allowed* to invest. For example, you can invest as little as you like in shares, but the commission you have to pay means that an investment of less than £1,000 to £1,500 or so may not be worthwhile.

Does it pay a regular income?
Some investments pay income direct to you at regular

intervals. With others, the income is added to the value of what you first invested.

Of course, with some investments which don't pay an income out to you, such as single-premium bonds and National Savings Certificates, you may still be able to give yourself a regular income by cashing part of your investment at regular intervals. Indeed, with some investments (such as single-premium bonds) there are often standard schemes to allow you to do this.

With some investments which pay out a regular income, the income is fixed when you take out the investment, e.g. guaranteed income bonds. With other investments, such as deposit accounts offered by banks and building societies, the income can vary after you've invested your money.

If you need to be sure of getting a regular number of £££ from your investment each year, go for one that pays out a fixed income, but see *Keeping up with inflation* on p. 17.

Note that if you go for a fixed income, you may regret your decision if interest rates in general rise; investments with interest rates which vary may turn out to have been better bets. On the other hand, if interest rates in general fall, you will feel pleased with yourself for putting your money in a fixed income investment.

How long is the investment meant to be for?
This row tells you how long you should expect to have to leave your money invested in order to get the best return.

Can you get your money back quickly?
In some cases, you can't. So don't put your money in one of these investments unless you're certain you'll be able to leave it there for the agreed period.

With other investments, you may be able to cash in early but not get back (or not be sure of getting back) what you paid in. So, if you want a certain amount of money at a certain time, e.g. to go on holiday in two years' time, you'd be wise to steer clear of these investments too.

Does the value of your capital fluctuate?
Investments can be divided into two types:
■ the value of the capital you invest stays the same (but see *Keeping up with inflation* on p. 17)
■ the value may fluctuate. Unit trusts, single-premium bonds and property are examples of investments where the value of the capital invested will fluctuate. With investments like these, you stand a chance of making a capital gain, but also run the risk of losing some of your money.

And because the value of the capital fluctuates, the success of your investment depends very much on *when* you invest and *when* you cash in your investment. For more about how to reduce the risk of doing very badly see p. 19.

Points about tax
This row picks out particular tax points for the various investments. More details on tax are given in Chapter 7, and in the chapters dealing with each investment.

   For example, some investments, where the return is tax-free, look more attractive if you're a higher-rate taxpayer. This also applies to investments where you get tax relief on the payments you make, e.g. contributions to an employer's pension scheme or payments to a personal pension plan.

Where can you get the investment?
This row tells you where to go to put your money in these investments.

Other comments
This gives snippets of information about how some of the investments work, who might find it worthwhile to consider or to avoid a particular investment, and so on.

type of investment (and where to find more details)	Alternative investments (e.g. stamps, antique furniture, diamonds, gold . . .) *Chapter 25, p. 393*	Annuities *Chapter 22, p. 349*
regular saving or lump sum?	lump sum	lump sum
minimum investment (but see p. 121)	varies	depends on age and income required
does it pay a regular income?	no – in fact you have to pay for insurance etc	yes, normally arranged at time you buy the annuity. The older you are at that time, the higher the income
how long is investment meant to be for?	in the main, long-term investment	until you die
can you get your money back quickly?	as quickly as you can find a buyer. But may get back less than you invested	you can't – once you've made investment you can't cash it in
does value of capital fluctuate?	yes	not applicable – can't get capital back
points about tax	no capital gains tax unless value of item at time of disposal more than £6,000 (post-1837 UK gold sovereigns and Britannia coins are free of capital gains tax). If you count as a trader, you may have to pay income tax	you get interest and return of part of capital. Only interest taxable – normally paid after deduction of basic-rate tax. With annuities you *have* to buy, e.g. as part of a personal pension – it's *all* taxed as income
where can you get investment?	auctions, dealers, other collectors, sometimes investment companies too	life insurance company or adviser
other comments	needs expert knowledge. Watch out for dealer's mark-up	only worth considering for older people (around 70, say). Man gets higher income than woman of same age

type of investment (and where to find more details)	Banks and building societies *Chapter 10, p. 160* – **instant access accounts**	Banks and building societies *Chapter 10, p. 159* – **term and notice accounts**
regular saving or lump sum?	either	either
minimum investment (but see p. 121)	often £1	varies – £500 to £5,000 (or more)
does it pay a regular income?	no – but interest is reinvested and can be withdrawn. Interest varies	yes – if you choose. Interest varies on notice and some term accounts
how long is investment meant to be for?	any period: suitable for emergency funds and a temporary home for other funds (unless interest rate is high)	varies from a few days to a few years
can you get your money back quickly?	in practice, can cash in at any time (but sometimes only balance over a set amount) and you may lose some interest	not until end of agreed term or notice period, or after a period (e.g. one or three months notice) or immediately, but you'll lose some interest
does value of capital fluctuate?	no	no
points about tax	basic-rate tax normally deducted from interest before you get it. Non-taxpayers can get interest paid gross, higher-rate taxpayers will have extra tax to pay	see *instant access accounts*
where can you get investment?	banks, building societies, finance companies	see *instant access accounts*
other comments	often, the more you invest, the higher the interest rate	normally pays higher interest rate than instant access accounts. May get higher interest the more you invest. Some pay a monthly income

type of investment (and where to find more details)	Banks and building societies Chapter 10, p. 161 – savings accounts	Banks and building societies Chapter 10, p. 162 – Save-As-You-Earn (SAYE)
regular saving or lump sum?	regular saving	regular saving
minimum investment (but see p. 121)	varies – could be as low as £1 a month	£1 a month (maximum £20 a month)
does it pay a regular income?	no – interest is reinvested	no
how long is investment meant to be for?	normally at least one year to get higher interest	5 or 7 years
can you get your money back quickly?	may be able to cash small amounts once or twice a year	can withdraw at any time (but if cashed in before 5 years are up, return is lower). No interest at all on withdrawals in first year
does value of capital fluctuate?	no	no
points about tax	see *instant access accounts*	return tax-free
where can you get investment?	see *instant access accounts*	building society or bank
other comments	not common nowadays	at end of 5 years you get bonus of extra monthly payments – and a further bonus if you invest for another 2 years. Conditions are identical whichever society you go to, but not many societies offer them. May be hard to find

type of investment (and where to find more details)	**Building societies** *Chapter 10, p. 165* **– Permanent Interest-Bearing Shares (PIBS)**	**Banks and building societies** *Chapter 10, p. 163* **– Tax Exempt Special Savings Accounts (TESSAs)**
regular saving or lump sum?	lump sum	either
minimum investment (but see p. 121)	varies from £1,000 to £50,000	varies (maximum £9,000 over 5 years)
does it pay a regular income?	yes – interest fixed at the time you buy	no, but interest is reinvested and can be withdrawn (although withdrawals over a certain amount will lose you the tax concessions)
how long is investment meant to be for?	no set period	5 years
can you get your money back quickly?	in theory, yes, but you may get back less than you invested	an account must last for 5 years to get the tax concessions
does value of capital fluctuate?	yes	no
points about tax	paid after deduction – basic rate tax – *accrued income* scheme applies, see p. 104. Free of capital gains tax	return tax-free
where can you get investment?	building society	see *instant access accounts*
other comments	relatively new and available from only the largest societies	watch out for penalties on transferring to another bank or building society

type of investment (and where to find more details)	British Government Stocks *Chapter 17, p. 291* – conventional stocks	British Government Stocks *Chapter 17, p. 299* – index-linked stocks
regular saving or lump sum?	lump sum	see *conventional stocks*
minimum investment (but see p. 121)	none if bought on National Savings Stock Register; otherwise £1,000 sensible minimum	see *conventional stock*
does it pay a regular income?	yes – income fixed at the time you buy the stock (except with a few stocks)	yes – and income increases in line with Retail Prices Index
how long is investment meant to be for?	until stock due to be redeemed (paid back) by government – but some stocks can also be short-term speculation	see *conventional stocks*
can you get your money back quickly?	can sell stock at any time. Can take a day or two to get money if sold through stockbroker, a week or so through National Savings Stock Register	see *conventional stocks*
does value of capital fluctuate?	yes – but if you hold stock until redemption, you know for certain what you'll get back	yes – but at redemption, government pays back *nominal value* (see p. 292) increased in line with Retail Prices Index since time of issue
points about tax	interest is taxable – paid without deduction of tax if bought through National Savings Stock Register, normally after deduction of basic-rate tax if bought through stockbroker. Free of capital gains tax	see *conventional stocks*
where can you get investment?	stockbroker, post office, high street bank or other agent, e.g. accountant	see *conventional stocks*
other comments	best stock for you depends to large extent on rate of tax you pay. Get advice on which stock to choose, e.g. from stockbroker or bank. Buying and selling costs less for small investments if made through National Savings Stock Register	see *conventional stocks*

type of investment (and where to find more details)	**Commodities** *Chapter 23, p. 359*	**Endowment policies (with-profits)** *Chapter 19, p. 309*
regular saving or lump sum?	lump sum	regular saving
minimum investment (but see p. 121)	several thousand £££ for direct investment; £3,000 say, for commodity fund or trust	£20 a month, say
does it pay a regular income?	no, with direct investment. Some funds and trusts pay an income – with others you can get income by cashing units	no
how long is investment meant to be for?	long-term investment or short-term speculation	10 years or more – period usually agreed at outset
can you get your money back quickly?	if direct investment, can sell at any time. With fund or trust, a few days or a month	can surrender policy at any time but what you get back is often at discretion of company (and in first year or two may get little or nothing)
does value of capital fluctuate?	yes	get at least a guaranteed amount at end of policy (or if you die), usually bonuses too
points about tax	gain may be taxed as income or as capital gain, depending on circumstances – see *Chapter 23*	because insurance fund pays tax, return is tax-free as long as you pay tax at no more than the basic rate – always tax-free if you keep policy going for at least 10 years or three-quarters of its term, whichever is less
where can you get investment?	commodity broker; direct from fund or trust or through intermediary	life insurance company or insurance adviser
other comments	investing directly in commodities not sensible for most people. Very risky – consider commodity fund or unit trust instead. For legal and tax reasons, funds may be based offshore – Isle of Man or Channel Islands, say	can be used as a way of repaying a mortgage

type of investment (and where to find more details)	Home *Chapter 9, p. 143*	Home income schemes *Chapter 22, p. 355*
regular saving or lump sum?	lump sum	lump sum (raised from mortgaging your home)
minimum investment (but see p. 121)	often at least 10 per cent of price of home	normally £15,000
does it pay a regular income?	no (unless you let it out)	yes – income (from an annuity) arranged at the time you take out the scheme (amount depends on age and sex)
how long is investment meant to be for?	any period	until you die
can you get your money back quickly?	may take several months or longer to sell your home – unless you can raise a loan on it	you can't get your money back at all
does value of capital fluctuate?	yes	with schemes based on loans, you benefit from increases in value of home. With schemes where you sell part or all of your home to the company ('reversions'), you don't
points about tax	get tax relief at the basic rate on interest on up to £30,000 of loans to buy your only or main home – and capital gain is normally tax-free	you get basic rate tax relief on interest on up to £30,000 to buy a scheme. Part of income tax-free
where can you get investment?	estate agent, newspaper ads, *For sale* signs	life insurance company, insurance adviser, building society
other comments	a very poor *short-term* investment recently, although a good *long-term* investment in the past	only worth considering for people over 70

type of investment (and where to find more details)	Guaranteed income and growth bonds *Chapter 21, p. 345*	Investment trusts *Chapter 16, p. 283*
regular saving or lump sum?	lump sum	either
minimum investment (but see p. 121)	£1,000 to £10,000 but may be more particularly for income bonds	£1,000 to £1,500, say
does it pay a regular income?	income bonds – yes growth bonds – no	yes – most companies pay dividends. These can vary
how long is investment meant to be for?	fixed period, varying from 1 to 10 years	long-term investment or short-term speculation
can you get your money back quickly?	with some companies, at the end of agreed period only. With others, can cash in early, but return up to company	can sell and get money back in 2 to 4 weeks, but may get less than you invested
does value of capital fluctuate?	no	yes
points about tax	tax treatment depends on how bonds work – can work in one of several ways. Check with company before investing	dividends are taxable, paid after deduction of basic-rate tax. Liable for capital gains tax on any gain
where can you get investment?	life insurance company or insurance adviser	stockbroker, bank or other agent, e.g. accountant; savings schemes direct from investment trust company
other comments	return may be lower if you or your spouse is over 65 when you cash bond in (see p. 347), because tax bill could rise	you buy shares in an investment trust company – a company whose sole business is investing in other companies' shares

type of investment (and where to find more details)	National Savings investments *Chapter 11, p. 177* – Ordinary accounts	National Savings investments *Chapter 11, p. 178* – Investment accounts
regular saving or lump sum?	either	either
minimum investment (but see p. 121)	£5 (maximum £10,000), though you get twice the normal rate of interest if you invest £500 or more	£5 (maximum £25,000)
does it pay a regular income?	no – but interest can be withdrawn. Interest can vary	no – but interest can be withdrawn. Interest can vary
how long is investment meant to be for?	for emergency funds and a temporary home for other funds	any period over a month
can you get your money back quickly?	£250 at once (about a week to withdraw all money)	1 month
does value of capital fluctuate?	no	no
points about tax	first £70 interest each year is tax-free – all interest paid without deduction of tax	all interest is taxable – paid without deduction of tax
where you can get investment?	post office	post office
other comments	interest paid only for complete calendar months money is invested	worth considering if you don't pay tax

type of investment (and where to find more details)	National Savings investments Chapter 11, p. 170 – National Savings Certificates (40th issue)	National Savings investments Chapter 11, p. 173 – index-linked National Savings Certificates (6th issue)
regular saving or lump sum?	either	either
minimum investment (but see p. 121)	£100 (maximum £5,000)	£100 (maximum £5,000)
does it pay a regular income?	no – but can be cashed in to provide income	no – but can cash certificates to get an income
how long is investment meant to be for?	for best return, 5 years	initially for 5 years (get overall return of at least 3.25% plus inflation at end of 5 years)
can you get your money back quickly?	within 8 working days (but return lower if cashed in within first 5 years)	within 8 working days (but certificates not index-linked if cashed in before held for 12 months)
does value of capital fluctuate?	no	yes – but won't get back less than invested
points about tax	return is tax-free	return is tax-free
where you can get investment?	post office, high street bank	post office, high street bank
other comments	can also reinvest up to £10,000 of 'matured' Certificates (i.e. over 5 years old)	value goes up in line with Retail Prices Index

type of investment (and where to find more details)	National Savings investments *Chapter 11, p. 180* – Capital Bond (Series G)	National Savings investments *Chapter 11, p. 185* – Children's Bonus Bonds
regular saving or lump sum?	lump sum	lump sum
minimum investment (but see p. 121)	£100 (maximum £100,000)	£25 (maximum £1,000)
does it pay a regular income?	no	no
how long is investment meant to be for?	5 years	5 years
can you get your money back quickly?	allow 8 working days. But you lose interest if you cash in before 5 years are up (no interest at all if you cash in during year 1)	1 month, but for best return need to keep for 5 years
does value of capital fluctuate?	no	no
points about tax	no tax deducted for non-taxpayers. Interest added yearly, but you can't get it until bond is repaid. If you're a taxpayer, you'll pay tax each year on the interest, at your highest rate	return is tax-free
where can you get investment?	post office	post office
other comments	rate of interest rises on yearly scale. Goof for non-taxpayers	can be bought for any child under 16 by anybody aged 16 or over. Can be held until child is 21

type of investment (and where to find more details)	National Savings investments Chapter 11, p. 179 – National Savings Income Bonds	National Savings investments Chapter 11, p. 182 – National Savings Yearly Plan
regular saving or lump sum?	lump sum	regular saving
minimum investment (but see p. 121)	£2,000 (maximum £50,000)	£20 a month (maximum £400 a month)
does it pay a regular income?	yes – each month	no
how long is investment meant to be for?	any period over a year. Return lower if cashed in first year	for best return, 5 years
can you get your money back quickly?	3 months	around a couple of weeks (but no interest on withdrawals in first year)
does value of capital fluctuate?	no	no
points about tax	all interest is taxable – paid without deduction of tax	return is tax-free
where can you get investment?	post office, high street bank	post office, high street bank
other comments		

type of investment (and where to find more details)	National Savings Investments *Chapter 11, p. 184* **National Savings FIRST Option Bond**	Pension schemes – employers' schemes *Chapter 12, p. 200*
regular saving or lump sum?	lump sum	regular saving
minimum investment (but see p. 121)	£1,000 (maximum £250,000)	some schemes are non-contributory (i.e. employee pays nothing); with others you pay a fixed % of your earnings
does it pay a regular income?	no	yes – from time you retire. Can often choose to have lump sum on retirement instead of part of pension
how long is investment meant to be for?	1 year at a time	from time you join scheme until you retire or leave job (income carries on for life)
can you get your money back quickly?	around a couple of weeks (but no interest on withdrawals before end of first year, and low interest on withdrawals part-way through a year after that)	contributions must normally stay invested until the scheme's pension age (unless you leave job within 2 years of joining scheme)
does value of capital fluctuate?	no	depends on scheme
points about tax	interest is taxable but paid without deduction of tax	you get tax relief on payments. Lump sum taken instead of part of pension is tax-free. Actual pension is taxable
where can you get investment?	post office	employer
other comments	withdrawn in November 1992, though could be reintroduced	you can choose to make *additional voluntary contributions* (see p. 203)

type of investment (and where to find more details)	Pension schemes – personal pension plans *Chapter 13, p. 213*	Pension schemes – state schemes *Chapter 12, p. 189*
regular saving or lump sum?	either	regular saving (through National Insurance contributions)
minimum investment (but see p. 121)	£10 to £50 a month or £250 to £1,000 for lump sum plans	depends on what you earn and whether you are employed or self-employed
does it pay a regular income?	yes – normally from any age between 50 and 75. Can choose to have lump sum on retirement instead of part of pension	yes, from state pension age (later if you choose)
how long is investment meant to be for?	from time you begin payments until income starts (income carries on for life)	you normally make payments until state pension age (income carries on for life)
can you get your money back quickly?	you can't cash investment in, but with some schemes you can get a loan (see p. 221)	you can't cash investment in
does value of capital fluctuate?	with some schemes, yes	not applicable – can't get capital back
points about tax	get tax relief on payments (see p. 235). Lump sum taken instead of part of pension is tax-free. Actual pension is taxable	don't get tax relief on payments. Pension taxed as earnings, currently paid without deduction of tax
where can you get investment?	bank, building society, life insurance company, unit trust company, investment adviser	payments made through employer, or through Inland Revenue if self-employed
other comments	better the younger you are, as longer time for investment to grow	if you're earning, normally no way you can opt out of the state scheme altogether, but you may be able to contract out of SERPS (see p. 191)

type of investment (and where to find more details)	Personal Equity Plans (PEPs) *Chapter 14, p. 262*	Premium bonds *Chapter 11, p. 185*
regular saving or lump sum?	either	either
minimum investment (but see p. 121)	minimum varies; maximum £6,000 (plus £3,000 in a single company PEP)	£10 for people under 16, otherwise £100 (maximum £10,000)
does it pay a regular income?	varies – it depends on the plan	no – but might win prizes
how long is investment meant to be for?	in the main, long-term investment, otherwise costs may outweigh gains	any period – but can't win prize until bond held for 3 months
can you get your money back quickly?	yes, but you may make a loss	around a couple of weeks
does value of capital fluctuate?	yes	no
points about tax	no income tax or capital gains tax payable on the return from PEPs	prizes are tax-free
where can you get investment?	stockbroker, bank, building society, unit trust company, investment trust company or other agent, e.g. accountant	post office, high street bank
other comments	charges can be high	prizes worked out to give return of 6½% on all bonds held for 3 months or more.

type of investment (and where to find more details)	Shares *Chapter 14, p. 241*	Single-premium investment bonds *Chapter 20, p. 328*
regular saving or lump sum?	lump sum	lump sum
minimum investment (but see p. 121)	£1,000 to £1,500, say, in each company	varies – but often £1,000
does it pay a regular income?	yes – most companies pay dividends. Amounts can vary	not usually – but most com- panies have schemes which let you cash in part of investment (can cash up to 5% a year without paying tax at the time)
how long is investment meant to be for?	in the main, long-term investment. But can also be short-term speculation	in the main, long-term investment
can you get your money back quickly?	you can sell shares and get money in 2 to 4 weeks – but you may get less than you invested	varies – can be straight away, sometimes up to a week or month. May get back less than invested
does value of capital fluctuate?	yes	yes
points about tax	dividends are taxable – paid after deduction of basic-rate tax. Liable for capital gains tax on any gain	when you cash in bond, may have to pay tax on the gain you've made (including any amounts you got earlier on, not taxed at the time) if you pay tax at the higher rate. Fund pays capital gains tax on gains
where can you get investment?	stockbroker, bank or other agent, e.g. accountant	life insurance company or insurance adviser
other comments	buying shares of just one or two companies is very risky (see p. 243)	value of investment depends on performance of fund of investments, e.g. property fund. Limited appeal except to higher- rate taxpayers or people who want to switch funds frequently

type of investment (and where to find more details)	Unit-linked regular premium plans *Chapter 20, p. 325*	Unit trusts *Chapter 15, p. 265*
regular saving or lump sum?	regular saving	either
minimum investment *(but see p. 121)*	varies – £15 to £50 a month	for lump sum, often £250 to £1,500; for regular saving £20 to £50 a month
does it pay a regular income?	normally no	yes, with many trusts – amount can vary
how long is investment meant to be for?	at least 10 years	in the main, long-term investment. But can also be short-term speculation
can you get your money back quickly?	can cash at any time but may get back less than you invested (and in first year or two, may get little or nothing)	varies between trusts – can normally sell each day (but may get back less than you invested)
does value of capital fluctuate?	yes	yes
points about tax	return tax-free as long as you pay tax at no more than the basic rate – always tax-free if you keep policy going for at least 10 years, or three-quarters of its term, whichever is less. Fund pays capital gains tax on gains	income is taxable – paid after deduction of basic-rate tax. Liable for capital gains on any gain
where can you get investment?	life insurance company or insurance adviser	direct from unit trust company or via insurance adviser, stockbroker, bank
other comments	money invested in unit trust or insurance company fund (as for *single-premium investment bonds*). Limited appeal except to higher-rate taxpayers or people who want to switch funds frequently	value of investment depends on performance of fund of investments selected

Where to Put Your Money First

9

YOUR HOME

Your home is first and foremost a place to live in, but you can look upon it as probably the largest single investment you'll ever make.

The diagram on p. 144 shows that house prices have, on average, increased 16 times since 1965. On the diagram, we've also shown the Retail Prices Index (RPI), which measures increases in prices in general. You can see that for most of the period, house prices increased more quickly than the RPI. This means that the real value of a home in terms of the buying-power of what it's worth has, on average, gone up over this period. Of course, part of the increase in house prices is due to better standards of housing. For example, more houses now have central heating than in 1965, and many dilapidated properties have been brought up to scratch. And there have been times, particularly after boom periods, when house price increases haven't matched inflation; this happened in 1980 and 1981. It has also happened since the end of the last boom in 1988. If you bought a home at the height of the boom, in the summer of 1988, you may even make a loss if you sell now (January 1993). It seems likely that property prices will eventually pick up, though no one can say for sure that property will be as good an investment in the future as it has been in the past. And no one can say for sure *when* prices will start to take off again, though there is no shortage of speculation in the press.

Of course, not all property values have gone up by the amounts shown in the diagram. The values of some types of home and in some areas will have risen more than average, others less. The map on p. 146 shows how prices varied in the UK in the second quarter of 1992, and the rate at which they'd gone up over the previous five years. For each region, we've shown prices for three different types of property: detached, semi-detached and terraced.

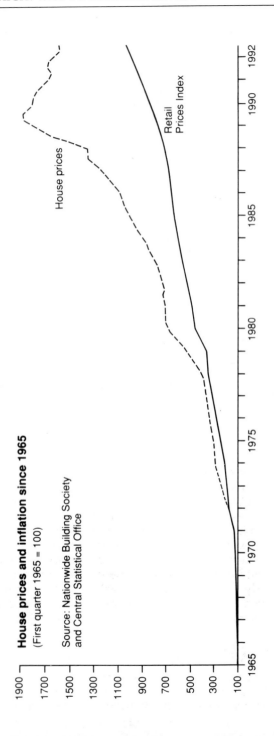

House prices and inflation since 1965

(First quarter 1965 = 100)

Source: Nationwide Building Society
and Central Statistical Office

House prices

Retail
Prices Index

Within the regions prices vary considerably, because of factors like size, number of rooms, how big the garden is and whether there's a garage, central heating and so on. But other things, like the age of the house and its condition, architectural style, the area it's in, may also affect prices and the rate at which they change.

For example, in rural areas houses in a pretty village may become expensive because people increasingly want to buy them as second homes, or as first homes if, say, they are near an improved railway service making commuting easier. But property in a less attractive village a few miles away may be cheaper than average for the region because there are few jobs for the locals and people want to move away.

Local redevelopment or major transport schemes such as the Channel Tunnel can have a significant impact on prices. And if you have to sell your home quickly (because your job moves, say) you may also have to accept a cut in price.

A house as an investment

For how investing in a house has compared with other investments, see the diagram on pp. 20 and 21. This shows that over the long-term houses have on average proved a worthwhile investment, when compared with conventional homes for your money, but over the past five and ten years have failed to match inflation. Bear in mind that, over the periods we've looked at, houses have improved in quality, which artificially increases the return. And, of course, the gain on a house is not easy to get at. You may have to sell and rent, or trade down to see your money.

With a house, you have to pay various running costs, e.g. decorating, repairs, poll tax, council tax and so on. If you weren't buying your own home, but renting one instead, you would be paying some of these costs anyway (perhaps indirectly in your rent). But with a second home, these running costs are additional ones (unless you can rent the home out to cover them).

A hedge against inflation?

There is a traditional belief that investing in property offers protection against the ravages of inflation, as property tends to hold its value in real terms. The diagram opposite

House prices in the UK

Average house prices in second quarter 1992 and average regional yearly rates of increase since first quarter 1987 [1].

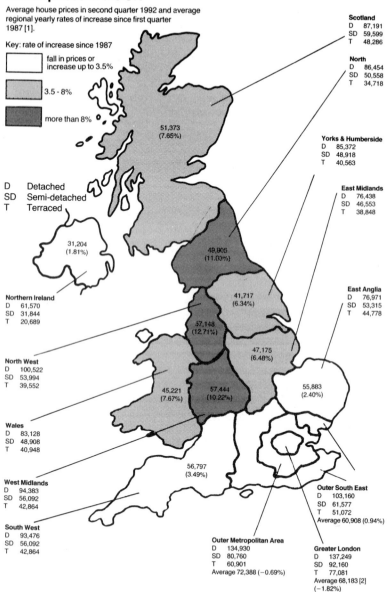

Key: rate of increase since 1987

	fall in prices or increase up to 3.5%
	3.5 - 8%
	more than 8%

D Detached
SD Semi-detached
T Terraced

Scotland
D 87,191
SD 59,599
T 48,286

North
D 86,454
SD 50,558
T 34,718

Yorks & Humberside
D 85,372
SD 48,918
T 40,563

East Midlands
D 76,438
SD 46,553
T 38,848

East Anglia
D 76,971
SD 53,315
T 44,778

Northern Ireland
D 61,570
SD 31,844
T 20,689

North West
D 100,522
SD 53,994
T 39,552

Wales
D 83,128
SD 48,908
T 40,948

West Midlands
D 94,383
SD 56,092
T 42,864

South West
D 93,476
SD 56,092
T 42,864

Outer South East
D 103,160
SD 61,577
T 51,072
Average 60,908 (0.94%)

Outer Metropolitan Area
D 134,930
SD 80,760
T 60,901
Average 72,388 (−0.69%)

Greater London
D 137,249
SD 92,160
T 77,081
Average 68,183 [2]
(−1.82%)

51,373 (7.65%)

31,204 (1.81%)

49,905 (11.03%)

41,717 (6.34%)

57,148 (12.71%)

47,175 (6.48%)

45,221 (7.67%)

57,444 (10.22%)

55,883 (2.40%)

56,797 (3.49%)

[1] Based on information from Nationwide Building Society for houses on which mortgages have been approved.

[2] The average is low because of the large number of flats in London.

supports this belief. Of course, when you invest, where you invest and when you sell are crucially important. If, for example, you'd bought a house in the South-East in 1988 (when prices were booming) and sold again in 1990 or later, you could probably have *lost* money – even before allowing for inflation, or even the costs of buying and selling.

What makes property prices change?

House prices are influenced by several factors, both in the long-term and the short-term.

Long-term factors include:
- people's earnings, particularly in terms of buying-power
- the availability of homes to buy
- trading-up (i.e. the tendency for owner-occupiers to move on to more expensive homes).

In the short-term, relatively sudden increases in earnings (compared with prices in general) and in the numbers of first-time buyers, temporary shortages of houses to buy (e.g. not enough new houses being built), and speculation about house prices can fuel short, sharp booms of perhaps a few years' duration. On the other hand, lack of confidence in the economy as a whole – and likely employment prospects in particular – can depress house prices. And the availability (or otherwise) of loan finance (mortgages from building societies, banks, etc.) has played a part.

Other factors help to make housing a more attractive investment. These include:
- tax relief on mortgage interest – see below
- exemption from capital gains tax on your only or main home – see p. 148
- the effects of *gearing* – see p. 149.

Tax relief on mortgage interest

In general, you can get tax relief on the interest you pay on up to £30,000 of loans to buy your only or main home (normally the one you live in most of the time).

To get tax relief on a loan you must, in general, be buying an interest in the home, e.g. the whole of it, a half share, or buying out someone else. The home must be in the UK or Eire. If you pay your mortgage under the MIRAS (Mortgage Interest Relief At Source) scheme, you get the tax relief even if you're a non-taxpayer.

What tax relief is worth

Tax relief reduces the amount you have to pay for your mortgage by 25p in each £ (in the 1992–3 tax year). This means that borrowing can be much cheaper than it seems at first sight. A mortgage rate of, say, 10 per cent costs in effect only three-quarters of that: 7.5 per cent.

However, the tax benefits have been reduced: the £30,000 limit is gradually being eroded by inflation and from 6 April 1991 higher-rate taxpayers have no longer had extra tax relief. Note that there are some loans you can't get relief on even if they are used for buying your only or main home. These include overdrafts and borrowing on credit cards.

The £30,000 rule

The £30,000 limit applies to the total amount you and any other person buying with you owe on one property (for mortgages taken out since 1 August 1988). If you are 65 or over, you can also get tax relief on the interest on up to a futher £30,000 of loans to buy an annuity, if the loan is secured on your only or main home –see p. 356.

Moving home

You may be faced with paying out on two loans at once – one on your new home, and one on your (unsold) old home. Under the normal rules, you get tax relief on £30,000 of loans on your new home. But for a year (longer in deserving cases) you carry on receiving tax relief as before on your old home also.

Capital gains tax

Unlike many other forms of investment, any profit from the sale of your only or main home is, in most cases, exempt from capital gains tax. When house prices are rising, this helps existing owner-occupiers to trade up, i.e. to move to a better house. The non-taxable profit from the first home can be ploughed back into the next home together with a bigger mortgage, in the hope of reaping a higher capital gain. For more details, see *Gearing* opposite.

If you have two or more homes, you can choose which one should count as your main home for capital gains tax purposes (but married couples can have only one main home, regardless of who actually owns the homes). Make your choice within two years of acquiring the second home, otherwise the Revenue can choose for you. You can alter the choice at any time, simply by telling the Revenue (your new choice can be back-dated by up to two years).

In addition, one home owned by you or your husband or wife, bought before 6 April 1988 and occupied rent-free by a dependent relative since before that date, may be exempt from capital gains tax (but, normally, not if the relative gave you the house in the first place).

You may not get full exemption from capital gains tax if any of the following apply:
- you let all or part of your home
- you use part exclusively for work
- the home wasn't your main one for capital gains tax purposes for all the time you owned it
- you were away from the home because of your work for periods totalling over four years (though you get full exemption for any period in which you were an employee working entirely abroad)
- you were away from the home for reasons unconnected with your work for periods totalling over three years
- you were away from the home for longer than the last three years you owned it
- your home is one of a series of homes you bought, or spent money on, in order to make a profit
- your garden is bigger than half a hectare.

For more details, see Inland Revenue leaflet *CGT4* – available free from your tax office. For how capital gains tax works, see p. 107.

Gearing

In the investment world, borrowing money to buy an asset, and only putting down a small part of the money yourself, is called *gearing*. This is a shrewd move – *if* the asset increases in value at a greater rate than the rate of interest you have to pay on your loan. If house prices go up by more than the after-tax relief interest on the mortgage, you'll get a relatively high return for your money.

Suppose, for example, that you had bought a home in December 1966 for £3,820 and sold it in December 1986 for £41,150. With an 80 per cent mortgage, your initial investment would have been 20 per cent of £3,820, i.e. £764. Your gain in 1986 (after buying and selling costs) would be £35,677 and the return on your investment (initial investment plus mortgage repayments, allowing for tax relief at the basic rate) works out at about 12.84 per cent a year. If you'd bought a home for cash, your investment would have been £3,896, and your rate of return 11.92 per cent a year. If you'd had a 90 per cent mortgage instead of an 80 per cent one, gearing would have been even more profitable.

If you sell your home at a profit and use that profit to buy another home, the size of your mortgage relative to the cost of your home is likely to decrease. So a first-time buyer might get a 90 per cent mortgage, then sell the home and get a 70 per cent mortgage on the new home. This lessens the effect of gearing, and means that the return on the investment will be smaller (of course, if house prices were to fall, the *loss* would also be smaller).

But, be warned, your investment may come adrift if the mortgage rate (after tax relief) exceeds the rate of increase in the price of your house. And when house prices are falling, you might even end up owing more on your mortgage than your house would fetch (known as 'negative equity') – potentially disastrous if, for any reason, you had to sell.

House prices in the future

If you've owned a home over the last 20 years, you will almost certainly have seen its value increase. Indeed, you may well have seen it do better than many other forms of investment. Is this likely to remain the long-term trend?

It's impossible to say for certain. In the short term at least, the high cost of houses in relation to what people earn and a lack of confidence in the economic future have put a stop to the house price boom.

While this is not the first housing market recession, it is probably the most complex of recent times. As the graph on p. 144 shows, it has been rare for house prices to fall in money terms – although they have fallen quite dramatically in real terms (i.e. compared with inflation, or average earnings). This housing recession has been partnered by a savage general recession; a sometimes dramatic fall in money prices of houses; a significant number of home-owners facing negative equity; an alarming number of homes repossessed by mortgage lenders; and a severe lack of economic confidence. Optimism by mortgage lenders and house sellers and builders has all but dried up, as each previous attempt to talk up the market has turned out to be a false dawn.

At the end of 1992, the consensus seems to be that a

sustained upturn – or even levelling-out – isn't imminent unless the market is artificially stimulated – not only with more cuts in interest rates, but also an increase in the mortgage relief limit, bailing out home-owners with negative equity, and so on. As that sort of interventionism is politically unlikely, the housing recession looks like remaining for some time.

In the long run, the signs are not all gloomy. Several surveys and analyses in mid-1992 suggest that owner-occupation remains most people's goal – so it's unlikely that a large housing rental market will develop, as in some other European countries. If there's to be no large-scale alternative to buying, it's difficult to see how the housing market can remain in slump for ever.

10

SAVING IN BANKS
AND BUILDING SOCIETIES

Banks, and especially building societies, are very popular homes for people's savings. Both types of organisation offer a range of *deposit-based* savings schemes, and the difference between the two types is becoming smaller and smaller. Banks will use the money they borrow in this way to finance all their lending activities; building societies still use most of their borrowings to lend to individuals who want to buy their own homes.

Most organisations which offer deposit-based accounts that aren't building societies are properly called banks (including many 'finance companies'), and are authorised to do business under the Banking Act of 1987. A bank is a *limited company*, owned by its shareholders; a building society is a *mutual* organisation, owned by its investor members and regulated by the Building Societies Act 1986.

The largest of the building societies can, if they and their members wish, 'convert' into banks: Abbey National did this in 1989.

A safe home for your savings?

Building societies have traditionally been very safe places to invest; they rarely run into difficulties and those that have were quietly bailed out by others.

This safety is partly because societies' traditional business has been restricted to lending on mortgage securities. But societies, particularly the large ones, are now diversifying into many different financial products, and some observers worry that this might in time shake their tradition of security. But there are limits on what proportion of 'riskier' business societies can undertake, and your investment is protected by law to the same degree, no matter how large or small the society with which you invest.

153

If a society gets into difficulties, you are guaranteed to get back 90 per cent of up to the first £20,000 of your savings in that society; with a joint account each account holder is separately protected up to £20,000.

Legal security for money saved with a bank is similar to the security offered by a building society, although the bank deposit protection scheme guarantees you slightly less: 75 per cent of the first £20,000 invested with that bank.

Offshore accounts
Money placed in most offshore locations and held in branches of UK banks or subsidiary companies of building societies is not covered by the bank and building societies protection schemes. But building societies are required by law to make good any losses that a subsidiary fails to cover. The Isle of Man runs a compensation scheme for building societies and banks similar to the UK bank scheme.

There is also a problem with probate should you die: it may cost several hundred £££ and take a month or two for your savings to be released to your executors.

What's on offer

Building societies and banks offer a wide range of different investment schemes. Though many accounts have descriptive names these can be a very misleading guide to the actual terms and conditions of the account. A single account may have a number of 'variations' which can quite change it. And account types vary from time to time.

So it is more useful to look at the features generally available on accounts: most 'new' account types are composed of different selections of these basic features. Armed with this knowledge, you can go on to see how these features are applied in practice to the account types currently available, and then decide how to go about choosing an account for your particular needs.

Basic features

Although schemes vary, they are all based on variations of three main factors:

- how you intend to *pay money in*, when and in what form
- how easily and quickly you want to be able to make *withdrawals*
- arrangements for paying *interest*.

Paying money in

Some schemes have no restrictions on how you pay your money in – you can open the account with a modest pound or two, and pay in what you like, when you like. But many do have some restrictions:

- the minimum investment to open an account can vary from £1 up to tens of thousands of £££
- you may not be allowed to make any additions to the account once it's opened
- you may be allowed to make additions only in certain multiples, e.g. in lumps of £100
- you may have to make regular additions, usually every month
- you may be restricted to a maximum investment level (though rarely less than around £20,000, except perhaps for children's accounts).

There are also practical aspects to making investments. Most organisations will accept money over the counter at their branches or through the post, and most are linked to a network of cash machines which allow you to make deposits outside normal opening hours. Some building societies have agents such as solicitors, insurance brokers and estate agents through whom you can deposit money. Some building societies market special 'postal-only' accounts. But apart from the fact that these societies should be geared up to dealing with quantities of postal transactions efficiently, there's no intrinsic difference between them and any other bank or society which will deal by post.

There is no formal limit on how much you can invest in any one organisation, but some set their own limits, which may vary from account to account. Occasionally this may be as low as £30,000, but it's usually not less than £100,000.

Withdrawals

Some accounts let you get at your savings instantly, on demand; others require you to give some notice or lock your money away for a period of time (a *term*).

To make these *notice accounts* and *term shares* more attractive, accounts may offer a number of concessions:
■ easy access to the balance over a certain amount in your account. The 'balance-over' figure is often £10,000 and the access usually instant: that is, if you have £12,000 invested you can withdraw up to £2,000 on demand whatever the normal conditions for withdrawals
■ instant access, in spite of the normal withdrawal conditions, if you pay a penalty charge (e.g. three months' interest, or so much for every £100 you withdraw)
■ instant access without a penalty, restricted, for example, to £3,000 or one-tenth of your balance once or twice a year.

There may be other restrictions on withdrawals:
■ withdrawing only part of your savings may not be allowed; you may have to close the account if you want to take any money out
■ you may have to withdraw in fixed multiples of, say, £100, or even £1,000.

Interest

How often is interest paid?

Accounts are available which pay interest yearly (occasionally even less frequently), half-yearly, quarterly or monthly. For an explanation of how the frequency of interest affects the true rate of interest you get, see p. 27.

In most cases you can choose to have the interest:
■ paid out to you, or directly into another account with the same or a different organisation
■ kept in the same account to roll up (so that you get compound interest). This option is not often available where the interest is paid monthly.

Some accounts offer a choice of interest payment frequencies, e.g. half-yearly or monthly. If they do, there may be penalties such as lower interest rates or higher minimum investments if you choose to have your interest paid more frequently.

How are interest rates quoted?

Banks and building societies mostly think in terms of gross (before-tax) rates – despite the fact that for most customers they have to deduct tax first, before adding it to the account.

Advertisements and rates cards will often quote up to four rates:
■ **gross** – the *flat rate* before taking into account how often interest is paid, and without deduction of any tax. This is the 'contractual' rate – the rate on which (subject to the

account conditions) the bank or society is obliged to base its calculations for paying you

- **net** – the *flat rate* after deduction of basic-rate tax. You'll usually find a phrase in the literature along the lines of 'net rates are illustrative only, and are based on the deduction of tax at 25 per cent'. So, if the basic rate of income tax changes, the bank or society isn't obliged to pay you on the basis of the net rate shown
- **gross CAR** – or compounded annual rate: a true rate of return taking into account how often interest is compounded within the account. The gross CAR is the rate at which a non-taxpayer will earn over a full year, provided the interest remains in the account
- **net CAR** – the net rate compounded, and what a basic-rate taxpayer will earn over a full year. Higher rate taxpayers will have to pay extra tax, so reducing their effective interest rate – see p. 158.

If a CAR figure is not quoted, it usually implies that interest is paid once a year, and the compounded rates are the same as the flat rates.

Variable or fixed interest?

Most accounts are *variable*, which means that a building society or bank can change interest rates (up or down) on any of its accounts, whenever it likes, without giving any notice, and without making any special concessions to its existing account holders.

An overall increase or decrease in bank rates is usually triggered by a change in the bank base rate, and most banks will respond to such a change quite quickly, while building societies move more slowly. A general change in their savings rate is usually signalled by one of the largest societies and often linked to a change in mortgage rates and a sustained change in bank base rates. Over the following couple of months almost all other societies will move their rates in line with the signallers.

Some accounts offer a *guaranteed premium* (or differential), guaranteeing to pay at least a set amount above the rate of one of the other accounts offered by the bank or building society, whatever happens to rates generally (though perhaps only for a year or two after you take up the offer). In practice, almost all accounts act as though they had a guaranteed premium, so this is not something you need look out for especially.

There are also accounts where the rate is *fixed* for a period; whatever happens to interest rates generally during that time: see p. 160.

How is interest taxed?
Building societies and banks will normally deduct basic-rate tax from your interest before adding it to your account.

If you're a *higher-rate* taxpayer, you'll have to pay additional tax of the difference between the basic rate and the higher rate. This isn't collected by the banks and building societies; the Inland Revenue will send you a tax bill later.

If you're a *non-taxpayer* you don't have to pay tax on your building society and bank interest. Get form R85 from a building society, bank, or tax office: if you can declare that your total income from all sources (including interest) is likely to be less than your total tax allowances for the coming year, sign the form and take it to your building society or bank, who will then pay you interest gross.

If after the end of a tax year you find that you've had more tax deducted from your savings than you are liable for (for example, if you are a *lower-rate taxpayer*), you can claim a repayment from the Inland Revenue.

If all holders of a joint account are non-taxpayers, they will each need to complete a form R85. If not all are, the bank or building society may allow the non-taxpayers their share of interest gross; otherwise they will have to claim a repayment of tax from the Inland Revenue. Joint accounts are almost always deemed to be held by their owners in equal shares.

For more on tax, see pp. 100 and 102.

How much interest?
As a rule of thumb, the longer your money is tied up, and the larger the investment required, the higher the interest rate.

Tiered interest accounts stick to this rule: the larger your investment the higher the interest. Usually you get the higher interest automatically if your balance grows enough to tip you into a higher tier (the rate is cut automatically if it falls), but watch out for accounts that do not do so. You usually get the highest rate your investment level entitles you to on the *whole* of your balance, but watch out for accounts that pay you the higher rates only on the amount of your money in each tier (which results in a lower average rate overall).

A tiered interest account can be linked to notice periods rather than investment levels. For example, some years ago there were very complicated accounts in which your interest rate depended both on how long you *intended* to leave your money invested, and how long you *actually* left it invested.

Some accounts pay a bonus if you satisfy particular conditions, such as not making any withdrawals for a year.

Interest is usually calculated on the balance in your account each day, but in a few cases it may be worked out on a less advantageous basis, e.g. your lowest balance over a month.

Types of account

Term shares

These are accounts which lock your money up for a period of time, which can be anything from a few days to perhaps five years. The term is usually fixed at the time you open the account, either as a fixed amount of time (e.g. six months or two years), or as a fixed date (e.g. a term ending on 1 December 1994).

Normally, you will not be allowed to withdraw until the account *matures* at the end of its term; if you are allowed withdrawals, then you will have to pay a *penalty charge* and perhaps give some months' notice as well, or be restricted to withdrawing only the balance over a certain amount. You may not be allowed to add to the account, though normally you can start another one.

Check what happens to your investment at the end of the term. It may be:

■ automatically cashed in – you'll be sent a cheque

■ automatically transferred to another account, which pays a different rate of interest

■ left where it is, paying the same rate of interest, and converted into a notice account (in which case check whether you can give the required notice *before* the end of the term, otherwise the term will be longer than you originally thought, e.g. if you have to give three months' notice at the end of a one-year term share you've effectively got a 15-month term share)

■ automatically re-invested for a further term (though not necessarily at the same rate). This is more likely to happen with the shorter-period bank term shares.

Notice accounts

Accounts allowing you access to your money at three months' notice are very popular, but there are many others with shorter notice periods (down to one week) and a few with longer (four to eighteen months) notice periods.

Most notice accounts allow instant access if you pay a *penalty charge* of, usually, the same number of months' interest as the notice period. For example, on a three-month account you can give either three months' notice, or have instant access and lose the equivalent of three months' interest on the money you're withdrawing. These are useful in an emergency, but can reduce drastically the effective interest rate you get.

You may have access to the balance over a certain amount in a notice account without notice or penalty. And some accounts are *tiered interest* accounts with minimum investment levels and tiers ranging anywhere from £1 (though £500 is more common) to tens of thousands of £££.

A penalty charge trap

Watch out for accounts that *always* operate a penalty charge. Some of these are term shares, so you don't suffer the penalty if you leave your money invested for the full term. But some are not: if you have no way of escaping a penalty charge, it means you'll never get as high an interest rate as that quoted, taken over the whole period of your investment.

Instant access accounts

Many instant access accounts have *tiered interest* rates, with minimum investment levels and tiers ranging anywhere from £1 to tens of thousands of £££. Even though instant withdrawals are allowed, there may still be some restrictions with building society accounts: often you can draw no more than £250 in cash, perhaps as little as £5,000 as a cheque; larger cash sums or cheques take up to three days to arrange.

Beware of accounts that give you instant access, but only if you pay a penalty charge. Beware, too, of accounts which give you instant access only to the balance over a certain amount (though if this amount is low, these accounts can still be useful if you have a large amount to invest).

Fixed rate accounts

Accounts that offer a fixed rate of interest for a fixed term are a gamble. If rates fall during the term you may do well; if they rise you might have been better off with a variable rate account. You can't normally withdraw before the end of the term, and certainly not without suffering a penalty.

Beware of interest rates which are fixed for only part of the term of the account: such rates can fall dramatically when the fixed-rate period ends, leaving you locked into a poor-paying account.

Monthly income accounts

These are accounts which pay out interest monthly, to help you boost your income. They come with all sorts of minimum investment levels and notice periods. Though your capital is as safe as in any other building society or bank account (see p. 153) your monthly income will fluctuate up and down as rates vary – unless you go for a *fixed-rate* monthly-income account.

Monthly income accounts are often variations of other accounts, but with perhaps a higher minimum investment and a lower interest rate, so make sure that you are looking at the right version of the account.

Regular savings accounts

Once the only high-interest account available, regular savings accounts (sometimes called subscription accounts) are now few and far between. They are not available from all banks and building societies, and have not recently paid particularly high rates. But they could be useful if you really have only a few £££ a month to invest and you need to discipline yourself to save it regularly.

Regularly savings offer perhaps the most complicated conditions of any account type, so check carefully that what you are being offered suits your needs. Ask:

■ what are the minimum and maximum amounts I can save each month?

■ can I vary the amount I save as I wish each month, or only by agreement with the society?

■ can I miss payments? How many can I miss, and how often?

■ can I withdraw part of my savings? How much can I withdraw, and how often?

■ are there any restrictions (such as a notice period) for closing the account?

In general, the more restrictive the conditions you accept, the higher the interest rate.

Save-As-You-Earn (SAYE)

SAYE is also a regular savings scheme, offered by some building societies: banks can offer them, too. The conditions are identical no matter which society you go to, and you can invest in only one scheme. They may be difficult to find, since they're not publicised.

You make a fixed investment of £1 to £20 a month for five years. Interest is added as a tax-free bonus of 14 months' savings at the end of the term (equal to a fixed rate of 8.3 per cent). Leave your money and the bonus invested for two more years and you get a bonus of another 14 months' savings, boosting the return to 8.62 per cent.

You can stop payments and withdraw at any time, but do this in the first year and you'll get no interest at all. After the first year you'll earn interest of 6 per cent a year (8 per cent if the reason for stopping is the saver's death). You can miss up to six payments over the five years provided you make them up in the months directly following the end of your five-year term.

Cheque accounts

There are now quite a few savings accounts which include the use of a cheque book. Some of them are full current accounts which pay interest and offer: a cheque book which allows you to write as many cheques as you like; a cheque guarantee card; cash machines; and access to overdrafts, standing orders and direct debits. But note that you may be able to get higher interest from an account which does not offer all these extras.

At the other end of the scale are instant access accounts which simply include a cheque book as your means of making easy withdrawals. You get none of the other facilities of a current account; there may be a minimum investment of £500 or more; and you may have to pay a fee for all or some (e.g. after the first half-dozen a quarter) of the cheques you write. In return for these restrictions you should get a better rate of interest than from an interest-bearing current account, but you may get a higher rate still from an account without a cheque book at all.

Money market accounts

With many bank accounts (and very occasionally a building society account) the interest is linked to the rates paid on the money markets. The rate can fluctuate quite frequently, in some cases every day; and often it is reviewed every week.

These accounts come with all sorts of minimum investment stipulations and notice periods, although instant access high-minimum investment types are perhaps the most common. Many offer the use of a cheque book.

TESSAs

Anyone aged 18 and over may hold one Tax Exempt Special Savings Account (TESSA) with a bank or building society. They are designed as a savings scheme parallel to share-holding Personal Equity Plans: stick to the scheme conditions and the interest you earn will be free of both basic-rate and higher-rate tax.

Here are the main features of TESSAs:

- a TESSA lasts for five years
- you can save up to £3,000 in the first year, and up to £1,800 in each of the following four years, provided you don't exceed £9,000 over the five years in total
- the interest earned will be tax-free *provided* you withdraw no more than the interest credited to your account at the time you want to make the withdrawal *less* the basic-rate tax you would otherwise have paid. If you want to withdraw more interest than this, or some of your capital, then the account is terminated. All the interest credited to the account then becomes taxable in the tax year that the account is terminated (even though some of it may have been earned in earlier tax years)
- provided you don't overstep the mark, you aren't taxed on any interest that you withdraw: the interest you cannot withdraw stays in your account (earning interest itself) until the TESSA matures, when it's paid out to you as a sort of bonus.

Apart from these tax rules, the other details of TESSAs are up to each building society or bank. Some schemes are for regular, equal, monthly savings (maximum £150 a month); others allow you to save as and when you like (sometimes subject to a minimum investment each time). Some may not allow any withdrawals; others do; some may automatically pay you a monthly income of as much as the Revenue (and the scheme's interest rate) allows.

Some banks and building societies offer a scheme which allows you to pay a single lump sum into a 'feeder' account which is then transferred into a TESSA as fast as the rules allow. Note that the interest earned on the money while it is waiting in the feeder account *will* be taxable, and may not pay as good a rate as the TESSA itself: so the true rate of interest earned may be significantly lower than that quoted in any advertisements.

Building societies and banks can set any rate of interest on their TESSAs, and this can be fixed or variable. Although you can hold only one TESSA at any one time, the Revenue will allow you to transfer from one organisation's scheme to another, e.g. to chase best interest rates. Organisations must allow you to transfer *out* (though they can impose any penalties or charges they like), but they're not obliged to let you transfer *in* to their TESSA.

You can close a TESSA whenever you like – you don't have to wait until the five years is up. You'll have to pay tax on your interest, and the organization might charge you a penalty. If your TESSA has no penalty for closure, it could be worth-while thinking about even for short-term savings.

Children's accounts

Many banks and building societies have an account aimed at children. This may offer little more than a colourful passbook with a cartoon character; or it may offer a wide range of extras, such as free gifts, membership to zoos and clubs, magazines and so on.

Interest rates vary from amongst the lowest of any account to some of the higher rates; usually the higher payers offer the least extras. But high interest might not be the most important factor for a child in deciding where to save. See Chapter 4 for more on investing for children.

Combination accounts

A few building societies have offered accounts combined with other investments such as unit trusts or life insurance. They are also available from to time as 'special offers' from financial advisers. The money you invest can be split in various ways, e.g. half going into a building society account, half into, say, an insurance company investment bond, or all your money going into a building society account, but with the interest used to buy unit trusts.

Often, the building society investment will sport a very high rate of interest (usually because the society has split its commission on the other investment with you), but this rate may apply for only a relatively short period. There is nothing magical about the other investment, which will be as good or as bad a buy as any other investment of its particular type, despite its building society connection.

Don't go for a combination account purely on the strength of a high initial building society rate; check that both parts of the account look like good buys over the investment period (which is likely to be relatively long compared with most building society accounts).

Permanent Interest-Bearing Shares (PIBS)

Building societies were first allowed to offer these from 1 June 1991, but so far only a few of the biggest societies have done so. They don't bear any relation to building society 'share' accounts (as the simplest instant access accounts are often called): instead, you buy a share in the building society, which then pays you a fixed rate of interest for an unlimited period.

PIBS are traded like ordinary stocks and shares – they're bought through a stockbroker. The value of the share will depend on what the market will pay for it. The minimum amount which can be purchased varies from £1,000 to £50,000.

The interest rates in September 1992 compared well with many other fixed-interest investments (at about 11.5 per cent before tax), but it's not yet clear how much the price will fluctuate, although so far fluctuations have been relatively low. Like fixed-interest British Government stocks, they're likely to be bad value in times of high inflation.

If the building society goes bust, the last person in line for the remaining assets will be the PIBS-holder. And they're not covered by the compensation arrangements which normally apply to building society investments, nor by the Investors' Compensation Scheme (unless you bought through an investment adviser or manager who goes bust).

It may be less likely that a building society will go under than other types of institution, but it's early days for PIBS so proceed with caution.

Friendly society bonds

Some (very few) building society accounts are linked with friendly societies which are allowed to offer a very restricted tax-free regular savings scheme. You pay a *maximum* of £18 a month (or £200 a year) for 10 years and the friendly society invests the money with the building society. Because the scheme is tax-free, you make a little more interest than you would by investing directly in the building society, but not as much as you might think (only 1 to 2 per cent or so extra) because of the friendly societies' management charges. The scheme is free of higher-rate tax, too, so is more appealing to higher-rate taxpayers (but the actual number of £££ involved is small because the savings limits are so restricted).

If you cash in within the first 7½ years, you get back, at most, only your gross premiums; if you cash in between 7½ and 10 years you may get a little more.

A version allowing you to pay in a lump sum (maximum £1,145) is also available: the money goes into a building society account from which the regular premiums are automatically paid. Because you have to pay tax in the normal way on the interest on this pool of money, the lump sum scheme has a lower effective rate of interest. To a basic-rate taxpayer it could be little better than the best normal building society account, which should offer better access and fewer restrictions.

Other friendly society investments

Friendly societies don't invest only with building societies. With some regular savings schemes, your money is invested in, say, unit trusts, with the same tax advantages (and same restrictions). And there are some schemes which *are* taxable, where your money is invested, say, half in shares and half in safer investments such as British Government stocks or building societies. Some of these plans (whether involving building society investments or not) may be available through building societies.

Making your choice

Too little income to pay tax?

You can get your interest without deduction of tax from any bank or building society account provided you can sign a declaration stating that you're likely to be a non-taxpayer in that tax year (see p. 158).

Looking at a large tax bill?

Consider offshore accounts. You still have to pay tax – but you may be able to arrange things so that the tax bill falls due in a year that suits you.

Investing for the long term?

Building society and bank investments are safe, but over the long term may not make as much as more risky forms of investment. If you have a very large sum to invest for a long period, think about putting some of it into other investments – see Chapters 1 and 2.

Don't need your money for a year or so?

Term shares look tempting, but you may get as good or better rates of interest (especially on large sums) from a *notice* account, as well as easier access to your money, There's always the possibility with variable rate term shares that the rate may go down significantly once you're locked in.

TESSAs look inviting if you can keep one up for the full five years and collect the interest tax-free. But they're worth thinking about even over a shorter period provided you don't have to pay a penalty for early closure – the best can match or beat the best term shares.

Think interest rates will fall?

Check *fixed rate* accounts – but compare them with the best variable rates on offer before you decide whether the gamble is likely to be worthwhile. Consider British Government stocks or guaranteed income bonds.

Prepared to wait a while for your money?

A *notice* account may give higher interest than one offering instant access – often, the longer the notice period, the higher the interest will be. But don't tie up money you think you may need to get out quickly. Consider a TESSA, provided it has no penalties for early closure.

Can't wait, won't wait?

Try an *instant access* account. If you have a large investment and need instant access to only part of your money, look at a notice account which gives you instant access to money above a certain amount. Or can you make do with a short notice account (say up to a month)?

Want a regular income?

You can draw a monthly income from any account, but it is easiest to do so from an account offering *monthly interest* – many different types offer this. If you want a fixed income, think also about other investments like British Government stocks or guaranteed income bonds.

Want to save regularly?

A *regular savings* account is a possibility, if you need to be disciplined. But, especially if you have a few hundred £££ to start you off, you could make more interest and have better access to your money from any other type of account (except those that don't allow you to add to your original investment). A regular savings TESSA is worth considering if you can save for five years (especially if you are a higher-rate taxpayer). Use the flowchart on p. 36 to guide you to the other types of savings and investment available.

Expect your savings to fluctuate?

Think about an account with a *tiered interest rate* structure. But if you do, keep an eye on your balance and what it is earning.

Choosing a home for your savings

With over 3,000 accounts and variations on accounts on offer, from scores of banks and building societies, picking the best buy is not easy. Consider first *convenience*: if you want to withdraw *and* deposit money quickly and frequently (and especially if you want current account facilities) then you will need a branch or a cash machine close to your home or place of work; this will restrict you to the larger high street organisations and whichever local ones are in your area.

For larger, more infrequent transactions, you can deal by post. This gives you a wider range of organisations from which to choose. When comparing rates:

■ note that slight differences in interest rate are important only with large investments. For example, on an investment of £1,000, 1 per cent extra on a rate will make you only between £10 and £10.47 extra in a full year

■ make sure you are comparing the right rate. The CAR or 'true' rate applies strictly only to money that is invested for a full year or more. If you are investing for a period much shorter than a year, the 'flat' rate is a better comparative guide.

You can find information on the best buys from several sources, including *Which?* from time to time; the financial pages in newspapers; and *MoneyGuides* which publishes monthly lists of the highest-paying bank and building society accounts in various categories (details from Riverside House, Rattlesden, Bury St Edmunds IP30 0SF).

11

NATIONAL SAVINGS INVESTMENTS

One way in which the government raises money is to borrow it from the public. It offers various forms of investment in the hope that people will put their money in them. One such investment is the wide range of British Government stocks, dealt with in Chapter 16. Here, we look at National Savings investments.

National Savings Certificates

The first National Savings Certificates – then called War Savings Certificates – were issued in 1916. Since then, governments have brought out a new issue whenever the rate of interest on the old issue seemed too high, or too low, in the prevailing circumstances. Normally, you can buy only one issue – the current one – at any one time. In all, various governments have brought out 40 issues of National Savings Certificates (by November 1992). Once you've bought a certificate you can in practice hold it indefinitely. Moreover, you don't have to have been alive and investing in 1916 in order to own some of the first issue, because certificates can be inherited. So you could hold quite a wide range of certificates. Here we tell you about conventional National Savings Certificates – see p. 173 for index-linked certificates.

How interest is paid

With all National Savings Certificates, interest is not paid out to you: it's added on to the value of your certificate, and you get it when you cash in the certificate. The interest is free of income tax and capital gains tax doesn't apply.

With the early issues (up to and including the 6th) interest is added *ad infinitum* to the value of your certificates at a fixed rate of five-twelfths a month (or, with some of these issues, 1½p or 1¼p every three months). Because the amount of interest is fixed, it follows that the rate of interest – expressed as a yearly percentage return on the value of your investment – is going down, year by year. These now offer a miserly rate of return of well under 2 per cent a year.

For issues after the 6th, the interest paid used to vary depending on the issue and the year; the exact rates were fixed for a certain number of years at a time, e.g. five or seven years. But in 1982, the government announced that when a particular certificate got to the end of the period for which interest rates had been set, a common rate of interest called the *general extension rate* would be paid. The general extension rate was 3.75 per cent as we went to press.

Below, we give details of the 40th issue, the one available when this book went to press in November 1992. And then we look in detail at whether you should cash in any old certificates you have.

Investing in National Savings Certificates (40th issue)

Anyone can invest, irrespective of their age. You can invest anything between £100 and £5,000, in units of £100, so certificates are suitable for both lump sums and savings. A husband and wife can invest up to £5,000 each; if the certificates are in their joint names, however, they can invest only £5,000 between them.

If you are cashing in earlier issues of National Savings Certificates (or Yearly Plan – see p. 182) which you've held for at least five years, you can invest up to £10,000 in *Reinvestment Certificates* on top of the ordinary £5,000 limit. The terms are the same as for other 40th issue certificates, except that if you cash reinvestment certificates within one year of having invested you will get interest equivalent to 4.0 per cent a year for each complete three months of investment.

How to invest
Fill in an application form available from most post offices and banks. Your certificate showing how many units of £100 you have bought will be sent to you later.

How much interest?

Interest is added to the value of your certificate over the period of its life (which is five years at the outset). The amount of interest added increases as time goes by, giving you an added incentive to hang on to your certificates. Table 1 below gives the details, and shows the rate of interest for each year. Within any year, it's the rate of interest in the right-hand column which you should compare with, say, the after-tax (or, for non-taxpayers, the gross) rate of interest on building society accounts. If you hold the certificate for the full five years, the overall yearly rate of return works out at 5.75 per cent.

Table 1   How a unit of the 40th issue grows

during year	£100 certificate increases by	for each complete	value at end of year	rate of interest for year
1	£4.00	12 months	£104.00	4.0%
2	£1.14½	3 months	£108.58	4.4%
3	£1.56	3 months	£114.82	5.75%
4	£1.93¼	3 months	£122.57	6.75%
5	£2.42	3 months	£132.25	7.9%

How do you cash your certificates?

Get *form DNS502MA* from a post office. You shouldn't have to wait more than a couple of weeks for your money. You can cash in any number of units, e.g. if you hold 40 units each bought for £100, you can cash in 20 of them.

What happens to your certificates should you die?

Your heirs can either cash in the certificates or transfer them into their own names. *Form DNS904* from most post offices will get things underway.

What about your old certificates?

Because interest is not paid out, but added on to the value of your certificates, working out what return you are actually getting from your investment isn't an easy matter. Moreover, besides needing to know the rate of interest you are getting now, you need to know what interest will be paid on them in the next year or two, in case the interest, though low this year, will get better later on.

First, find your Savings Certificates. Next, check which issue (or issues) your certificates are. This is printed on the certificates, e.g. *sixth issue, decimal issue.* Next, look at the date stamp on each certificate to find out when it was bought.

If you are still holding certificates from one of the very earliest issues – from the 1st to the 6th (on sale from 1916 until November 1939) – the interest rate you are getting on these is betweeen 1.1 and 1.8 per cent a year.

For later issues you should look at the table opposite. If there isn't an entry which matches the age and issue of certificates you hold, you are earning interest at the *general extension rate* – see p. 170. At present, this is a few per cent higher than the lowest rate paid by the big building societies. However, depending on how much money you have in old certificates you may be able to increase your return by investing your money elsewhere.

If there is an entry which relates to a certificate you hold, then column 3 gives the value of each certificate in 1992 on the anniversary of the date it was bought. For example, a 33rd issue certificate bought on 16 November 1987 will be worth £35.06 on 16 November 1992. This value is that for a single unit. The certificate documents you have may in fact say they are for multiples of 2, 3, 4 or more units, in which case the value is the figure in column 3 multiplied by 2, 3, 4 and so on, as the case may be.

British Savings Bonds

These are no longer earning any interest. If you still have bonds you should surrender them for repayment as soon as you can. Write to the Bonds and Stock Office, Blackpool FY3 9YP.

Interest
■ **Column 4** tells you the rate of interest paid for the year ending during 1992, on the anniversary of the date the certificates were bought. As the interest is tax-free, this is, in effect, the after-tax rate of return.
■ **Column 5** tells you the rate of interest due to be paid in the year ending during 1993 on the anniversary of the date the certificates were bought.
■ **Column 6** tells you the rate of interest for the year ending during 1994.

Value for money
As we have said, all the early issues from the 1st to the 6th give a very low return – it varies between 1.1 and 1.8 per cent. Other investments can give a much better return. So

if you've any of these early issues, cash them in at once and reinvest elsewhere.

With certificates of the later issues, compare the return you're getting with that available on other investments (taking your rate of tax into account). Don't forget to look at the rate of return next year, and the year after next, before coming to a decision. For example, with 34th issue bought in 1989, although the rate of return in 1992 is 7.02 per cent, in 1993 you'd get 8.5 per cent, and the year after 9.52 per cent. So it may be worth hanging on to them.

Table 2 Old National Savings Certificates

1	2	3	4	5	6
name of issue (and issue price)	year bought	value in 1992 at anniversary of date bought	interest now	interest next year	interest year after next
			rate of interest for year ending at anniversary of date bought in:		
			1992	1993	1994
		£	%	%	%
32nd (£25)	1987	38.03	11.23		
33rd (£25)	1987	35.06	9.02		
	1988	32.16	7.99	9.02	
34th (£25)	1988	32.77	8.51	9.52	
	1989	30.20	7.02	8.51	9.52
	1990	28.22	6.49	7.02	8.51
35th (£25)	1990	28.62	7.51	9.26	10.81
	1991	26.62	5.25	7.51	9.26
36th (£25)	1991	26.38	5.50	6.48	8.26
	1992	n/a	n/a	5.50	6.48
37th (£25)	1992	n/a	n/a	5.50	6.17
38th (£25)	1992	n/a	n/a	5.25	6.20
39th (£100)	1992	n/a	n/a	4.60	5.25

Index-linked National Savings Certificates (6th issue)

These certificates are worth considering if you're worried about inflation. They guarantee that the buying-power of the money you invest will keep pace with the rising prices. For how they compare with index-linked British Government stocks, see p. 299.

How much can you invest?
You can invest anything between £100 and £5,000, in units of £25, so they are suitable for both lump sums or savings (regular or a bit at a time). A husband and wife can each invest up to £5,000 (i.e. up to £10,000 in all). If the certificates are in their joint names, however, they can invest only £5,000 between them.

If you are cashing in National Savings Certificates which you've held for at least five years, or mature Yearly Plan savings, you can invest up to £10,000 in *Reinvestment Certificates* on top of your normal £10,000 limit. The terms are the same as for other 6th issue index-linked certificates, except that if you cash in your investment within one year your investment will be increased in line with the Retail Prices Index for each complete month of investment.

How to invest
Go to a post office or bank and fill in an application form. You'll get a receipt, and your certificate, showing how much you've invested, will be sent on to you by post.

How index-linked certificates work

If you cash one in within a year of buying it, you get back only the money you invested in the first place. But after a year, its value is increased in line with the change in the Retail Prices Index (RPI) since you bought it. If you hold your certificate for the full five years, your overall return is 3.25 per cent a year on top of inflation. After five years, you should check what return you will get.

Table 3 How a £25 unit of the 6th index-linked issue grows

during year	interest paid in each year %	value at anniversary of date invested [1] £	effective rate in year [2] %
1	1.5	26.62	6.5
2	2	28.48	6.98
3	2.75	30.69	7.76
4	3.75	33.38	8.76
5	6.32	37.16	11.32

[1] This is the sum of money you would get if you cashed in your unit having held it for exactly this number of years, assuming inflation runs at 5 per cent a year
[2] Assuming inflation runs at 5 per cent

Which month's index applies?

The level of the RPI for the previous month is announced on the second or third Friday of each month, and reported in the newspapers the following day. When you buy a certificate or cash one in, the RPI figure that applies is the one announced in the previous month, which, in turn, refers to the cost of living in the month before that. See p. 111 for a list of RPI figures since March 1982.

Working out how much you'd get if you cashed in now

The easiest way to find out the present value of your holding in 6th issue index-linked certificates is to look at the chart on display at post offices. But to decide whether or not your return is worthwhile compared with other risk-free investments, you should also consider the rate of return you are getting. The effective rate you get varies, depending on the rate of inflation and on how long you hold the certificate. For example, if inflation runs at 5 per cent, during the fourth year you will, in effect, earn over 10 per cent on your investment – see Table 3.

Is there any tax to pay on the gain?

No, there isn't. The gain is free of both income tax and capital gains tax. This makes these certificates particularly attractive to people paying higher-rate income tax, or who have used up their yearly tax-free slice for capital gains tax.

What happens to your certificate if you die?

The certificate can be transferred into your heir's name, even if he or she already has the maximum holding of certificates.

How to cash in certificates

Get *form DNS502MA* from a post office. Fill it in and send it off in the pre-paid envelope provided with the form. You shouldn't have to wait longer than a couple of weeks for your money.

Can you cash in only part of your money?

Yes, you can. When you bought your certificate you bought a number of £25 units. You can cash in any number of units you wish.

What happens if the Retail Prices Index actually falls?

The value of your certificate goes down in line with the fall in the Retail Prices Index though interest is still added. But it is guaranteed that when you cash your units in, you'll get back at least as much as you originally invested (plus the extra supplements).

Any old National Savings Stamps?

Remember them – 10p each (or 6d and 1/- in pre-decimal days)? They were withdrawn on 31 December 1976, but you can still cash in any you've got knocking around. Send them to National Savings, Boydstone Road, Glasgow G58 1SB and ask for their value to be refunded.

What happens if the rate of inflation goes down?

A fall in the *rate* of inflation means that the Retail Prices Index is still going up, but not as fast as before; the value of your certificate will continue to increase, but at a slower rate. The value of your certificate will not fall. What's important from the point of view of your investment is how the rate of inflation, plus the interest, compares with the rate of return you could get on other comparatively safe investments, e.g. bank and building society accounts.

Should you cash in old index-linked certificates?

You don't have to. You can keep your money where it is, and your investment will continue to be index-linked. In addition, you may get tax-free interest. For example, if you have money invested in the 2nd index-linked issue (sold between 1980 and 1985), and your investment is coming up to its tenth anniversary, you have an added incentive to hang on to your certificates until that date is past. That's because a bonus of 4 per cent of the value on the fifth anniversary of your purchase will be added on the tenth anniversary of your purchase – you'll get this in 1993 if you bought 2nd issue index-linked certificates in 1983.

Apart from these bonuses, your investment, for example in 3rd issue index-linked certificates, will simply grow along with inflation. To decide whether or not to leave your money invested you need to guess what will happen to inflation over the next year or so and compare this with the after-tax rate you could expect by investing elsewhere, e.g. in a bank or building society or in another National Savings scheme. For example, if you think that inflation is likely to be around 4 to 5 per cent in the next year, it is only worth moving your money if you know you will get a higher rate than this elsewhere.

If you have certificates of the 4th or 5th index-linked issue, Table 4 shows what interest to expect on top of index-linking. It is calculated monthly and added on the anniversary of purchase. Your overall return will depend on the rate of inflation over the year. So when you're deciding whether to cash in your investment, consider what may happen to inflation. If you think it is on the increase, you should be less keen to cash in your investment and vice versa. Also look at the return on the current issue of index-linked certificates to see if it is higher.

Table 4   Index-linked National Savings Certificates

name of issue	year bought	interest added at end of year to value at start of year (on top of index-linking)		
		1992 %	1993 %	1994 %
4th	1987	6.00		
	1988	4.50	6.00	
	1989	3.50	4.50	6.00
5th	1989	2.00	5.00	15.00
	1990	1.00	2.00	5.00
	1991	–	1.00	2.00
	1992	–	–	1.00

Other National Savings investments

National Savings Ordinary account

Who can invest?
Anyone can open an account. For young children, the account can be opened by a relative or friend.

How much can you invest?
You must invest a minimum of £5 to open an account, while the maximum is £10,000, no matter how many Ordinary accounts you have. Further deposits must be at least £5 (£10 from February 1993).

How to invest
You can open an account at most post offices – you'll be sent a bank book where a record is keep of all your transactions.

How much interest?
The rate of interest can vary, though it tends to be fixed for at least one year at a time. For 1993, if your account is kept

open from 31 December 1992 to 1 January 1994, you'll get interest at a rate of 3.75 per cent for each calendar month in which the balance is £500 or more. Otherwise you'd get the standard rate of interest – 2.5 per cent. Interest is worked out on each complete £1 in the account for a full calendar month. Money in your account doesn't start earning interest until the start of the month following the one in which it is deposited. And it stops getting interest from the start of the month in which it is withdrawn. So you'll get most interest if you put your money in on the last day of a month, and take it out on the first day of a month.

Interest is added to your account on 31 December. The first £70 interest is tax-free and a husband and wife can each have this much interest tax-free (see p. 104 for more on tax).

Getting your money out

You can withdraw up to £250 at once by taking your bank book to most post offices. If you want more than £250, you have to apply in writing on an application form available from most post offices; getting your money could take about a week. If you withdraw more than £50, your bank book has to be sent to the Savings Bank headquarters (the limit is £250 if you have a *Regular Customer Account* – check at your post office).

What happens if you die?

The money in your account can be cashed in or transferred to your heir's account. *Form DNS904* gives all the details.

National Savings Investment account

Who can invest?

The same people who can invest in the Ordinary account.

How much can you invest?

You must invest a minimum of £5 to open an account. The maximum is £25,000, no matter how many Investment accounts you have. Each time you put money in, you must deposit at least £5 (£20 from February 1993).

How to invest?

Follow the procedure for the Ordinary account.

How much interest?

The rate of interest varies (8 per cent in November 1992, due to drop to 7 per cent from December 26).

Interest is added to your account on 31 December. All interest is taxable, but is paid without tax having been deducted, which makes the account particularly suitable for non-taxpayers.

Getting your money out
You have to give one month's notice to withdraw your money. You can get an application form from most post offices. You'll have to send your bank book in with your application form.

What happens if you die?
Follow the procedure for the Ordinary account.

National Savings Income Bonds

Who can invest?
Anyone, irrespective of age, can invest. Income Bonds may be particularly suitable for non-taxpayers who want a regular income from their savings.

How much can you invest?
Income Bonds cost £1,000 each. The minimum number you can buy is two, and the maximum holding is £50,000 (50 bonds). A husband and wife can have £100,000 even if the investment is in joint names. They are suitable only for lump sum investment.

How to invest
You can get an application form from a post office, which you send to the *Bonds and Stock Office*. A certificate showing the value of the bonds you have bought will be sent to you.

How much interest?
The rate of interest varies, depending on how much the government feels it needs to offer to attract investors (in October 1992, the rate was 8.0 per cent a year). Interest is paid out to you monthly (on the fifth day of each month). When you first invest, you will have to wait at least six weeks for your first payment. All interest is taxable, but is paid without tax having been deducted.

Getting your money out
You have to give three months' notice if you want to cash one of your bonds. If you cash a bond within a year of purchasing it, you'll get only half the normal rate of

interest on it. After a year, there is no penalty and your bond will be repaid in full. Get *form DNS201* from a post office if you want to cash a bond.

What happens if you die?
Your heirs can cash the bonds without notice and with no loss of interest. *Form DNS904* gives details of what to do.

National Savings Deposit Bonds

Who can invest?
You can't now buy deposit bonds as they were withdrawn from sale in November 1988. However, if you bought bonds before that date you can continue to hold them and withdraw part or all of your savings.

How much interest?
The interest rate varies depending on how much the government feels it needs to offer to get the amount of money it wants from investors (7 per cent a year from 26 December 1992). Interest is added to the value of your bond each year on the anniversary of your investment. This interest is taxable, but it is paid without tax having been deducted.

Getting your money out
You can withdraw any amount above £50 as long as at least £100 of your original investment remains. You have to give three months' notice. Forms for withdrawals are available at post offices.

What happens if you die?
Your heirs can withdraw your investment without notice and with no loss of interest. *Form DNS904* gives the details of what to do.

National Savings Capital Bonds Series G

Who can invest?
Anyone, irrespective of age, can invest. Capital Bonds could be particularly attractive to non-taxpayers who don't want income from their savings. But they are worth considering only if you are prepared to tie up your money for five years.

How much can you invest?
You have to invest at least £100 in multiples of £100.

There is a maximum investment of £100,000. In addition, your total investment in National Savings Capital Bonds (excluding Series A) can't be more than £100,000. A husband and wife can each have £100,000 invested in Capital Bonds; if the Bonds are held in joint names, they can invest only £100,000 between them. Capital Bonds would be suitable for lump sum investments or occasional savings.

How to invest

You can buy your bond at a post office, although your certificate will be sent to you later from the *Capital Bond Office*; or you can get *form DNS151* from a post office and apply by post.

How much interest?

Interest is added to the value of your bond over its five-year life and the amount is fixed at the time of purchase. The interest added increases each year giving you an incentive to hold on to your bond. Over the full five years your return at the rates which applied 7 December 1992 works out as 7.75 per cent a year before tax, 5.8 per cent after basic-rate tax.

At the end of the five years your Bond will be repaid together with the full amount of interest earned. No tax will be deducted, which is good for non-taxpayers. If you are a taxpayer you have to pay tax each year on the interest even though you won't receive the interest until your bond is repaid. If you cash in your bond early you get a lower rate – see Table 6 below.

Table 5 How a £100 Capital Bond (Series G) grows

during year	interest rate	after-tax return: basic-rate taxpayer	higher-rate taxpayer
	%	%	%
1	5.3	3.97	3.18
2	5.9	4.42	3.54
3	7.7	5.77	4.62
4	9.0	6.75	5.40
5	10.95	8.21	6.57
Average:	7.75	5.81	4.65

Table 6 Interest when you cash in your Bond early

year in which you cash bond	interest rate
1	No interest
2	5.3%
3	Year 1 see Table 5, 5.9% for remainder
4	Years 1 and 2 see Table 5, 7.7% for remainder
5	Years 1, 2 and 3 see Table 5, 9.0% for remainder

Should you cash in old Capital Bonds?
If you invested in the earlier Capital bonds (Series A, B, C, D, E or F) you may be wondering whether it is worth cashing them in and investing in the current Bonds (or another National Savings scheme). If you hold them for the full five years your return over the whole period will be between 13 per cent gross (Series A), and 9 per cent gross (Series F).

Whatever Bond you have invested in, if you have not yet held it for a full year, you should not cash it in as you will get back only your initial investment with no interest. In general, it's not worth cashing in your original bonds and investing in the new series as you will, over the length of your investment, receive a lower rate of return.

Getting your money out
You don't have to give notice to cash in your bond, but it will take at least eight days to get your money. You don't have to cash in your whole investment; part of a bond can be repaid as long as you withdraw at least £100 and at least £100 remains invested. You can get forms for withdrawal at a post office. After the five years, your bond plus interest will be repaid automatically.

What happens if you die?
Your heirs can either cash in your bond or transfer it to their own names using *form DNS904* (available at post offices).

National Savings Yearly Plan

Who can invest?
Anyone, irrespective of age, who wants to save regularly.

How much can you invest?
You have to save a regular monthly amount of between £20 and £400 in units of £5 by standing order for one year. After the first year you can either continue paying the same amount on the same date each month for another year, or start a new plan if you want to alter the amount and/or the date of payment.

How to invest
Get an application form from a post office and send it to the *Savings Certificate Office, Yearly Plan*.

How does Yearly Plan work?
At the end of the year you get a Yearly Plan Certificate

showing a value equal to your 12 monthly payments plus interest on each – in November 1992 this was paid at a rate of 4 per cent a year. If you hold this Certificate for a further four years, you get a higher rate of interest (6 per cent a year in November 1992). If you keep the Certificate for the full four years, the overall rate of return works out at 5.75 per cent. If you hold your Certificate for more than four years it will earn interest at the general extension rate – see p. 170. The interest is free of income tax and your gain is not liable to capital gains tax.

Getting your money out
If you want to stop saving before having made your 12 monthly payments, you get back only what you have paid in. Once you have your Certificate, the interest you get depends on how long you hold it before cashing in. With the rates as they were in November 1992, you'd get interest at a rate of 4.5 per cent a year if you had held the Certificate for at least one month but less than two years. If you cashed it in when you'd had it for more than two years, but less than four, you'd get a higher rate of 5.25 per cent.

What happens if you die?
Your heirs can cash in your Yearly Plan or, if a certificate has been issued, they can transfer it to their own name. Get *form DNS904* from a post office.

Index-linked Save-As-You-Earn (3rd Issue)

All savers will now have finished making a regular monthly payment for five years, as the scheme closed in May 1984. In addition to the index-linking of each payment from the time it was made, the accumulated value was increased by the addition of a bonus of two monthly contributions after a further two years. Your investment is now increased in line with inflation, so the decision to cash in really depends on how inflation compares with the return you could get elsewhere.

There is no tax to pay on the returns from index-linked SAYE. To cash in your savings you should get *form DNS699MA* from a post office.

National Savings and Premium Bond gift tokens

You can get gift tokens worth £5, or in multiples of £5 up to £60, from most post offices. These can be deposited in National Savings accounts as if they were money, or can be used to buy Premium Bonds or National Savings Certificates.

National Savings FIRST Option Bonds

These bonds were introduced in July 1992, but withdrawn later in the year. It's not impossible that they may be reissued at some point in the future. The information below is useful for people who already hold the bonds.

Who can invest?
Anyone aged 16 or more.

How much can you invest?
You have to invest at least £1,000 but can then invest any amount up to £250,000. A husband and wife can each invest £250,000 but if the investment is in joint names they can invest only £250,000 between them.

How to invest
Get a form from a post office.

How much interest?
The interest rate is fixed for 12 months at a time; at the end of the 12 month period you can either cash in your investment or leave the money invested at a fixed rate for another 12 months. This rate will be the fixed rate applying at that time. In October 1992 the fixed rate was 8.67 per cent gross for sums between £1,000 and £20,000; as interest is credited to the bond after deduction of basic rate tax the return for a basic rate taxpayer is 6.5 per cent. If you invest £20,000 or more you get a higher rate of 10.07 per cent gross or 7.55 per cent after deduction of basic rate tax.

If you are a non-taxpayer you can reclaim the tax deducted from your interest; if you pay higher-rate tax you will have to pay more.

Getting your money out
You can cash in your investment on the anniversary date without any penalty. If you withdraw during the first period of 12 months you will get no interest and will simply get your initial investment back; after the first 12-month period you can withdraw at any time but will get the value at the most recent anniversary plus half the fixed rate of interest for the period since then. You don't have to cash in your whole investment and can take any amount as long as you leave £1,000 or more.

What happens if you die?
Your heirs can cash in your bond or transfer it to their own names.

National Savings Children's Bonus Bonds

Who can invest?
These can be bought for any child under 16 by anybody aged 16 or over. Once purchased, the bonds can be held until the child is 21.

How much can you invest?
Bonds are sold in units of £25. You can invest a minimum of £25 and a child can't have more than £1,000 of bonds in his or her name.

How to invest
Get a form at your post office. The bond will be sent to the child's parent or guardian who will have control of the investment until the child is 16.

How much interest?
The rate of interest is fixed for five years. In 1992 the rate is 5 per cent a year. A bonus is added on the fifth anniversary of purchase which takes the full return over the five years to 7.85 per cent.

After the first five years another offer of five years fixed interest and a bonus will be made. If the child is 16 or more when the first five years is complete, the next offer of interest and bonus will be for whatever length of time remains until he or she is 21, when the final bonus will be added.

The interest is free of income tax and capital gains tax. Although parents usually have to pay income tax on interest gained by their children as a result of their investing gifts from the parents of £100 or more, this does not apply to National Savings Children's Bonus Bonds.

Getting your money out
You can cash any number of units of £25 (plus interest) and need to give one month's notice. No notice need be given at the end of the five year period or when the holder reaches 21. Until the child is 16, the parent or guardian will have to apply for repayment and the money will be paid to him or her. Once the holder is 16, control is passed to him or her.

Premium Bonds

Who can invest?
Anyone aged 16 or over can buy Premium Bonds. And they

can be bought in the name of someone under 16 by parents, grandparents or legal guardians.

How much can you invest?
Premium Bonds cost £1 each, but you have to buy a minimum of £100 worth (until February 1993 the minimum is £10 if you're buying for someone aged under 16). You can hold up to £10,000 of bonds in multiples of £10.

How to invest
You can get an application form from most post offices and banks. Your bonds will be sent to you by the *Bonds and Stock Office* (which keeps all the records).

How do you know if you've won a prize?
You'll be contacted by post at the last address the Bonds and Stock office has for you. So make sure you let them know if you move – get change-of-address forms from a post office. There's over £4 million in unclaimed prizes because the winners can't be traced.

How do you cash your bonds?
Get *form DNS303* from a post office or bank. For each £1 invested you'll get £1 back (but, of course, if you've had your money invested for some time, inflation will have eaten away at its buying power).

What happens if you die?
Your bonds will remain eligible for prizes for 12 months after your death. To cash in the bonds, your heirs should get *form DNS904* from a post office.

How do Premium Bonds work?

You don't get interest on your money as such. Instead you get a chance of winning prizes. The total value of the prize money is equal to interest on all bonds that have been held for at least three months (over 2,060 million of them) calculated at a rate of 6.5 per cent a year (5 per cent from March 1993).

Once you've held a bond for three clear months it has a chance of winning one of the monthly prizes, ranging from £50 to £250,000, and the once-a-week prizes of £100,000, £50,000 and £25,000. All prizes are free of both income tax and capital gains tax.

There are rules about how the total prize money is divided into prizes of different amounts. For example, in

October 1992, the prize money for Premium Bonds was split up as shown in the box below.

Premium bond prizes in October 1992	
1 prize of	£250,000
4 prizes of	£100,000
4 prizes of	£50,000
4 prizes of	£25,000
5 prizes of	£10,000
25 prizes of	£5,000
125 prizes of	£1,000
375 prizes of	£500
12,658 prizes of	£100
206,170 prizes of	£50

PENSIONS FROM EMPLOYERS AND STATE

Your pension is one of the most important ways of saving for the future. Understanding how state pensions work is particularly important. Unless you know roughly what you are going to receive from the state, you'll be ill-prepared to sort out the rest of your savings and investments.

In recent years the government has made changes to the state pension scheme, and created new choices which you must make between the state system, a pension from your employer and a personal pension plan. In this chapter we explain the choices facing you concerning the state and employers' schemes; for your personal pension plan choices see Chapter 13. For how pensions in general tie in to planning your savings and investments for retirement, see Chapter 3.

The state pension system

There are three main parts to the state system. Your state pension may be made up of:
- a flat rate *basic* pension
- a *graduated* pension based on your earnings from 1961 to 1975
- an additional pension based on your earnings since April 1978, usually known as the *State Earnings Related Pension Scheme (SERPS)*.

The amount of these pensions is increased each year in line with changes in the Retail Prices Index.

Basic pension

Anyone who has paid enough full-rate Class 1, Class 2 or Class 3 National Insurance contributions, or has been given credits, qualifies for this pension. There are complicated rules to work out whether you have paid enough in contributions; but you are pretty certain to qualify for the full basic-rate pension (£54.15 a week for a single person in the 1992–3 tax year) if you have paid full-rate contributions for nine-tenths of your *working life* (broadly, between ages 16 and 64 for a man, or between ages 16 and 59 for a woman). Even if you don't qualify for the full pension, you may qualify for a reduced one, if you have contributed for a quarter of the years in your working life or more. If there were periods when you were not working, but receiving a National Insurance benefit such as Unemployment Benefit, Sickness or Invalidity Benefit, Maternity Allowance, or Invalid Care Allowance, you would have been credited with contributions for these years.

Since April 1978, if you've stayed at home to look after children, or an elderly or sick person, the number of years needed to qualify are reduced. This is called *home responsibilities protection*.

You can check on your basic pension and your graduated and SERPS pensions too by using the DSS Retirement Pensions Forecast and Advice Service. You need to get form BR19 from your local DSS office, fill it in, and send it to RPFA Unit, Room 37D, Newcastle upon Tyne NE98 1YX. The service can tell you how much pension you're entitled to so far, how much you might get by the time you retire, and anything you can do now to increase your entitlement. For example, it's possible in some cases to make up gaps in your contribution record by paying voluntary Class 3 contributions.

You can find the address of your local DSS office in the telephone book under *Social Security, Department of*.

Graduated pension

People who were employed in a job between 1961 and 1975 and had reached 18 before 1975, are likely to have a small amount of graduated pension payable on top of the basic pension.

Between April 1961 and April 1975, there were two kinds of National Insurance contribution: a flat rate one paid by almost everyone in employment, and a graduated one paid by people who earned more than £9 in any one week.

For each £7.50 he contributed during those years, a man gets a unit of pension, which is now worth 7.09p a week (in 1992–3). If you're a woman, it will have taken £9 of contributions to earn that 7.09p a week. The rules were set in this way because women have an earlier state pension age than men, and live longer on average.

The graduated pension has been increased in step with rising prices since April 1978. But it's never going to be very large. In 1992–3, the maximum graduated pension is £5.11 a week for a woman and £6.10 a week for a man.

The DSS keep records of how many *units* of pension each person has earned. You can check with them for your own position using the Retirement Pensions Forecast and Advice Service (see opposite).

Many people were *contracted out* of the old graduated scheme because their employers ran their own pension schemes. But when the scheme was wound up, many employers paid the money back into the state scheme in order to get rid of their liabilities. Again, you can ask the DSS about this. If it turns out that your employer did not buy you back into the state scheme, ask the employer for details of how much is owing to you.

State Earnings Related Pension Scheme (SERPS)

This is a supplement to the basic pension for employed people paying the full National Insurance contribution. It started in 1978, but the government has cut back on it for people retiring after April 1999.

What you get, and what you pay, depends on your earnings. We tell you how the scheme works and how to find out what you'll get on p. 193 onwards. If you are *contracted out* of SERPS, the benefits from your contracted out scheme replace SERPS. We explain the different methods of contracting out on p. 196.

Married women

If you pay the full rate National Insurance contribution, you are treated in exactly the same way as a man or a single woman. If you have had to spend time at home caring for children, or elderly relatives, you can qualify for a basic pension with a shorter contribution record, under *home responsibilities protection* (see opposite).

However, there are still many married women paying the reduced rate contribution, which used to be called the *small stamp*. No one has been able to *start* doing so since 1977. Reduced rate contributors qualify for a state pension only on a husband's record (in the same way as married women who have paid no contributions), and they have to wait until a husband starts to receive his pension. These woman don't quality for SERPS. The pension for a dependent wife is approximately 60 per cent – three-fifths – of the rate the husband is getting.

If the man has retired, and his wife is under 60, he can draw a dependant's allowance for her too, provided he is not earning or drawing an occupational pension of more than £43.10 a week. If she is over 60, then the pension is the same amount (three-fifths of his pension) but it is paid directly to her. Occupational pension is not taken into account once she is over 60.

Widows

If your husband paid enough National Insurance contri-butions, you qualify for a number of benefits, including state retirement pension when you reach pension age. For details, get leaflet NP45 from your local social security office. All widows' benefits, except the state retirement pension, stop if you re-marry. They also stop if you live with a man as his wife, but re-start if you subsequently live alone again.

Widows' benefits increase in the same way as the basic retirement pension.

If you're over 60 when your husband dies, you'll normally get the basic retirement pension. If you were under 60 and your husband was not getting the retirement pension when he died, you will also get a tax-free lump sum *widow's payment* of £1,000. You will also be entitled to an additional pension based on your husband's SERPS record.

Is it worth putting off claiming?

You can earn extra state pension by putting off drawing your state retirement pension for up to five years after pension age. For each week you postpone drawing the pension, your total state pension is increased by one-seventh of a per cent. But you have to put off your retirement for at least seven weeks before the pension is increased, because the minimum increase is 1 per cent. For each *year* that you postpone your retirement, the pension is increased by 7.5 per cent. You won't get any increases in the state pension for any weeks when you are drawing other state benefits such as unemployment benefit. Any graduated pension, and any SERPS benefits (see pp. 190 and 191) will be increased in the same way.

Once you're 65, if a woman, 70 if a man (i.e. five years over state pension age), you have to start taking your state pension, and continuing work won't increase it any further.

A wife can't claim a pension on her husband's contributions until he starts drawing the state pension. If he puts it off, her part of the pension will be postponed too, and increased by the same percentage as her husband's.

If you've already started drawing your state pension, you can cancel your retirement *once*, and earn increases in your pension from then on.

Is it worth deferring your pension in this way? By deferring your pension you are, in effect, giving up capital (your pension) in order to earn interest at a rate of 7.5 per cent a year (without compounding). It depends on your view on interest rates: you may feel you couldn't achieve a better return by drawing your pension and investing it to spend later. Things were different when the earnings rule applied. You can now get your pension in full at the age of 60 for a woman, 65 for a man, no matter how much you earn. Until 1 October 1989, your pension was reduced if you earned more than £75 a week during the first five years after reaching pension age.

How SERPS works

If you earn more than a certain amount, the *lower earnings limit* (£54 a week in the 1992–93 tax year), you pay National Insurance on the whole of your earnings up to a given ceiling, the *upper earnings limit* (£405 a week in 1992–3). These contributions qualify you for a SERPS pension.

The DSS has a record of your earnings from employers for each year since 1978–9. Your SERPS pension is related to the earnings recorded for all those years, revalued in line with the way average earnings have increased between the date when they were earned and the date you retire. So it is largely protected against inflation.

Who's not in SERPS?

You can be in SERPS only if you count as an employee; so you're not in SERPS during periods when you're self-employed. There are also several groups of people who, though they are in SERPS, are not building up a SERPS pension. These are:

■ low-paid people earning less than the lower earnings

limit (£54 a week in the 1992–3 tax year). They don't pay any National Insurance and, as a result, will get a lower, or no pension at retirement
■ people paying only voluntary National Insurance contributions
■ people whose earnings aren't taxed under the Pay As You Earn (PAYE) system. If you are in the 'black economy' and not declaring your income to the Revenue, you will not build up a SERPS pension either
■ people who are unemployed. If you are unemployed, you receive credits for the *basic* state pension only. But for SERPS purposes, for a year of unemployment you would have an earnings record of zero, which will reduce your pension at retirement
■ people who are at home looking after children or dependent relatives. However, if they are covered by *home responsibilities protection* (see p. 190) those years are not counted in their SERPS record at all, and so don't reduce their pension at retirement.

How much pension will SERPS give you?

Contributions on earnings up to the lower earnings limit count towards the basic pension, but not towards SERPS. So an amount equal to the lower earnings limit for the tax year in which you are 64 (59 if you a woman) is knocked off each of the revalued figures. What's left is the amount of earnings counted towards your SERPS pension. The original idea was that after the scheme had been running for more than 20 years, the best 20 years would be picked out and averaged together, but this has now been dropped. Now, the pension is based on the average of *all* your revalued earnings, less the lower earnings limit. This will include years of unemployment and part-time work; so, for many people, this new formula will significantly reduce their SERPS pension. If you are earning more than the upper earnings limit (£405 a week in 1992–3) these higher earnings are ignored.

How fast the SERPS pension builds up depends on when you are due to retire.

For anyone retiring before, or in, April 1999, the SERPS pension builds up at one-eightieth (1.25 per cent) of your revalued earnings for each year since 1978. So the maximum available is twenty-eightieths, or 25 per cent. But for people retiring after April 1999, SERPS will be gradually reduced. The pension earned before 1988 is always 'safeguarded' by being worked out on the one-eightieth basis, though as time goes on it will be a smaller and smaller fraction of your total SERPS pension.

For anyone retiring after April 2008, the SERPS pension will be 20 per cent of earnings between the lower and upper limits for the years after 1988. During the transitional years, 1998–2008, the SERPS pension earned after 1988 drops by 0.5 per cent a year, for those retiring in that year. So someone retiring in 2000–1 gets 24 per cent, someone retiring in 2001–2 gets 23.5 per cent and so on. Note that it's always state pension age that matters, not the age at which you choose to retire.

Working out your SERPS pension

It's not possible to work out your own SERPS pension accurately, because you don't know what your earnings pattern is going to be in the future. A few bad years, or a few good ones, would change the average over your working lifetime considerably. The safeguarding for the years between 1978 and 1988 also complicates the arithmetic.

But you can get a *rough* idea, in today's money, by ignoring the safeguarding and assuming that your current earnings are what you will always earn, in real terms. This means you are ignoring the effects of inflation or changes in your earnings pattern. What it will give you is an idea of what *proportion* of your earnings you can expect from SERPS.

■ **Step one** Decide on the figure for your total weekly earnings before tax in the current tax year (1992–3). Deduct the lower earnings limit (£54). If your earnings figure is above the upper earnings limit (£405), then ignore the extra earnings as well. For example, Fred Hurst's earnings are £209 a week, so he deducts £54, leaving £155 as the slice of earnings used for calculating SERPS. Mary Henson, however, is earning £420. She ignores the last £15 and assumes that her earnings are £405 (the upper earnings limit). So she deducts £54 from £405, leaving earnings of £351 a week.

■ **Step two** Work out in what tax year you will reach state pension age. If it's the 1998–9 tax year or earlier, go to **Step three.** If it's the 2008–9 tax year or later, go to **Step four.** If it's between 1998–9 and 2008–9 (the transitional years) go to **Step five.**

■ **Step three** Work out how many full tax years there are between 1978–9 and your retirement date. If you are a man who reaches 65 in May 1993, for instance, there will be 14 full tax years. For each year since 1978–9, you get one-eightieth of your earnings. So someone retiring in May 1993 would get fourteen-eightieths. This means that you divide the earnings figure you worked out in **Step one** by 80 and multiply by 14.

■ **Step four** If you will reach state pension age in 2008–9 or later, you get 20 per cent, or a fifth, of your earnings between the lower and upper earnings limit. So this means that you divide the earnings figure you worked out in **Step one** by five.

■ **Step five** This is for the people reaching state pension age during the transitional years, who have the most complicated sum. You need first to work out how many full tax years there are between 1998–9 and state retirement age. Then you take the 25 per cent figure (the amount of SERPS pension you'd have had if you'd been retiring in 1998–9) and deduct 0.5 per cent for each year after 1998–9. So if you'll retire in 2003–4, you deduct 2.5 per cent. This leaves you with 22.5 per cent, and you now work out 22.5 per cent of the earnings figure already calculated in **Step one.**

The DSS always starts by working out your SERPS pension as if you have been contracted in to SERPS since it began in 1978. But if in fact you have been contracted *out* (see below), the DSS will assume that part of it is coming from other sources.

Remember, what you have worked out is an *approximate* figure, based on some fairly crude assumptions, and in today's money values. See p. 225 for some points on how inflation will affect the calculations.

For a more sophisticated estimate of your SERPS entitlement, use the Retirement Pension Forecast and Advice Service – see p. 190.

Contracting out of SERPS

If you are contracted out, then a lower percentage of your National Insurance goes toward the state pension scheme. The remainder, called the *rebate*, is intended to be used for the contracted out pension. Until 6 April 1993, the rebate is 2 per cent of the employee's contribution on earnings between the lower and upper earnings limits (explained on p. 193), plus 3.8 per cent of the employer's contribution on the same slice of earnings. This makes a total of 5.8 per cent which is expected to go towards the replacement pension.

From 6 April 1993, the rebate will be reduced from 5.8 per cent to 4.8 per cent.

Contracting out with a pensions guarantee

This is the original way of contracting out. Broadly speaking, a contracted out employer's scheme must guarantee that the pension it pays (including the deferred pensions of early leavers) is generally equivalent to the SERPS pension that you would have had from the state if your employer's scheme had not been contracted out. This is called the *guaranteed minimum pension*, or *GMP* for short. In return for giving these guarantees, both employer and employee pay less National Insurance.

The GMP will go up to take account of inflation both before and after your retirement. Before retirement, this is the responsibility of the employer's scheme; after retirement, the first 3 per cent increase each year (on pension earned after April 1988) will be provided by the scheme, and the state will provide the rest. If you have a *preserved* pension (see p. 205), increases in the GMP are provided partly or wholly by the scheme, and any extra that is necessary is added by the state.

Contracting out with a Contracted Out Money Purchase (COMP) scheme

Since April 1988, employers have been allowed to contract out their workers in a new way, with what's called a *Contracted Out Money Purchase* (*COMP*) scheme. Here they guarantee only the amount of money going *in*, as contributions: there's no guaranteed minimum pension.

This money is used to create *protected rights* to a money purchase pension (explained on p. 207) payable at state pension age, and to a spouse's pension, based on the fund that has built up so far, when you die. If only the minimum contribution (see over) is going in, no other benefits are possible. There are special restrictions on how the money is invested to cover your protected rights, and each person must have an individual account which can be identified. You give up your SERPS rights for those years, and the COMP pension could be greater than what you would have had from SERPS, or it could be less. The DSS calculates the pension you would have had from SERPS, and then deducts a theoretical amount for each year you were in a COMP scheme. If the COMP in fact provides less than the theoretical amount, you bear the shortfall.

The employer and employee both pay less National Insurance than if the scheme were contracted in to SERPS.

But at least as much as the rebate (see p. 196) must go into the COMP scheme, plus, in some cases, a 2 per cent incentive (see box below). The employer makes the payments, and can (but need not) recover the 2 per cent from the employee. It is the employer who chooses whether to run a COMP scheme or not, and what contributions to charge the employee. But you don't have to join (or stay in) a COMP scheme or any other employer's scheme if you don't want to.

The 2 per cent incentive

At present the government is paying an extra 2 per cent of earnings, above the lower earnings limit and up to the upper earnings limit, towards the pensions of people who have not been contracted out before. From 6 April 1993, the bonus will be withdrawn for people under 30 and reduced to one per cent for people aged 30 or over.

Contracting out with a Minimum Appropriate Personal Pension (MAPP)

This was introduced in July 1988, and allows you to contract out of SERPS, outside your employer's scheme. You can take out a MAPP if:

■ your employer doesn't have a contracted out pension scheme *or*

■ your employer has a contracted out scheme, but you don't belong to it *or*

■ your employer has a contracted in scheme, whether or not you are a member of it.

If you take out a MAPP, your National Insurance rebate of 5.8 per cent, plus the incentive as appropriate (see above), goes into the scheme and buys you *protected rights*, on a money purchase basis (see p. 207). These entitle you to a pension at state pension age (no earlier) and a spouse's pension on your death. If you want extra pension or a different pattern of benefits, you must pay extra. You *give up* your SERPS rights for the years you are in a MAPP. The resulting pension may be bigger than what you would have got under SERPS – if the MAPP you choose has done well – or it may be less. As for COMP schemes, the DSS calculates the pension you would have had from SERPS, and then deducts a theoretical amount for each year you were in a MAPP scheme. If the MAPP in fact provides less than the theoretical amount, you bear the shortfall.

If you have a MAPP, you pay full-rate National Insurance contributions. You (and the organisation you take out the MAPP policy with) notify the DSS that you have taken out a MAPP. At the end of each tax year the DSS calculates what your rebate is, and pays it over to the *provider* (i.e. the organisation running the MAPP for you). But if anything is wrong with the DSS records, or the provider's records, there will be a delay while it's sorted out, and the rebate will not reach your account (and so start earning interest or dividends) until then.

Is contracting out a good idea?

If your employer is contracting you out and replacing SERPS with a *guaranteed minimum pension,* GMPs plus the remaining SERPS pension will always equal what you'd have got if you'd been in SERPS all along. But the wisdom of contracting out via a COMP or a MAPP depends very much on your age and circumstances.

Since SERPS is going to be reduced for people retiring after 1998, it may seem that anyone retiring after that date would be better out of it. But this is not so. The National Insurance rebate is the same percentage of your earnings, 5.8 per cent (4.8 per cent from 6 April 1993), whatever age you are, and it is likely to be reduced further in the future. But a *money purchase* pension (i.e. a COMP or a MAPP) can build up a much greater sum for a younger person than for an older one. This is because the contributions made in the early stages have far longer to build up compound interest, so are much more valuable.

So what matters is, firstly, the age at which you put the contributions in (the younger, the better) and, secondly, how fast you think your contribution will grow. If you are optimistic about how investments will do generally in the future, the rebate for a man in his early forties, and a woman in her mid thirties, might be enough at least to equal the SERPS pension that would build up during that year. If you are not too optimistic about investment returns, then the age at which you believe SERPS will beat a MAPP or COMP will be lower. If you are very optimistic, it will be higher. However optimistic you are, it is highly unlikely that anyone in their 50s will see their rebate beating SERPS.

Even if you think contracting out will give you a better pension that staying in SERPS, you will reach an age when it will make sense to re-join SERPS. If you contract out via a MAPP, in April 1993 you should review your decision. If you're unsure of what to do, you could pay for advice from a pensions consultant or an actuary (the Association of Consulting Actuaries will provide a list; tel 071-248 3163). Fees could be steep, so find out how much it costs before committing yourself.

So if you want to take no risks at all, SERPS is the place for you. If you are willing to take some risks, then, if you are young enough, contract out. But don't regard it as a once-and-for-all decision. Think again at least every five years.

A pension from your employer

Since April 1988, membership of employer's pension schemes has been voluntary. So if you are starting a new job, you can choose whether or not to join. Even if you are already in a pension scheme, you always have the option to leave your scheme and make your own provision. But if the employer provides a scheme which is any good, then your best bet will be to stay within it, and receive the benefits of the employer's contributions as well as your own.

An employer's pension scheme may be *contributory* which means you pay in a proportion of your pay to the scheme each week or month. Four or five per cent are common contribution rates (normally your employer will be paying the same, or more). Alternatively, the scheme may be *non-contributory*. In either case, the employer makes contributions into the scheme on your behalf. Provided the scheme meets certain conditions laid down by the Inland Revenue, it gets very favourable tax treatment (as do personal pension plans – see Chapter 13). You get tax relief on any contributions you make, you pay no tax on any contributions made by your employer, and the pension fund itself pays no income tax or capital gains tax.

To work out how much you will get from your pension scheme, you need to know what kind it is. There are five main kinds. The type covering most people is a *final pay* scheme, explained below. The other kinds are summarised from p. 207 onwards.

Final pay scheme

With a final pay scheme, the number of years you've been a member of the scheme, and the yearly amount you're earning at the time you retire or averaged over the few years before then, decide the size of your pension. Many schemes pay one-sixtieth of your final pay for each year of membership. Others pay, for example, one-eightieth of final pay.

Under the Inland Revenue's rules, the maximum pension you can get is two-thirds of your final pay. There is no limit on the final pay that can be taken into account if the pension scheme was set up before 14 March 1989 and you joined it before 1 June 1989. Otherwise, there is a limit of £75,000 in the 1992–3 tax year; it will be increased each year in line with price inflation.

Employers can set up 'top-up' schemes for highly paid employees to cover earnings over the limit, but such schemes have none of the tax advantages of normal pension schemes.

Employer's pension schemes usually set a normal retirement age. It can vary widely, between the ages of 50 and 70.

In what's known as a *fast accrual* scheme, you can get the maximum pension after only 10 years' service, if you were in the scheme before 17 March 1987. But if you changed employer after that date, this maximum can be reached only after 20 years.

For most people, the benefits are assumed to build up over 40 years. So if you reach normal retirement age after 40 years' membership of a scheme which pays one-sixtieth of your final pay for each year, you can retire on two-thirds final pay. But even if you retire after 45 years in the scheme, you can still only have a two-thirds pension.

In a scheme which works on eightieths, you would only have a pension of half final pay (i.e. forty-eightieths) after 40 years of membership.

The higher your final yearly pay, the higher your pension from the scheme. There are different definitions, though, of what 'pay' is. Sometimes the rules define it as including bonus, commission, overtime and such items as London Weighting, or some of these and not others. The Inland Revenue no longer allows income from *share option* schemes to be counted.

There are also differences in the way 'final' is defined. Common methods of definition are:
■ average pay in the best three consecutive years out of the last thirteen
■ basic salary in the last year before you retire (or the last but one year), plus the average of your 'fluctuating emoluments' such as bonus or commission over the last few years
■ average yearly pay over the last few years (most often three or five).

Check in your scheme booklet exactly how your employer's scheme works. You have a legal right to up-to-date details of your scheme.

Taking account of the state pension

Some final pay schemes make a deduction either from the final pay used to work out your pension, or from the pension itself, to allow for the fact that you'll be getting some money from the state. Often the way this is done is to take away an amount equivalent to the lower earnings limit (explained on p. 193), or more or less than that level, from your pay before the pension and contributions are calculated. But schemes vary, so check what yours does. If the normal retirement age in your job is earlier than state pension age, the deduction for the state pension ought not to be applied until you reach the official retirement age for the state pension. It's particularly important that it should not apply if you're forced to retire early because of ill-health.

Inflation proofing

Retirement can last a long time, particularly for women. On average, men retiring at 65 can expect 13 years of retirement; women retiring at 60 have 21 years. You want an adequate pension not just at the time you retire, but later in your retirement too. A pension of, for example, only half your final pay but with inflation proofing, will soon overtake an apparently better pension of two-thirds of your final pay with no protection against rising prices.

In public sector jobs, such as employment in the Civil Service, most pensions increase in line with the rise in the Retail Prices Index. In the private sector, not many schemes do this. Many, though, do promise to increase pensions by a certain percentage each year. Often this is 3 per cent or 4 per cent, or the increase in the Retail Prices Index if less. While this isn't too bad when inflation is low, it provides poor protection at even modest rates of inflation.

Some schemes, particularly those run by large companies, have in practice given increases which don't fall far short of inflation. In the last few years, when pension schemes have been flush with money, many have done a 'catching-up exercise' for older pensioners, increasing their pensions to the real level they were at when they retired. But how far pension funds can continue to do this, especially if inflation rises again or the funds do not grow fast enough, is uncertain.

From a date still to be decided, *future* final pay pension you earn will have to be increased by 5 per cent (or the rate of inflation if less). But this won't apply to pension rights you have already accrued. So when you retire, unless your pension is guaranteed to be inflation-proof, you should make some allowance for a fall in its buying power when you retire.

Tax-free lump sums

When you retire, you can normally exchange part of your pension for a tax-free lump sum. With some schemes, especially in the public sector, you automatically get a smaller pension and a lump sum, which you may be able to exchange for a pension. You can have up to one and a half times your earnings as a lump sum, subject (where it applies) to the £75,000 earnings limit – see p. 201. You may also be subject to a limit of £150,000 if you joined your scheme between 17 March 1987 and 1 June 1989.

If you have a choice, should you go for a tax-free lump sum or more pension? If the pension is inflation-proofed, be wary of exchanging any of it for lump sum. But if you don't expect any worthwhile increases in your pension after retirement, it may pay you to exchange as much as possible of your pension for a lump sum, and then buy an annuity – see Chapter 22. Your after-tax income from the annuity may be worth more than the pension you are giving up. It would be worth checking, close to the time you retire, what income you'd get from an annuity. The size of the annuity available to you will depend on interest rates at the time. If they are high, you could do very well. If they are low, you could do badly.

Additional voluntary contributions (AVCs)

All employers' pension schemes allow members to make *additional voluntary contributions (AVCs)*, over and above those they have to make to belong to the scheme, in order to build up extra pension. Some employers offer a range of AVC schemes, and some – but not many – will match the members' extra contributions with some of their own. The most you can put into an employer's pension scheme and AVC scheme altogether is 15 per cent of your total earnings in any one tax year (or 15 per cent of £75,000 if you earn more than this and the £75,000 rule applies – see

p. 201). However much you put in, you cannot have more than the final two-thirds pension allowed by the Inland Revenue – see p. 201. But if you over-contribute, any 'excess' AVCs will be returned to you at retirement after a tax deduction of 35 per cent for basic-rate taxpayers.

You are entitled to make contributions to another scheme run by a commercial pension provider, such as an insurance company, outside your employer's scheme. These schemes are called *free standing AVCs*, or *FSAVCs* for short. You are still not allowed to go over the two-thirds limit on pension, but 'excess' FSAVCs will be returned at retirement after a tax deduction. You can also use an FSAVC for contracting out of the state scheme, if your employer's scheme is contracted in. This is an alternative to a MAPP (see p. 198), but it is less tax-efficient because you do not receive tax relief on the National Insurance rebate this way.

Anyone who starts an AVC or FSAVC scheme now can use it to provide only a pension, not a lump sum. The rules on this changed from 8 April 1987, and so anyone who was already paying in before that date still has a right to take a lump sum. The rules also changed then to say that *if your scheme allows it*, you can start and stop contributions as you like, reduce the amount or pay in windfall amounts in odd years (before that, once you'd started you were not allowed to stop or reduce the amount). Check whether the rules of your scheme are flexible in this way.

Should you make AVCs?
Before deciding whether to make AVCs to your employer's scheme, check what will happen to them. Will they build up solely on your behalf, e.g via an account in your name with a building society, or will they go into the general pension fund, which might mean that you don't get the full benefit from them? Find out next what benefits you'd get from the AVCs. It could be only a fixed amount of pension at retirement age, which won't go up as time passes. But with some schemes, you may be able to use your extra contributions to buy extra years on your main pension, to add to the rate at which the pension increases, or to provide a pension for your spouse.

Your extra contributions are normally treated in the same way as ordinary ones for tax purposes. That is, you get tax relief on them at your top rate of tax, and they go into a fund which pays no tax on its income or capital gains. But you can't get them out until you draw your main pension, though in many cases you will be able to transfer them, along with your main pension, to another provider. AVCs can be a very good way of saving, particularly for higher-rate taxpayers and those close to retirement age. But they are less flexible than other forms of saving.

With an employer's AVC scheme, the employer almost always pays the setting up and administrative costs. With an FSAVC scheme, *you* do so, and pay the commission to the plan provider. But you may still want to take this route.

Other benefits from your employer's scheme

An employer's pension scheme may provide other benefits besides a retirement pension, such as:

- a pension if you are forced to retire early because of ill health; this is usually more generous than the pension if you retire early of your own accord. Or there may be a permanent health insurance scheme, which provides a long-term benefit for anyone who is off sick for a long spell, even right up to retirement
- a pension for your husband or wife if you are the one who dies first
- pensions for children or other dependants you leave on death
- life insurance, which can be as much as four times your earnings, if you die before leaving or retiring.

In some cases, the permanent health insurance and the life insurance will be paid to all employees whether they are a member of the pension scheme or not. More often, employers provide these benefits only for those who are actually in the scheme, although they may provide a reduced rate of life insurance for everyone.

Changing jobs

People who left a final pay pension scheme before retirement used to get a very raw deal. It's now been improved by a change in the law, though it is still a final pay scheme's weak spot compared to a money purchase scheme – see p. 207. The position now is:

- if you leave the scheme (whether or not you leave the job) within two years of joining, you can have a refund of your contributions, if the scheme allows it. But if you were contracted out of SERPS, part of your contributions will be used to buy you back into SERPS. You'll also pay 20 per cent tax on what's left
- if you leave after longer than that, you must be given a *preserved pension*. Any guaranteed minimum pension

(explained on p. 197) is increased either at a fixed rate or in line with inflation, and the state picks up any shortfall. If you leave a final salary scheme on or after 1 January 1991, your pension rights must be increased in line with the Retail Prices Index up to a maximum of 5 per cent. If you left a scheme before then, any pension built up since 1 January 1985 must be revalued in the same way. There is no obligation to increase pre-1985 preserved pensions. Your scheme may do better than the legal minimum, e.g. by giving 5 per cent even if that is more than the increase in prices

■ alternatively, you can take a *transfer value*, worked out according to standard tables, to a new employer's scheme, a personal pension plan, or a *Section 32* policy. A Section 32 policy is a special type of deferred annuity (roughly speaking, another type of pension) which you buy with a single premium. Other names for it are *buy-out plan* or *transfer plan*. You have the right to contact any employer whose scheme you left after January 1986, and with which you have a preserved pension, at any date up to a year before retirement, and say that you now want a transfer. You lose the right to a transfer if the employer's scheme is wound up; instead, the administrators must buy you an annuity.

A transfer between two public sector jobs is governed by special rules, which mean you are unlikely to lose out. With a transfer to a private sector employer, your new employer will either:

■ agree to pay you extra pension in your retirement; this is normally fixed in £££ and not increased in line with future pay increases

or

■ give you a credit of so many years' membership of the scheme. This may not be the full number of years that you had been in the old employer's scheme, because the benefit you get from it may be different. If you are offered credited years, try to negotiate a guarantee of the minimum pension in £££ from the transfer payment. This should not be less than the preserved benefits you're giving up, but will help if you change jobs again.

If you are transferring a pension that has been contracted out of SERPS, then there are special rules. If you are transferring a preserved-guaranteed minimum pension (see p. 197) into a Section 32 policy, it must guarantee to pay at least as much. On the other hand, if you are transferring it into a personal pension plan, then its money value is turned into *protected rights* (see p. 197) within the personal pension plan. This means that it can only be used in certain ways, and you are giving up the guaranteed benefits the guaranteed minimum pension gave you.

Other sorts of scheme

Money purchase schemes

In the past, few large employers ran this type of scheme, but now, with the new way of contracting out via a COMP (see p. 197), a number of new schemes have begun.

You and your employer pay contributions which are fixed as a percentage of your pay (and only pay up to £75,000 can count – see p. 201). The bulk of these contributions is invested for you (the rest goes to pay the expenses of the people running the scheme). On retirement, the proceeds are used to buy a pension. How much pension you get depends on how the investments have done, and what level the interest rates are at when you retire.

The Inland Revenue has special rules for *simplified* money purchase schemes. For example, if a scheme limits the total contribution to 17.5 per cent of earnings, on top of the National Insurance rebate, there need be no limit on the amount of benefit. So, in theory, if a simplified scheme did exceptionally well, you might end up with a pension bigger than your earnings (not normally allowed). Only up to a quarter of the total pension fund accumulated for you, however, may be taken as cash, the rest must be pension. There are also various restrictions on the way a scheme like this is run, and when the benefits may be taken.

With a money purchase scheme, you don't lose out on leaving your job; the fund simply continues to receive interest and dividends on the amount already in there, though no more will be paid in. You could transfer it to a new employer's scheme or a personal pension plan, if you felt that they were going to produce a better return on your investment than the current managers. But you would need to look carefully to see how much you would lose by leaving the existing scheme, especially if you have been in it for only a few years.

Though they are nothing new, *hybrid* schemes are now being introduced by more employers, either final pay schemes with a guarantee that you will not do worse than on a money purchase basis with a given level of contributions, or money purchase with a guarantee of at least a certain growth rate on the final pay basis. If the guarantees are at a reasonable level, these hybrid schemes can give you the best of both worlds. They protect the pensions of early leavers (still the weak spot for final pay schemes), and provide protection against inflation, in line with increases in earnings, for those who stay to claim their pensions.

Average pay schemes
With these, your pension is based on your pay in each year you belong to the scheme; there is usually a graded scale of earnings. For each year that your pay is in a particular earnings band, you get a fixed amount of pension. As you move up the earnings scale, the amount earned in pension will rise, as will any contributions you pay. The yearly pension you're eventually paid will be the total of all the little bits of yearly pension you've earned in each band, so there is no protection against inflation in these schemes.

For example, for each year your earnings are between £3,000 and £4,000, you may get £50 in pension a year. For each year your earnings are £4,000 a year, you may get £60 a year.

Revalued average schemes
These work in a similar way to SERPS (explained on p. 193). Your earnings are revalued to take account of the rise in earnings (or sometimes only prices) between the date when you earned them and the date when you retire. Then an average is taken and a fraction given, depending on the rate at which the pension builds up, for each year you are in the scheme.

Flat rate schemes
Flat rate schemes provide a fixed amount of pension, perhaps £5 a year, for each year's membership of the scheme.

How safe is your pension?

In late 1991, after Robert Maxwell's death, large numbers of people who were contributing to or getting a pension from the Maxwell Communications Pension Scheme were horrified to learn that over £400 million had been stolen from the scheme. As we went to press in late 1992, a major Government review was addressing the issues raised by the Maxwell affair, including how pensions are regulated.

Don't be tempted to leave your employer's scheme just because of the Maxwell affair: pension scheme frauds are very rare, though their effects can be very serious indeed for those who are unlucky enough to be victims. But do take an interest in your scheme and the way it is run, by reading the information sent to you, asking to see copies of the accounts and putting questions to the trustees (and making sure that you know who the trustees are). If you don't get the answers you need, you can contact the *Occupational Pensions Advisory Service (OPAS)* (tel: 071-233 8080) for help.

Verdict: employer's scheme or personal pension plan?

Employers' final pay schemes (contracted out)

If you are in a good employer's scheme that is based on final pay and *contracted out* of SERPS, you should think very seriously before deciding to leave and go it alone with a personal pension plan. It would mean that you were giving up the guarantees made by your employer about the level of retirement benefits. Your pension will be less certain, because it is not based on final pay, and it will depend instead on two other uncertainties: how well your money has been invested up to your retirement date, and interest rates at that time. A sudden change in the fortunes of the stock market, like the crash in share values in October 1987, or a drop in the interest rates which dictate *annuity rates* (i.e. the pension you can actually buy with your fund), could mean a big change in your pension. (Of course, all this applies also to employer's money purchase schemes as well as to personal pension plans.)

It's likely that if you go outside the scheme your employer will say that you must also provide death in service benefits and disability benefits for yourself. Find out about this before taking any decision, and shop around to compare the costs; if you are over a certain age, you may well find that replacing the benefits costs more than your contribution to the employer's scheme as a whole.

Before taking any decision, find out whether the employer will allow you to rejoin the pension scheme if you change your mind. In many cases, an employer allows you one change of mind, but says that if you leave again, you stay out. Other employers put an upper limit on the ages at which people will be allowed to join or rejoin, say age 45. Still others say that if you leave, you will be out for good.

Employers' final pay schemes (contracted in)

If your employer's scheme is contracted in, then as a younger person you may want to contract out of SERPS. Again, you can do this with an FSAVC or a MAPP (see p. 198), without leaving the employer's scheme. The arguments in favour of employers' final pay schemes are much the same whether they are contracted in or out (see p. 209).

Personal pensions

Employers who have their own schemes are unlikely to contribute to a personal pension plan, unless you are in a sufficiently senior position to bargain for special treatment. As many employers contribute twice as much as the members to the employer's pension scheme, only the very young or very lucky are likely to have more pension from a personal pension plan than from an employer's scheme (unless the benefits from the employer's scheme are very poor).

For a personal pension plan, there will be administration and commission charges, while employers normally pay the running costs of their own schemes. In any case, the administration charges are likely to be higher for a personal pension plan than for an employer's scheme, because there won't be the same economies of scale in running the scheme. All this means that if you are in a personal pension plan for only a short time, it is likely to be poor value, because the administration charges will be deducted at the beginning of the policy.

On the other hand, the attraction of a personal pension plan is that there is no loss on changing jobs. There is also no limit on benefits, only on contributions – see Chapter 13. So full advantage can be gained from favourable investment conditions; in an employer's pension scheme, the employer tends to reap the benefits in terms of lower contributions. You also have the freedom to choose who will provide the pension.

Employers' money purchase schemes

If the employer runs a money purchase scheme, you may feel that you could do better with your own money purchase personal pension plan. But find out how much the employer is putting in to the scheme, and what administrative charges (if any) are being deducted. Doing your own thing is likely to mean paying your own charges as well. And with an employer's COMP scheme, the money goes straight in each month when the payroll calculations are done. With a personal pension, the National Insurance rebate is held back by the DSS until after the end of the tax year. It does not start earning interest or dividends until it reaches the personal pension plan provider.

Verdict

Overall, unless you are under 30 or so, intend to move jobs rapidly, and have no dependants, a reasonable employer's scheme is likely to be the best for you. If you take out a personal pension plan in the early years of your working life, you ought to aim to move back into an employer's scheme in your 30s, or when you get married. You can join an employer's scheme and still have your own visible pension 'pot' by setting up an FSAVC scheme (explained on p. 204) in addition, so taking out a two-way bet.

13

PERSONAL PENSION PLANS

Personal pension plans are a type of pension scheme for individuals; they can be provided by banks, building societies, friendly societies, unit trusts and insurance companies for anyone (employed or self-employed) who is not in an employer's pension scheme. Even if you are in an employer's pension scheme, you can take out a *Minimum Appropriate Personal Pension (MAPP)* to contract out of the *State Earnings Related Pension Scheme* or *SERPS* (see Chapter 12), *unless* your employer's scheme itself is contracted out. And, if you are in an employer's scheme for your main employment, but have some freelance earnings, or a second job from which you won't get a retirement pension, you can have a personal pension based on the earnings from these *non-pensionable* employments, while still remaining in your main employer's scheme.

If you have been in an employer's scheme in the past, you can transfer the money already built up in that scheme into a personal pension plan. Alternatively, you can set up a *Section 32* policy when you change jobs – see p. 206. Although transfers and Section 32 policies come under different rules from personal pension plans, the investment methods, and the sort of points to look out for, will be much the same. So although this chapter does not refer to transfers or Section 32 policies as such, read it if you are thinking of using one of these.

You take out a personal pension plan by paying a premium, or agreeing to pay a series of premiums, to whichever pension provider you've chosen. They invest the money and, when you retire, they pay you a pension for life, and usually a tax-free lump sum – see diagram overleaf.

For example, if you started paying £1,000 a year into a scheme at age 40, you might build up a fund of around £208,000 from age 65. Out of this you could have a pension

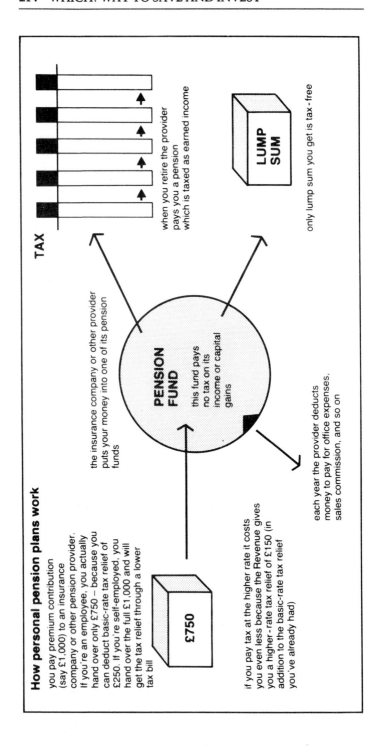

How personal pension plans work

you pay premium contribution (say £1,000) to an insurance company or other pension provider. If you're an employee, you actually hand over only £750 – because you can deduct basic-rate tax relief of £250. If you're self-employed, you hand over the full £1,000 and will get the tax relief through a lower tax bill

if you pay tax at the higher rate it costs you even less because the Revenue gives you a higher-rate tax relief of £150 (in addition to the basic-rate tax relief you've already had)

£753

the insurance company or other provider puts your money into one of its pension funds

PENSION FUND

this fund pays no tax on its income or capital gains

each year the provider deducts money to pay for office expenses, sales commission, and so on

TAX

when you retire the provider pays you a pension which is taxed as earned income

LUMP SUM

only lump sum you get is tax-free

of £23,000 a year. Alternatively, you could take a lump sum of a quarter of the fund, £52,000, and a pension of around £15,000 a year.

What are the advantages?

Pension schemes and plans get much more generous tax treatment than any other investment. You get tax relief on your premiums, provided you keep within certain limits, at the highest rate of tax you pay. So if you paid tax at the basic rate of 25 per cent, the £1,000 premiums in the example above would cost you only £750, or £600 if you paid tax at 40 per cent. The provider does not pay tax on the profits from investing your money and any lump sum you get is tax-free. This means that you are likely to get a higher income, after tax, from a pension scheme or plan than from a comparable investment in, say, investment-type life insurance used to buy an immediate annuity at age 65.

Whether a pension scheme or plan is a good investment for *you* depends mainly on how long you live. If you live to a ripe old age you get much better value than if you die shortly after retiring. But what you're paying for is the certainty of having a regular income as long as you live.

What are the disadvantages?

Once you've handed your money over you can't normally start to get it back until the retirement age written into your plan, which can't be younger than 50. Even when you reach retirement age, you can take only a limited amount as a lump sum (the rest has to be paid as pension). So if you decide later that another form of investment would give you a better return, you won't normally be able to switch. However, you can stop your payments, and you may be able to borrow money from the provider on the strength of the money already in your plan.

All this means that you shouldn't put money that you are likely to need in an emergency into any sort of pension scheme. But you should start paying in as young as possible, because the contributions you make when young have longest to build up compound interest.

Another disadvantage is inflation. You should always take account of inflation when planning how much pension you'll need. Suppose you're aged 40 now, planning to retire at 65, and the pension provider predicts that your contributions will grow enough to provide you with a pension of £15,000 a year. This may sound substantial as a pension today, but even if inflation averaged only 4 per cent over the 25 years you had been saving, your pension would be worth only about £5,630 (in today's buying power) in the year you retired. With 7 per cent inflation, it would be down to £2,760, and by the time you reached 75, it would be worth only £1,400. So if you are some way from retirement, the pension you'll need will be much more than seems sufficient now. We tell you how you can allow for inflation on p. 226.

Finally, a personal pension will give a lower pension to a woman, for the same level of contribution, than to a man retiring at the same age. This is because she can expect to live longer than he can, so the same amount of money has to be spread over a larger number of payments.

The exception here is the *Minimum Appropriate Personal Pension* (see p. 198), where the *annuity rates* which determine how much pension you get have to be 'unisex' at the same age, i.e. the same for men and women.

What happened to the old system?

Until 1 July 1988, self-employed people and those not in an employer's scheme could buy personal pensions in the form of policies called *Section 226* schemes or *Self-Employed Retirement Annuities*. No more of these policies have been sold since 1 July 1988, but if you already have such a plan, you are allowed to keep it in force and increase your payments to it, until you retire or decide you want to change it. And you can take out a new personal pension plan as well, if you wish.

With the old types of policy, the pension limits were less flexible than with new personal pension plans; in particular, you could not normally have a retirement age of below 60. But on the other hand the lump sum available was probably larger than under the new arrrangements. So if you already have one (or more) of these policies, it is worth maintaining it in its present form, and switching only at or near retirement date, if it then looks worthwhile.

When to start paying for a personal pension

The younger you are when you make contributions to a personal pension plan, the longer those contributions have to gather interest and dividends. If you paid the same amount in premiums each year, starting just one year earlier could increase your pension by over 10 per cent.

When can you start receiving the pension?

Generally speaking, at any time between the ages of 50 and 75, depending on the age which you specify when you take out the plan. People in certain occupations can retire earlier, and you may also be able to do so if you become too ill to carry on working, though the pension payable will be at a very much reduced rate. If you have several plans, you can start receiving the benefits from each at different times. You don't have to stop working to do so. (We use *retire* in this chapter to mean *start receiving the benefits of the plan*, whether or not you actually stop work at the time.)

The types of plan

There are several hundred different personal pension plans, but hardly two are the same. The main variations are in:

- who is providing the scheme
- how the pension you're entitled to is worked out
- how your money is invested
- how often you pay premiums.

Who is providing the scheme?

Pensions business was, until July 1988, strictly the provence of the insurance companies. Even if you thought you were buying a policy from someone else, like a building society, the small print would have revealed that they were either in partnership with an insurance company, or running the scheme through an insurance subsidiary.

In July 1988 this changed, and banks, building societies, unit trusts and the larger friendly societies were all allowed to join in. When the pension starts to be paid, however, the business might revert to an insurance company or friendly society, because only they are legally allowed to provide the annuities which are used to provide the pension payments.

So if you have a plan with one of the other providers, you select an insurance company or friendly society from which to buy the pension. This is called the *open market option*. (If you have a Minimum Appropriate Personal Pension, you will have the right to do this in any case.)

How your pension is worked out

Pension providers calculate benefits in different ways, depending on how your pension plan is worded.

A *deferred annuity* plan talks in terms of the pension you will get from a certain age. This will be based on the amount you've paid into the scheme. Taking the example on p. 213, if you pay in £1,000 for 25 years from age 40, the provider might quote a pension of £23,000 a year if you retire at 65.

A *cash-funded* plan (more common) talks in terms of the amount of money that accumulates to buy your pension with. For example, the plan may say that if you paid in the same amounts as in the example above, a cash fund of £208,000 would have accumulated by the age of 65.

When you retire, the cash is used to buy an *immediate annuity* which would pay you an income for life. The income you get will depend on the company's annuity rate for your age and sex when you retire. This will specify how much pension you get for each £ in your fund, usually in terms of pension per £1,000 in the fund. So, for example, your pension might be, say, £135 per £1,000 (13.5 per cent) for a 65-year-old man. Therefore, your pension might be 13.5 per cent of your cash fund of £208,000, which is £28,080. It all depends on the annuity rates at the time you retire. If annuity rates were lower, your pension, for the rest of your life, would be correspondingly lower. For more information, see *Annuities* on p. 349.

Your choice of investment

Below, we give the details of four main types of plan. For which type to choose, see p. 224.

With-profits

The premiums go into the provider's fund to be invested in, for example, shares, British Government stock and property. The plan guarantees from the outset the minimum pension it will pay you (if the policy is a deferred annuity one) or the minimum amount of money you'll have with which to buy an annuity (if it is cash-funded). These minimum amounts are low. But as the provider makes profits on its investments, it announces increases in the minimum pension (or fund) you're guaranteed at retirement. These are called *reversionary bonuses*, and once they've been announced – usually every year – they cannot be taken away.

With most policies, a one-off *terminal bonus* can be

added at the time you retire. You have no idea how much this will be until that time arrives. As a result of these bonuses, you're likely to end up with a pension or cash fund which is considerably higher than the minimum pension you're guaranteed.

Unit-linked and unit trust
Your premiums buy units in one or more of a number of funds offered by the insurance or unit trust company. The most common types of fund are:
- property funds – invested in office blocks, factories, shops and so on
- equity funds – invested in shares, directly or through unit trusts
- fixed-interest funds – invested in British Government stocks, company loan stocks, and other investments which pay out a fixed income
- cash funds – invested in bank deposit accounts and other investments whose return varies along with interest rates in general
- managed funds – invested in a range of the options listed above, in proportions decided by the investment managers.

Each fund is divided into a number of units. The price of each is, approximately, the value of the investments in the fund divided by the number of units that have been issued. So the unit price goes up and down as the value of the investments in the fund fluctuates.

With most providers there's a choice of funds to invest in, and you can switch from one to another. This could prove useful if you want to move your money around in the hope of getting the best return. But if you time things wrongly, you could end up doing rather badly. There's often a charge for switching, perhaps 0.5 per cent of the amount you're moving, if you switch more often than, say, once a year.

Nearly all unit-linked policies are cash-funded, so the amount of pension also depends on annuity rates at the time you start taking the benefits. If both the value of your units and annuity rates themselves are low at the time you retire, as they were for instance after the stock market crash in October 1987, you could find yourself having to make do with a low income, or putting off your retirement in the hope that things will improve.

A few unit-linked policies guarantee a minimum cash fund or a minimum annuity rate, but these guarantees tend to be at a pretty low level.

Unitised with-profits

This type is a cross between a unit-linked and a with-profits scheme. More and more providers are starting to offer this type, either as a completely separate plan or as one of the range of funds available with a unit-linked plan (in which case it is usually called a 'with-profits fund'). They work in a similar way to a with-profits plan: your contributions are allocated to units in a fund, but the return comes as bonus units which are added and can't then be taken away.

Deposit administration

This type of scheme is provided particularly by building societies, though other providers also offer it in some cases.

It works rather like a deposit account. Your premiums are put into an account with the provider, and interest is added from time to time. The interest rate will vary with the general level of interest rates, but there may be a guaranteed minimum amount, sometimes linked to the mortgage rate. The value of your fund, in £££, can't go down. With some providers you can switch between deposit administration and unit-linked policies. It is often sensible to switch your pension savings into this type of fund as you near retirement, if you think that your unit-linked fund might go down in value.

All deposit administration schemes are cash-funded, and a few guarantee a minimum amount of cash fund you'll have at retirement. The amount of pension will depend on annuity rates at the time you retire, though many policies do guarantee a minimum annuity rate at retirement.

How often you pay premiums

Most companies offer both regular- and single-premium policies. With a regular-premium policy you agree to make payments every month, quarter, half-year or year. With most providers, the terms you get are decided when you first take out the plan, and apply to all your regular premiums. So if the plan is cash-funded, and with a certain level of charges, this will apply for as long as the plan lasts.

With a single-premium policy, you pay in a lump sum which remains invested until you retire. The terms depend on when you pay the premium. So they could be worse, or better, than for a regular premium policy running at the same time. The distinction between single- and regular-premium policies is not always clear. For example, having paid in your first premium, a scheme may allow you to make any number of payments of almost any amount, at any time in the future. And with all schemes you can stop paying altogether at any time, as explained on p. 227.

Single-premium policies allow you to decide with no constraints what you want to pay, and when. You also have the chance to shop around each time for the company offering the best terms.

There is little point in going for a regular-premium policy that does *not* guarantee that the terms you get each year are the ones laid down at the outset – you'd be better off with single-premium policies. But regular premiums do provide the discipline of asking you to pay money regularly.

You may do best to go for a mixture of single-premium and regular-premium policies. At retirement you can use the *open market option* (see p. 232) to transfer the value of all your policies to the company offering the best annuity rates.

Borrowing back from the provider

A few schemes include what's called a *loan-back facility*, so that you can borrow from the provider up to the amount you've got in the pension fund. There is a minimum amount, usually £5,000, and you need to be able to offer security such as your house, business premises or shares. You can repay the loan when you like, perhaps from selling your business when you retire, or out of the tax-free lump sum you get on retirement if this is large enough.

There may be little advantage in borrowing in this way rather than, say, getting a loan from a bank. The bank's interest rates may be more competitive than those charged by the provider. But the facility could be useful if you wanted to borrow at a time when credit was difficult to obtain (though if you are turned down by a bank because you are not creditworthy, you are also quite likely to be turned down by the pension provider).

Pension mortgages

It is also possible to arrange to link your pension and your mortgage. Legally, there is no link, because you are not allowed to *assign* your pension benefit, i.e. use it as security for a loan. Instead, what happens is that you take out an interest-only mortgage, and receive tax relief on the repayments as normal. You also pay your pension scheme contributions, receiving tax relief on them. At retirement date, you use your tax-free lump sum to pay off the capital on the mortgage. A legal link is unnecessary, as the bank or building society holding the mortgage can foreclose on your house if you do not pay them back.

Pension mortgages have some disadvantages. They can tie you to one provider, who may not offer the best rates or returns, and you may have to take the pension at a fixed date, which may be inconvenient for other reasons. You commit yourself many years ahead to a particular use for your tax-free lump sum, though there may be other things on which you would prefer to spend the money.

You may find that having a pension mortgage creates problems if later on you join an employer who has a good pension scheme. You will be able to join that only if you stop paying into the personal pension plan. It should usually be possible to make a new arrangement for paying off the mortgage, however, so you are not locked in to the personal pension altogether.

There will also be difficulties in keeping up payments to the pension scheme if you become unemployed, and so have no earnings from which to pay. You can buy insurance to cover this, though at extra cost. With a mortgage linked to the employer's pension scheme (which is also possible), there is the added problem of rearranging the scheme if you leave that employment, though again, this will become easier if pension mortgages become more common.

Above all, taking a pension mortgage could reduce your income in retirement. If you're using part of your pension fund to repay a mortgage, there will be less available to provide a pension for you.

Although the tax advantages are considerable, they don't necessarily outweigh the disadvantages. Think carefully before deciding to take out a pension mortgage.

Minimum Appropriate Personal Pensions

These are policies, approved by the Occupational Pensions Board, which are contracted out of the State Earnings Related Pension Scheme (SERPS) and paid instead of part of your SERPS benefit – see p. 198. Only employees can take these out – the self-employed are not in SERPS.

You cannot have more than one Minimum Appropriate Personal Pension (MAPP) in any one tax year, but you can pay additional contributions to it and add as many ordinary personal pension plans on top as you like (if you are not in an employer's pension scheme). In practice, if your *only* pension provision was a MAPP policy you would get a very poor and inflexible pension, so it is not recommended. You would also forego the chance of a lump sum at retirement, or of retiring at any age earlier than state pension age. In most cases, the providers will sell a MAPP with the option of paying extra contributions as one package, and will be reluctant to let you buy only the most basic MAPP on its own unless you're also in an employer's scheme.

The contributions to a MAPP are made up of:

■ the National Insurance rebate – 5.8 per cent on your earnings between the lower and upper earnings limits (see p. 193) until 6 April 1993. After this, the rebate will be reduced from 5.8 per cent to 4.8 per cent

■ the 2 per cent 'incentive' until 6 April 1993, for people who have not already been in their current employer's contracted-out scheme for at least two years before they took out the personal pension plan, *and*

■ tax relief on your rebate which comes to roughly another 0.67 per cent of your earnings.

These contributions are paid over by the DSS after the end of the tax year, when they have sorted out the paperwork. They come to just over 8 per cent in all, and are not counted by the Inland Revenue against their limits for tax relief, explained on p. 235. For whether or not a MAPP would be a sensible choice for you, see p. 199.

What contributions to an Appropriate Personal Pension buy you

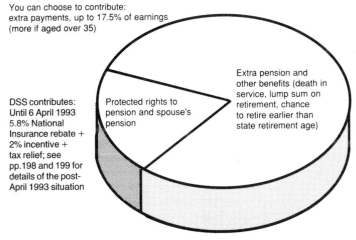

You can choose to contribute: extra payments, up to 17.5% of earnings (more if aged over 35)

DSS contributes: Until 6 April 1993 5.8% National Insurance rebate + 2% incentive + tax relief; see pp.198 and 199 for details of the post-April 1993 situation

Protected rights to pension and spouse's pension

Extra pension and other benefits (death in service, lump sum on retirement, chance to retire earlier than state retirement age)

Planning your pension

Which type of policy?

Deposit administration policies and the cash funds of unit-linked policies are very dependent on levels of interest rates. So they look good when interest rates are high, but less good when the rates are lower. Because the value of your fund or the price of your units (in £££) can't go down, these policies are useful for people nearing retirement who want to make sure they don't lose any money. If you have a unit-linked policy, switching into the cash fund or a deposit administration scheme can be useful if you're worried about units going down in value. But the pension will still be dependent on annuity rates when you retire.

For the longer term, the choice is between with-profits and unit-linked policies. With-profits schemes are the less risky. Although the guaranteed pension or cash fund is initially low, it is reasonably certain to be increased steadily over the period to retirement. But many insurance companies have been piling a large proportion of the 'profits' into the terminal bonus, which is not guaranteed and can be held static or cut, and even future rates of reversionary bonus can be reduced if a company falls on hard times.

If you go for a deferred annuity scheme, your pension will not suffer if annuity rates are low at the time you retire (though some companies will increase your pension if annuity rates are high). With unit-linked policies (apart from the small number of index-linked ones available), the return is much more dependent on when you make your payments and when you start taking the benefits. While you may do very well with a unit-linked policy, you could do rather badly.

One good compromise would be to take out a regular-premium with-profits policy for an amount you can fairly easily afford, at as young an age as possible – say, age 30. It is probably worth going for a policy which allows you to increase premiums on guaranteed terms in future years. But in years in which you can afford to pay a substantial extra amount, take out a single-premium policy, perhaps a unit-linked one. As time passes, in order to protect your pension from inflation you would need to take out further policies, which would help spread the risks, or to pay more into your existing policies.

This strategy should make sure that you have enough pension from with-profits policies whenever you want to retire. So you'll then be in a better position to choose a good time for taking the benefits of the unit-linked policies, when the prices of the units or annuity rates (or both) are high. Alternatively, in the few years before you intend to retire, switch into a cash fund or a deposit administration fund. You could do this when the price of the units reaches high levels or you think they are going to go down.

How much to pay in

With regular premium policies, most companies set a minimum regular premium of, say, £250 a year or £25 a month. The minimum for a single-premium policy could be £500 or £1,000, but can be a good deal higher for a scheme specially tailored for senior people on high salaries.

The maximum you can pay is the maximum amount you can get tax relief on, explained on p. 235.

Organisations selling pension plans give very accurate looking and impressive figures showing the pension you'd get from each £ you pay from a certain age. But these quotations are only estimates, based on set assumptions about future investment returns. For most plans, these assumptions are laid down under the Financial Services Act. The estimates take no account of inflation, which can be devastating over long periods of time (though you get a separate, and rather confusing, statement about inflation).

For example, if you started paying £500 a year into a regular premium policy at age 35, you might imagine yourself living in comfort on the £17,000 a year the insurance company quotes you. But if inflation averaged 4 per cent over the rest of your working life, the buying power of this pension at age 65 would be only £7,750 a year. Ten years after retirement it would be worth only about £5,240 a year, if inflation continued at 4 per cent.

This makes it extremely difficult to know how much you should be paying in to your pension. But you should consider the following points:
■ how much income you'll have after retirement from other sources, such as state retirement pension, from selling your business, or from part-time work
■ the age you intend to retire at – the older this is, the more pension you'll get for each £ you've paid in
■ inflation after retirement. If you live to age 65, you can expect to live to age 78, on average, if you're a man, 82 if you're a woman. You'll still want your pension to have reasonable purchasing power in your old age, so your

pension in the first year of retirement will need to be much
higher in £££ than you'd think. Alternatively you could
give up some pension in the early years of retirement
in order to have a pension which increases each year –
see p. 233

■ inflation between now and retirement. Over such a long
period of time, inflation can make mincemeat of your
pension.

You can use the table below to work out how many £££
pension you'll need for various rates of inflation. For
example, if you think you'll need a pension of £10,000 a
year (in today's money) in 30 years' time, and you reckon
inflation will average 7 per cent over that time, you'll need
to get £10,000 × 7.6 = £76,000 a year from the scheme to
achieve this.

yearly rate of inflation	£££ you'd need to get, for each £ (in today's buying power) of pension you want:				
	in 10yrs	in 20yrs	in 30yrs	in 40yrs	in 50yrs
4%	1.5	2.2	3.2	4.8	7.1
7%	2.0	3.9	7.6	15.0	29.0
10%	2.6	6.7	17.0	45.0	117.0

To take account of inflation both before and after
retirement, use the number of years up to your 70th or 75th
birthday, say, even if you intend to retire younger.

You may well find that you cannot possibly afford the
premiums for a pension of the amount you've worked out.
Your best approach may be to pay up to the limit allowed
by the Inland Revenue for tax relief each year (see p. 235)
or, if you are an employee, to try to persuade your employer
to put something in also. But if you're close to retirement,
it may be impossible to achieve anything like enough
pension, even if you do this.

When to start

If you are aiming at a pension at age 65 of two-thirds of
your final pay (which is the most that someone in an
employer's scheme would be allowed to have) you'll need
to pay the full percentage of earnings allowed by the Inland
Revenue each year from about age 44 onwards. This *might*
give you a fully index-linked two-thirds pension, plus a
pension of two-thirds of that for your spouse if you died in
retirement.

But you'd be unwise to leave starting a scheme as late as this. There may be years when you can afford to pay only a small amount in premiums; you may decide to use some of the premiums qualifying for tax relief to get life insurance or a pension for your dependants; you may need to retire before 65, perhaps because of ill-health; and inflation may be very high in the first few years of your retirement. So, unless you are confident you would have substantial income from elsewhere, you should certainly start paying for your pension by your early 30s.

If you stop paying

You may need to stop paying into a regular-premium policy, perhaps because you have no qualifying earnings in a tax year, or find yourself short of cash. Most providers will let you miss one or two payments, but there is usually a limit at which the policy has to be made *paid up*. This means that your money remains invested in the fund, and you'll get a pension when you retire, though it will be smaller than if you had kept paying. Check with the provider how they'd work out the pension.

You can often reinstate a policy within a year or so of its been made paid up. With with-profits policies, you'll normally have to pay all the premiums you've missed and perhaps a fee as well. But this could be worth doing if the guarantees on your old policies are better than they would be on a new one, or if the old policy is a Section 226 scheme with the higher level of lump sum available. Make sure you'll qualify for tax relief on the premiums – see p. 235.

When you plan to retire

You must start to take the benefits from a personal pension plan some time between your 50th and 75th birthday, unless your job is recognised as having a lower retirement age. There are now only a few of these, such as various groups of sportsmen and athletes with retirement ages of 35 or 40. Under the older, Section 226 policies, the minimum retirement age was 60, so there was a far longer list of exceptions.

If you have Section 226 policies and want to retire at an age between 50 and 60, it will be possible to alter them into personal pension plans, but you will lose the right to the greater lump sum if you do so.

There's no need to stop working in order to draw your pension and lump sum.

If you have become too ill to work before the lowest age at which you can retire, you can start taking the benefits then, but the amount will be much reduced. This is because you'll have been paying in for a shorter period and will expect to draw out for longer.

With some policies, you have to say at the outset when you intend to retire, though you can change your mind later. Other policies have a standard retirement age, but you can still retire when you like within the age range allowed. If you don't know when you'll want to retire, check that you won't lose out by retiring earlier or later than the date you name.

Phasing your retirement

You may not want to stop work suddenly but would rather slide out gradually over a period of years. If so, you may want to supplement your earnings over a number of years by drawing a small amount of pension, increasing year by year until you draw your full pension when you've stopped working altogether.

You could do this by having several policies and taking the benefits from each at a different time. Or you could invest with companies which design their policies as a series of separate units, each of which can start paying out at a different time. But check that this doesn't mean you are paying too much in administration charges.

If you die before retirement

With most policies, a lump sum will be paid to your heirs if you die before you have started taking the policy benefits. With some policies you have a choice about how much will be paid out, e.g. whether they just give back the premiums you've paid, or add interest to them.

The more you want paid out on your death, the less pension you'll get. It could be better to get the biggest pension you can and arrange extra life insurance separately (see box opposite), though you can get tax relief on life insurance premiums only if you use part of the overall contribution limit available for personal pension payments. To weigh up which is best for you, ask the insurance company (or other provider) to give you illustrations of the costs of both options.

A few providers will pay out a pension for a dependant instead of a lump sum. But the dependant might be able to get a better income by investing a lump sum.

See p. 234 for how personal pensions can be used to provide for dependants if you die after retirement.

Additional life insurance

If you qualify for a personal pension plan, you'll be able to use part of your contributions – up to 5 per cent of your earnings – to buy life insurance. This is particularly valuable because you get tax relief at your top rate on the life insurance premiums.

You don't have to get the life insurance from the same provider whose personal pension plan you are paying into though they may give you a discount. Shop around for a discount, or get a broker to do so for you.

For more on the important subject of life insurance for your family, see p. 313.

Choosing a policy

With so many different types of organisation now selling pensions, there are likely to be several hundred personal pension plans to choose from. Choosing among them isn't easy and, if this is going to be your main way of saving for retirement, it might be sensible to spread your investment over more than one plan, though each extra scheme you take out means an extra administration charge. Use the checklist in the box over the page to sort out the features you want in each plan.

To find out for yourself which policies offer which features, get hold of the most recent edition of *Choose Your Pension: an Action Pack from Which?* (available from bookshops or direct from Consumers' Association, PO Box 44, Hertford SG14 1SH) or the *Personal Pensions Handbook* published by *FTBI*, Greystoke Place, Fetter Lane, London EC4 1ND. These give useful comparative details on most plans.

You'll want to find a company which will give a better-than-average return on your investment. But there's no sure way of knowing how each company will perform.

With *with-profits* policies you could check what you'd get from different companies if current bonus rates were maintained, and how they've done in the past. However, there's no guarantee that companies that have done well in the past will continue to do well in the future and there is currently some doubt whether the high bonus rates of previous years can be maintained.

Pension Checklist

THE POLICY   **YOUR CHOICE**
deferred annuity or cash-funded

with-profits, unit-linked, unitised with-profits
or deposit administration

loan-back facility

pension mortgage

single-premium or regular-premium

if regular-premium:
■ do you want terms for future
premiums guaranteed at the outset?
■ do you want to be able to vary the
premiums?
■ do you need a policy that is flexible
if you stop paying?

YOUR PREMIUMS
if single-premium, amount (before tax
relief) you'd like to pay in

if regular-premium, yearly amount
(before tax relief) you can
commit yourself to

RETIREMENT
age at which you expect to retire

do you want to be able to phase retirement but still take out just one policy?

do you want to contract out via a MAPP?

IN CASE YOU DIE BEFORE RETIREMENT
be sure to find out what would be paid, and consider taking out
extra protection-only life insurance

With *unit-linked* and *deposit administration* schemes,
the past is, again, little guide to the future, nor are current
growth rates. The assumptions about future growth have
been standardised to some extent by the regulatory authorities, but probably the most important question to ask is

the level of charges made. These are worked out in complicated and varying ways. Plan providers now have to provide details of the amount by which their charges reduce the return on their policies – known as the *Reduction in Yield (RIY)*. It may be best to go for a company that keeps its charges down, though you can't be sure that it will continue to do so in the future. *The Personal Pensions Handbook* (see p. 229) gives comparable figures for the different plans with standard assumptions about future growth.

If you get an insurance adviser to do the work for you, bear in mind that he or she may be unlikely to steer you towards a policy which pays no commission (unless you are prepared to pay a fee for the advice). So check what commission is being given. The rule is that an adviser must tell you how much he or she will get, if you ask. You will be told the amount of commission, though not until up to 14 days after you've taken out the plan, and only as a percentage of your annual premium, not as a cash sum.

The clearer your own ideas of what you want, before you visit an adviser, the less likely you are to be persuaded by sales talk to buy something you don't want. You may also increase your chances of getting good advice if you go to more than one adviser.

The security of your policy

Insurance companies are covered by the Policyholders' Protection Act. If the company fails, then the Policyholders' Protection Board, set up by the government to administer the Act, has to try to get another company to take on the policy. Provided you carry on paying the premiums due, the Act guarantees that you'll get at least 90 per cent of the amount guaranteed at the time the company went bust, unless the Board considers this to be excessive.

But you get no guarantees of future bonuses from the new company that takes over your policy. So you could lose quite a lot if your company goes bust – it's prudent to stick with a large, well-established company.

Very few insurance companies do go bust. Sometimes they get taken over instead, and sometimes, if they get into financial trouble, they have to cut their bonus rates. In those cases, you won't lose the guarantees, but the rate of growth on the policies will be slower than you had expected.

Other pension providers are covered by compensation funds (though in some cases these cover smaller amounts than the Policyholders' Protection Act). Providers have to abide by rules laid down by the Financial Services Act or the laws for banks and building societies – see Chapter 5. In every case, therefore, at least part of your money is protected, but you could lose the rest.

Your choices at retirement

When to retire

Once you reach an age at which you can start taking the benefits under your plan (between 50 and 75 for a plan taken out on or after 1 July 1988, or between 60 and 75 for a Section 226 scheme), you can write to the provider at any time and tell them you want to start taking the benefits of your policy. Before committing yourself, find out what sort of benefits you'll get, so that you can postpone your decision if necessary.

Shopping around for a higher pension

With all minimum appropriate personal pensions and nearly all personal pension plans, you don't have to take your pension from the providers with which you have been saving. When you retire, you can shop around to see if you can get a better deal for the money that's built up for you. This is called the *open market option.*

If you want to do this, you first have to find out the value of your cash fund. If the policy is a deferred annuity, the provider will have to work out (using what is called its *commutation* rate) the number of £££ of fund you're allocated for the pension to which you're entitled. You then compare the benefits you would have got from this provider with the benefits you could get if you switched this amount to someone else. If, over the years, you've taken out a number of different plans, you could transfer them all at retirement to the insurance company offering the best package of benefits.

With some providers, the cash fund you can transfer is slightly lower than the one with which the original provider would have credited you.

To choose an insurance company yourself, get an up-to-date copy of one of the main pensions magazines, such as *Pensions Management* or *Money Management* (both published by *FTBI* – your library should have a copy), or ask an adviser to check on the most recent figures via the *Quotel* computer system.

Lump sum

When you retire, you can normally choose to have a reduced pension, and a tax-free lump sum. You may be glad to have a lump sum to spend at the start of your retirement, or you could invest the money and draw on it later. Even if you used the money to buy an *immediate* annuity, you could end up with a higher after-tax income than the pension you've given up. For more on immediate annuities, see Chapter 22.

The Inland Revenue rules on the size of the lump sum depend on whether you have a Section 226 policy (bought before 1 July 1988) or a personal pension policy (bought on or after 1 July 1988).

The Section 226 rules say that the maximum lump sum you can buy is three times the biggest remaining pension the company could pay you (though there is a cash limit for policies taken out on or after 17 March 1987). The personal pension rules, on the other hand, say that you can take a quarter of your fund (after some deductions) as a lump sum. If you have a *Minimum Appropriate Personal Pension* as part of the plan, you must not take any of that part as a lump sum – it must be paid as pension.

In most cases, the Section 226 rules give a larger lump sum. Exactly how much larger depends on your age, whether you are male or female, and what the annuity rates are at the time. But a typical insurance company quote is for a lump sum of about 29 per cent of the fund for a man of 65. So if you already have a Section 226 policy, and want to take a large lump sum, it's unwise to transfer it into a personal pension plan. If you exercise the open market option, you automatically get caught by the 25 per cent limit for personal pensions.

Level or increasing pension?

The buying power of a level pension will quickly be eaten away by inflation. You could instead choose a pension which increases each year. It will, though, be smaller to start off with. For example, a pension which increases by 5 per cent compound each year will start off at around three-quarters of the amount of a level pension. Although the increasing pension would catch the level pension up in about six years, it would take about twelve years before you'd actually received the same *total* number of £££ in pension.

A few providers offer pensions which are linked to an index – often the Retail Prices Index. But a pension which is increased in line with such an index will start off much lower than a level pension. If it started off at half as much when you retired at 65, it would have to increase by an average of 20 per cent a year if you were to have received the same total buying power by the time you were 75, or 12.5 per cent a year if you were to have received the same total buying power by the time you were 80.

With many unit-linked policies, you can choose to have the pension unit-linked as well. This means it will go up and down in line with the price of units in the fund. This could be a good idea for part of your pension, but it would be unwise to link too much of your pension in this way, in case the fund hits bad times.

If you have a Minimum Appropriate Personal Pension as part of your policy, that must be increased by 3 per cent a year compound. The smaller SERPS pension you are being paid will have its increases tailored (in a rather complicated way) to take this into account.

A pension for a dependant after you die

There are two ways in which you can provided an income for your husband or wife (or other person you name) if you die after you start drawing the pension. The first it to choose to have a pension paid as long as you or someone else is alive (called a joint life, last survivor annuity). The pension may continue at the same level, or it can be higher while you are both alive. A joint-life pension (if you're both 65 and the pension stays level) might be around 20 per cent lower than a pension payable on one life only for a man, 10 per cent lower than that for a woman.

Alternatively, you can choose to have the pension paid for a certain period (often five or ten years) whether you live that long or not. As this removes the risk of getting virtually nothing back if you die soon after retirement, the pension for a man aged 65 will be around 4 per cent less if it's guaranteed for 5 years (around 2 per cent less for a woman), or 10 per cent less if it's guaranteed for 10 years (around 5 per cent less for a woman). If you died, your dependant would receive nothing at the end of the guaranteed period, so don't look on this as adequate protection.

With a Minimum Appropriate Personal Pension, the policy must provide for a pension of half of what you would get, for your widow or widower after your death (even if you are not married at the time when you retire).

The tax rules

The main rules about how much you can pay into personal pension plans each year are given below. More details can be obtained from the Inland Revenue Superannuation Funds Office, Lynwood Road, Thames Ditton, Surrey KT7 0DP.

If you pay in more than the maximum you are allowed in any one year to a personal pension plan, the excess must be returned to you – but you get no interest on it.

How much tax relief

You get tax relief at your highest rate of tax on premiums of up to a percentage of your *net relevant earnings* for that year. The maximum contribution depends on your age, although there is also a limit on the earnings that can be taken into account of £75,000 (in the 1992–3 tax year). This limit will be increased each year in line with price inflation. The limits are:

up to 35	17.5 per cent
36–45	20 per cent
46–50	25 per cent
51–55	30 per cent
56 to 60	35 per cent
61 and over	40 per cent

Lower limits apply to Section 226 policies if you are aged 35 or more.

Husband and wife each have their own limit worked out on their net relative earnings and ages.

If your own contributions are below these limits, your employer is allowed to make contributions up to the balance (though they don't normally do so).

If you are an employee, you make payments *net* of basic rate tax: that is, you just pay the after-tax relief amount and the provider reclaims the tax from the Inland Revenue. So if you wanted to pay a total premium of £100, you would actually pay in £75, and the provider would reclaim £25 (with basic-rate tax at 25 per cent) from the Inland Revenue. If you're a higher-rate taxpayer, you have to reclaim the higher-rate relief through your tax office.

If you're self-employed, you make *gross* payments and claim back the tax relief through your tax return (i.e. if you want £100 to go into the plan, *you* pay in the full £100).

Your net relevant earnings

These will depend on the income used to work out your tax bill for that year. If you are in a job, your tax bill is worked out for the current year. That is, your tax bill for, say, the 1992–3 year is worked out on your pay during that tax year. This normally also applies if you have small freelance earnings. For employees, net relevant earnings will usually be any earnings you pay tax on under the Pay As You Earn system.

But if you are self-employed on a large scale, and your business has been going for some years, you will be taxed on a *preceding year basis.* That means that your tax bill for the 1992–3 tax year will be based on the taxable profit your business makes in your accounting year that ended in the 1991–2 tax year.

Your taxable profit from being self-employed is your takings (less certain debts to you) less certain costs you incur and deductions you can make. These are:
■ business expenses
■ capital allowances, for the cost of machinery and plant (including a car) used in your business
■ any business losses for earlier years which haven't been set against other income.

In the first two and last three years of a business, there are special rules about what income your tax is based on. Your net relevant earnings are your taxable profits, *minus* certain payments, such as patent royalties and annuities paid out from a business.

For more details, see the section covering tax and self-employment in the most recent *Which? Tax-Saving Guide.*

Unused relief for the last six years

You can get tax relief on premiums you pay on top of the normal limit, and up to the whole of your net relevant earnings in that tax year, if you didn't pay the maximum premiums allowed in any of the previous six tax years (though you can't count earnings from which you made contributions to an employer's pension scheme, unless your contributions were refunded). You have to use up the earliest unused relief first. You receive the relief at your current tax rate. So anyone now paying 25 per cent tax, who was on a higher rate in earlier years, can get relief only at 25 per cent.

Unused tax relief from longer ago

If an assessment becomes final for a tax year more than six years in the past, you *may* be able to claim some unused relief from that year. The rules are very complicated – check with your tax inspector.

Looking over your shoulder

You can ask in any tax year to have all or part of the premiums you pay in that year treated as if you'd paid them in the previous tax year. And, if you didn't have *any* net relevant earnings in the previous tax year, you'll be able to get the premiums treated as if you'd paid them in the year before that. Then you *can* get tax relief at the rate at which tax was payable in the earlier year rather than at the current rate.

Other Ways of Investing

14

SHARES

The number of private shareholders declined steadily from the early 1960s until the early 1980s. Then came the government's programme of selling off government-owned industries like British Gas and British Telecom. Largely as a result of privatisation, the number of private shareholders has grown quite dramatically.

Investing directly in shares is a risky business, as was demonstrated in the October 1987 stock market crash, when shares lost 20 per cent of their value in a few days. To reduce the risk, you need to be able to spread your money around a number of different shares, something you're unlikely to be able to do if you invest directly, unless you've got a lot of money to spare.

If you haven't got enough money to be able to spread your investment, and you don't fancy the risks of direct investment in shares, there are various ways of investing indirectly in shares. By investing indirectly and pooling your money with that of other investors, you can spread your risk, because your money will be invested in a wide range of companies. One way of indirect share investment is to put your money in unit trusts or investment trusts, dealt with in Chapters 15 and 16. For other ways of investing in shares, see p. 259 onwards.

Investing directly in shares is a way of investing in the performance of a company. You can expect two sorts of return:

■ income – the company will pay out an income (called dividends) to its shareholders. The hope is that this income will increase over the years as company profits rise

■ capital gain – the hope is that the share price of the company will rise over the years. This may happen if, for example, the company's prospects improve. But you shouldn't expect the share price to rise steadily.

Looking at what's happened in the past gives some sort

An investment in shares: 1982 – 92

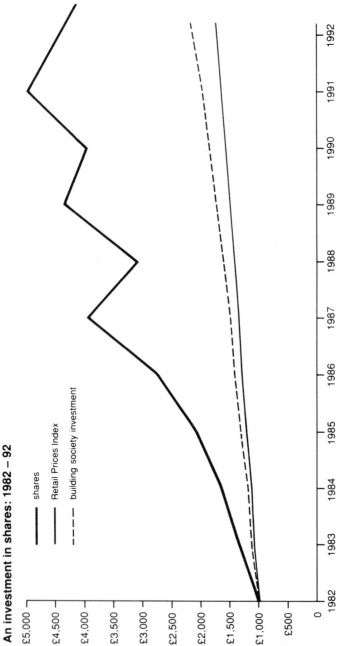

shares

Retail Prices Index

building society investment

Source: Micropal: based on *FT Actuaries All-Share Index*, offer to offer, net income reinvested

of idea of the ups and downs of investing in shares. The chart opposite shows how the value of an investment in shares has varied between 1982 and 1992. As you can see it's been a bumpy ride. The success of your investment depends crucially on when you buy the shares and when you sell. And no one has a cast-iron method of forecasting the right moment to buy and sell.

Over the years, however, the return on shares has, on average, been higher than with safer investments, e.g. an investment in building societies. Unfortunately, the past is not a guide to the future. The average investor should assume that investing in shares is a long-term business.

Spreading your investment

If you invest heavily in just one company's shares, or in those of a very few companies, you could do very badly, or very well indeed. But if you invest in a wide spread of different shares, the results you'd get from your investment are unlikely to be far removed from the results for shares on average.

If you buy the shares of just one company, there's a small chance, but not a negligible one, that you might achieve either a much above-average return, or lose most or even all of your money. If you buy the shares of more than one company, your chances of an extreme result become much smaller.

If you spread your money over the shares of as many as 16 or so companies, you'll be taking a very different sort of risk from that of an investment in shares of just one company. The chances of all of them doing much worse than average are small. Unfortunately, the chances of a much above-average return are also small.

It would be best to choose the shares of companies in different industries, because there's also the risk that a whole industry, and the shares of most of the companies in it, may hit the doldrums for a while. Similarly, it might be wise to spread your investments over different countries (see Chapter 24), so that the outcome of your investment doesn't depend entirely on the UK stockmarket.

But remember, share prices fluctuate both individually and on average. So, even if you invest in a wide spread of shares, you can't be sure that the value of your share investment won't fall, particularly in the short or even medium term.

Because of buying and selling costs, it doesn't make sense to invest small amounts in shares – less than about

£1,000 to £1,500 per company say. So to get a good spread – of shares in, say, five to ten companies – you'd need around £10,000 for this type of investment.

Ways of choosing shares

If you've made the decision to buy shares, you are still faced with the problem of choosing which ones.

Often, the amateur investor won't do the choosing entirely on his or her own, but will get professional advice (see Chapter 6) from a stockbroker, for example, or from the business pages of a newspaper. But in order to understand this advice, and to assess its worth, it would be helpful to know something about the different methods of choosing shares which may be used by advisers. There are four main ways of choosing shares:
- technical analysis
- fundamental analysis
- beta analysis
- hunch and inside knowledge.

Technical analysis (*chartism*)

Technical analysis is concerned with the behaviour of the stockmarket, i.e. the rises and falls in share prices, rather than the details of a company's management, earnings and so on. The method normally includes the study of charts (hence *chartism*).

The assumption is that investors, collectively, have all the available facts about companies, and that movements of share prices accurately and quickly reflect this knowledge. But technical analysts believe that share prices may not move instantly to take account of the information, and so believe they can predict price movements.

The method involves studying charts or graphs showing the range of prices at which each company's shares are bought and sold. The share price record of a company can indicate periods when investors have displayed confidence (or lack of it) in the company, and have built up (or sold) large holdings of its shares. Chartists argue that their graphs can tell them when such periods are about to recur, and they look for *trendlines*, and for significant shapes like *tops* and *bottoms*. If the chart of the share price of a company has completed a top formation (see chart opposite), a chartist would say this was the time to sell that share. A bottom formation (see chart) would be a signal to buy.

A typical chart

share price (p)

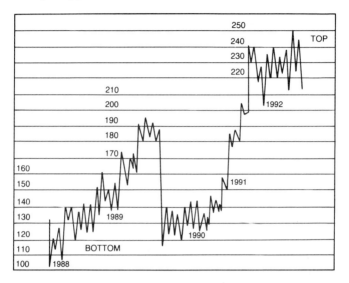

A few examples of common terms and ratios

Net working capital
First the value of what is owed by the company to suppliers, the Inland Revenue, shareholders (in the form of dividends), the bank (e.g. in the form of an overdraft) and so on is worked out. This value is then deducted from the sum of what is owed to the company by customers, cash held by the company or which the company can get at straight away and the value of items held as stock. This gives net working capital. A company needs to have sufficient working capital to keep going.

Profit margin
This is worked out by finding what the profit of the company is as a percentage of its sales.

Return on capital employed
This is worked out by finding what the profit of the company is as a percentage of its assets, i.e the sum of the value of its property, its stock, what it is owed by its customers and so on.

Fundamental analysis

The basic assumption here is that, at any given time, a company's shares have an intrinsic value. This value depends normally on the earning capacity of the company, which in turn depends on such things as the quality of management, and the outlook for the industry and for the economy as a whole. If the current market price of the shares is lower than what you suppose the intrinsic value to be, the share is one to consider buying.

Fundamental analysis will sometimes calculate a precise intrinsic value for a share, based on detailed estimates of the company's future earnings.

The analysis will use any information that can be obtained, e.g. by visiting companies, talking to the management and analysing the company report and accounts. Companies are obliged by law to publish the accounts of their business at least once a year, and to provide certain information. These accounts may reveal some important facts about the company's performance during the period covered by the accounts.

Specialists called investment analysts study these accounts with the idea of discovering how well the company is really doing. By working out the relationships between various factors (the *P/E ratio* described on p. 255 is probably the most commonly used – see box on p. 245 for some other examples) they build up a picture of the company's financial position. This can be compared with other companies in the same industry to assess the performance of the company and its management. In addition, by studying the economic background, this method is used to make predictions about how well, or badly, particular industries (e.g heavy engineering) or even whole countries are going to fare.

But there are problems. The information available is far from comprehensive and not sufficiently standardised. And information in accounts is out of date. For example, after the most skilful reading of a company's accounts, you may still not know whether one part of the company's business is making losses and is being subsidised by more profitable parts.

Beta analysis

This is a method of share analysis which concentrates on the riskiness of a share. It doesn't look at the risk of investing your money in the shares of only one company which does badly or even goes bust – the section on *Spreading your investment* on p. 243 shows how you can reduce this risk. Beta analysis looks at the *market risk* of a share. This occurs because the stock market goes up and down, roughly speaking, as the prospect for the economy goes up and down.

A share which has moved exactly in line with the FT-Actuaries All-Share Index is said to have a beta of one. But some shares and unit trusts go up and down more than average. These are described as *aggressive* – i.e. when the index goes up, the share or unit trust goes up relatively more, and when the index goes down, it goes down relatively more. The value of beta for aggressive shares or unit trusts is more than one. Some shares and unit trusts are described as *defensive* – i.e. they go up and down less than the average (and the value of beta is less than one). Other shares and unit trusts fall somewhere between the extremes. The beta of a share is a measure of how much the rate of return on that share is likely to be affected by general stock market movements. It's normally worked out from the past performance of the share, which, of course, is not necessarily a good guide to the future.

Some people use this analysis so that, if they think the general level of prices in the stock market is going to rise, they can invest in shares with high betas, because their prices will (they hope) go up correspondingly more. And if they think share prices in general are going to fall, they will switch to shares with low betas, whose prices should fall less than average. Another way of using this analysis is to find the right investment for people, taking into account the amount of risk they want to take.

Hunch and inside knowledge

Of course, you could choose your shares by hunch, i.e. when you have a feeling that things are going to go well for a particular company. Fortunes can be made or lost this way.

Investing as a result of a tip from an insider is a dodgy business. And if *you* are the insider and you use your knowledge to invest and make yourself or someone else some money, then it's probably against the law and you could be convicted.

Verdict

There is no effective, reliable, proven, and generally usable method of picking out which shares are going to be winners. Apart from hunch and inside knowledge, all the methods we've described depend, to some extent at least, on looking at how shares have fared in the past. But past performance is no guide to the future. A share can perform well for many months, then fall in value unexpectedly overnight.

This does not mean, however, that you cannot make a sensible choice of shares. A collection of shares which a person holds is called a *portfolio*; and a portfolio chosen to match *your* objectives and circumstances and preferred level of risk should certainly give you better results than one which hasn't been chosen in this way. In broad outline, choose your shares as follows:

■ decide what your objectives are, because different shares are likely to suit different objectives. For example, you may (or may not) attach importance to drawing an income from your investment, or you may be speculating with your money, in the hope of maximum gain, but accepting the possibility of a big loss

■ choose shares which carry the degree of risk you are willing to accept. If you want to speculate, you could put all your money into a collection of very risky shares. Alternatively, see p. 259 for other ways of investing in companies – *warrants, options* and *traded options*, in particular. On the other hand, if you are investing for the long term, divide your money among the shares of a fair number of companies and spread your investment over a number of carefully selected different industries

■ consider reducing the influence of the stock market on your investments by investing some of your money in other investments, which are less risky, e.g. building society accounts, British Government stock or company loan stock (see p. 259). And look at the possibilities of investing some of your money overseas and giving yourself a spread of geographical areas and currencies – see Chapter 24

■ in general, the best policy is likely to be *buy and hold*. Don't buy and sell shares too frequently. The costs of doing this will eat into any profits that you make.

Buying and selling shares

You can buy or sell shares by going to a stockbroker. *A Private Investors' Directory* is available from the Association of Private Client Investment Managers and Stockbrokers, 20 Dysart Street, London EC2A 2BX. Alternatively, you could go to a bank or building society, many of whom own or have agreements with stockbroking firms. For more details, see Chapter 6. Whichever you choose, the procedure is more or less the same.

There are a number of market places for buying and selling shares. Novice investors should probably stick to shares which are quoted on the main market place, i.e. those with a full listing on the Stock Exchange. However, the Stock Exchange also runs the *Unlisted Securities Market.* The procedure for buying and selling shares quoted on this market may vary slightly from that described below – a stockbroker should be able to advise you how it works.

Buying shares

Suppose that you have found a broker to deal with you, and that you decide you would like to buy 600 Slagthorpe Jam shares. You look at the share price lists in the morning paper and see that they are quoted at 300p.

There are two points which must be made at once about this price. Firstly, it is normally yesterday afternoon's price – the price being quoted towards the close of Stock Exchange business. Secondly, the price quoted in most of the newspapers is normally a middle price. If the newspaper says that Slagthorpe Jam PLC was 300p, it probably means that, yesterday afternoon, the *offer price* (the price at which you could have bought Slagthorpe) was 303p, while the *bid price* (the price at which you could have sold) was 297p. The difference between the two figures is called the *spread.*

You can give your order to your broker in one of two ways. One is simply to ring up and say, 'Buy me 600 Slagthorpe Jam'. The broker will take this as an order to buy this number of shares at the best (i.e. cheapest) available price *now*. The other way is to give the broker a *limit.* Suppose you decide the shares would be a good buy at 295p but no more. You ring up your boker and say, 'Buy me 600 Slagthorpe, at not more than 295p'.

So you lose nothing by setting a limit, and you protect yourself from the risk of buying at a higher price than you expected. However, it is no use setting too low a limit: you won't get your shares, and will have wasted your time, and the broker's. And make sure your broker knows how long you want your limit to stand (there may be a standard time limit, e.g. one month, or the broker may accept a limit only for the day you place your order).

Once you've placed your order, it's too late to change your mind: you've made a verbal contract. For most shares, the broker can call up SEAQ (Stock Exchange Automated

Quotation System) on a computer screen. This gives up-to-the-minute information on the prices at which a number of *market-makers* (share wholesalers) are prepared to buy and sell shares. The broker buys the shares on your behalf from the market-maker offering the best price. With some leading shares in lots of 1,000 shares or less, a broker can now buy (or sell) at the best price automatically, by computer; the deal can be done, and confirmed to you, while you wait on the telephone.

At the broker's office, a contract note will be made out for the shares you have bought. You should get this on the following day, or soon after, and check it at once to see that the details of what you have bought are correct. Keep this contract note safe, as evidence of what you have paid for the shares. It will look something like the example opposite.

Selling shares

As with buying shares, there are two kinds of order that you can give to your broker. You can simply ring up your broker and say, 'Sell 600 Slagthorpe Jam', or you can set a limit, e.g. say, 'Sell 600 Slagthorpe Jam if the price reaches 320p'.

The contract note for a sale looks much like the contract note for a purchase. Minimum commission rates used to be fixed, but now brokers can charge what they like, and rates and minimum charges vary widely. Charges usually range between 1 per cent and 1.9 per cent on a deal of up to, say, £7,000. A typical minimum commission can be £20 or £25. But with a sale there is no stamp duty. Some brokers may also charge a flat fee of around £5 which they call a 'compliance levy.'

When the contract note for your sale has been made out, the broker will send it to you. He or she will also send you a transfer form. All you will have to do is sign it at the place indicated and send it back to your broker, with your share certificate. Don't date this transfer form as the broker will do this for you. You should keep the contract note as evidence of how much you have sold the shares for.

If you have sent in the transfer form properly signed, together with your share certificate, you should get the balance due from your broker on settlement day (see p. 252).

CONTRACT NOTE

UNIQUE CODE NO.	F. MURRAY	DATE & TAX POINT	EXECUTED AT
6405/97Z		17 OCT 92	12.00

YOU HAVE BOUGHT, SUBJECT TO THE RULES AND REGULATIONS

OF THE STOCK EXCHANGE, FOR SETTLEMENT ON 29 OCT 92

600	SLAGTHORPE JAM ORD £1	295P	**1**	£1,770.00
....	BARGAIN OF PREVIOUS EVENING			....
600	** TALISMAN SECURITY **			£1,770.00

	TRANSFER STAMP	9.00	**2**	
	COMMISSION	29.21	**3**	
	TOTAL CHARGES			£38.21
				....
	DUE TO US			£1,808.21

COMMISSION DETAILS
£1,770 AT 1.65%

WE HAVE ACTED AS AGENT IN THIS TRANSACTION

UK RESIDENTS SHOULD RETAIN THIS CONTRACT NOTE AS THEY MAY
REQUIRE IT FOR CAPITAL GAINS TAX

BGN NO.	REFERENCE
0928	NO.01435

---

1 Consideration   The name sometimes given to the amount you pay for the shares (or get for them if you're selling) before the various deductions are made. In our example, the consideration is £1,770.

2 Stamp duty   This is the main government duty on the deal. It is $\frac{1}{2}$% of what you pay for the shares (rounded up to the nearest £50). In our example, the stamp duty is $\frac{1}{2}$% of £1,800 (i.e. £1,770 to the nearest £50 upwards).

3 Commission   The rate of commission varies depending on what you pay for the shares.

PTM Levy   If the cost of shares is £10,000 or more, an additional charge of £2 is made – this is a levy for the Panel on Takeovers and Mergers. This levy applies on both sales and purchases.

Settling up

All share deals on the Stock Exchange are done within a period called an *account*, usually lasting 10 working days. An account normally starts on a Monday, and ends on the Friday of the following week. Settlement day, or account day, is normally on the sixth working day after the final day of the account (i.e on a Monday). On settlement day, the broker pays the market-maker (or the reverse, for sellers) for all deals done during the account in question, and so the broker must have your money by that day.

Following the end of an account in which you have done business with him or her, your broker will probably send you a statement. This will set out the totals from all the contract notes which have been sent to you during the account. If the statement shows that, taking purchases and sales together, you owe money to your broker, you should send a cheque to arrive in time to be cleared by settlement day. If you are owed money, you should get it on settlement day or the day after, provided that you have sent the share certificate and signed transfer deed to the broker.

When you buy shares, anything from 10 to 21 days can elapse before you have to pay for them (but, of course, when you sell you may have to wait a corresponding length of time for your money).

The broker and market-maker settle most of their purchases and sales through a system known as Talisman. The broker who was sold shares will deliver a transfer form and share certificate to the Talisman office and Talisman gives the company registrar details of the new holder of shares. The registrar will send a new share certificate to your broker who sends it on to you.

How soon you get the share certificate depends on the company – it can be six weeks, or longer. But your contract note is evidence that you've bought the shares. Should you want to sell them again before you've received the certificate, there should be no problem with shares in UK companies. But you may have to wait until you can supply your broker with the certificate before you're paid since the market-maker won't pay the broker without it.

Changes in the pipeline

A new computerised system of share dealing is being developed by the Stock Exchange. It's called TAURUS (Transfer and Automated Registration of Uncertificated Stock). Shares will be held in accounts, and transferred automatically between accounts when they are bought and sold. You will no longer get a share certificate. It's hoped that the new system will start in 1993. An important advantage for the investor is that there will be no longer be any stamp duty on these 'paperless' transactions.

Another important change to be introduced at the same time will be in the system of two-week account periods (see opposite). The aim is to speed up the settlement time, so that you will have to pay for any shares bought much sooner than at present. The precise timetable and details of these changes were still being worked out as we went to press.

Shares in detail

What is a share?

When you buy ordinary shares you are literally buying a share in the company, and a right to benefit from its earnings (if any). You can go to general meetings and vote on matters to do with the company.

Some companies issue ordinary shares only. The net (i.e. after tax) profits of such a company all count as earnings available to the ordinary shareholders. This does not mean, however, that all such earnings will actually be paid to the ordinary shareholders – see *Dividend yield*, on p. 255.

Many companies, by contrast raise their capital in other ways, e.g. occasionally by issuing *preference shares*, or more commonly by issuing *loan stock* or *debentures* (see p. 259). The company's first commitment is to pay the fixed income to its lenders and preference shareholders, which is why all such payments commonly called prior charges. With such companies, the earnings available to the ordinary shareholders are the profits after deducting the prior charges and tax.

What the papers say

The shares page of a daily newspaper can be puzzling, but it contains a lot of useful information.

Let's suppose you wanted to find out about Slagthorpe Jam. The relevant section of the newspaper would look something like this:

Notes	Price	+ or -	1992 high	low	Mkt Cap£m	Yld Gr's	P/E
Arcolectric A NV.......	41	....	41	30	2.05	3.6	8.6
Arlen................................	14	....	22	12	4.21	–	–
ASEA B SKr.................	£32$\frac{1}{4}$	$-\frac{3}{8}$	£37$\frac{3}{8}$	£26$\frac{3}{8}$	785.1	2.1	15.0
■BICC.............................	244	−3	360	235	813.5	10.8	13.9
Cap Fin 10$\frac{3}{4}$ pc.....	96$\frac{1}{2}$	$-\frac{1}{2}$	121	90	170.8	11.1	–
Beales Hunter.............	230	....	*292	230	22.6	5.4	φ
■Benn't & F'tain.......	5$\frac{1}{2}$	$-\frac{1}{4}$	20	2	5.83	–	3.7
■Bulgin A.....................	6	....	8$\frac{1}{2}$	6	1.56	2.2	–
Burnfield.................g	148	....	*226	142	29.0	5.2	21.3
■Chloride.....................	9$\frac{1}{2}$	....	14$\frac{1}{2}$	7	22.6	–	–
Clarke (T).....................	70	....	104	70	10.3	12.5	10.2
Dale.................................	65	....	106	64	8.77	10.5	6.5
■Delta.......................✢	407	+2	506	385	599.5	4.6	15.7
✢Denmans................. †	168	....	190	148	7.28	4.6	7.6
Dewhurst A.............†	38	....	46	35	2.74	6.3	8.2
■Dowding & M.......†	49	....	66	47	70.9	6.5	14.3
Electrolux B SKr.......	£19	$-1\frac{1}{2}$	£27	£18	1,399	6.6	23.4
■Emess.........................	10	....	25$\frac{1}{2}$	10	10.6	13.3	–
6.25pc Pf.................	31	....	56	25	22.6	26.9	–
Ericsson (LM) SKr....	£11$\frac{1}{4}$	$-\frac{3}{8}$	£14$\frac{1}{2}$	£9	2,108	3.0	33.8
Fujitsu Y......................	256	+11	368	217	4,641	1.6	φ
✢Hilclare.....................	45	....	57	45	1.31	1.5	14.3
Jones Stroud..............	233	....	273	190	43.1	4.6	φ
♥Johnson El HK$.....	90	$-\frac{1}{2}$	101	63	277.2	1.6	31.0
■Kembrey.....................	11	−1	21	11	3.14	4.5	4.2
■Kenwood Appliances..W	263	....	290	263	96.5	3.8	13.9
✢LPA Inds...................	45	....	55	45	3.76	10.4	11.9
Lec Refrig....................	268xd	....	315	265	16.2	7.2	20.5

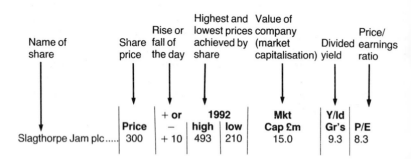

Name of share	Share price	Rise or fall of the day	Highest and lowest prices achieved by share		Value of company (market capitalisation)	Divided yield	Price/ earnings ratio
	Price	**+ or −**	**1992 high**	**low**	**Mkt Cap £m**	**Y/ld Gr's**	**P/E**
Slagthorpe Jam plc.....	300	+ 10	493	210	15.0	9.3	8.3

The share price

This is usually the previous day's middle market (i.e. halfway between offer and bid) closing price.

Market Capitalisation

This is the value put on the company by the stockmarket – i.e. the cost of buying all the shares in the company at the share price quoted. In our example, Slagthorpe Jam has issued 5 million shares and the current share price is 300p. So the market capitalisation of the company is £15 million.

Dividend Yield

Shareholders receive their share of the company profits as dividends. Dividends will be sent to you at the address which your broker puts on the transfer form. Dividends come in the form of dividend warrants. These are in effect cheques, which can be paid into your bank account. Slagthorpe Jam last year declared dividends of 21p per share. Basic-rate tax has already been deducted (in other words, it is a *net dividend*), so it is equivalent to 28p per share before basic-rate tax. For more details of how dividends are taxed, see p. 102.

The dividend of 28p is 9.3 per cent of the share price – 300p. Therefore the yield on your money would be 9.3 per cent a year (provided future dividends are the same as last year's). This yield is called the gross dividend yield.

Companies usually pay dividends twice a year (as long as they have earnings to distribute). About six to eight weeks before each dividend is paid, the company declares a dividend, i.e. announces what the next dividend will be. A week or two later, the company's shares go *ex-dividend* (and the share price is marked 'xd') and the register of shareholders is temporarily closed. The coming dividend will be paid only to those people who are on the register of shareholders on the day it was closed. Anyone who buys shares in the company after they have gone ex-dividend will not get the coming dividend.

A company normally keeps back part of its net profits (in our example on p. 257, £1,800,000 – £1,050,000 = £750,000) to finance expansion of its business, or to build up cash balances, or both. Amounts kept back are called retained profits or earnings, or retentions.

Price/earnings ratio

A common way of looking at share prices is to say that in buying a share what you are really doing is buying a right to benefit from a corresponding share in the company's yearly stream of earnings. The price/earnings ratio (or P/E ratio for short) is a way of saying at what expense (or how cheaply) you're buying that stream of earnings.

To work out a P/E ratio, first work out how much earnings there are for each share, i.e. divide the total after-tax earnings of the company by the number of shares. The P/E ratio is found by dividing the current market price by the earnings per share.

Take our Slagthorpe Jam example. Suppose the company's earnings in the last reported year were £1,800,000, which, since the company has five million ordinary shares (see opposite) works out at 36p for each share. Each share actually costs 300p at current prices, so to buy earnings of 36p a year, you have to pay 300p. Slagthorpe Jam would, therefore, be said to have a P/E ratio of 300 divided by 36 = 8.3.

Dividend cover

Some newspapers also show the *dividend cover* – i.e. how many times the company could have paid its dividend out of the profit for that year.

New issues

If a company is not quoted on the Stock Exchange, it may be difficult to buy or sell its shares. You have to find an individual or an organsation who is prepared to deal with you. When the company decides it wants to make a better market in its shares, it may offer its shares to the public and become quoted on the Stock Exchange.

The most usual method for marketing a new issue is an *offer for sale* by an *issuing house*, often a merchant bank. The issuing house puts advertisements in newspapers giving details of the company and offering a stated number of shares at a stated price (the *prospectus*). The advertisements normally include an application form. If you want to buy some of the shares, fill in the form saying how many you want, and send it with a cheque for the value of the shares.

If the terms on which a new issue is made look attractive to the investing public, the issue may be over-subscribed, i.e. more shares may be asked for than are on offer. In that case, the shares will be allocated by the issuing house (there are a variety of methods for doing this).

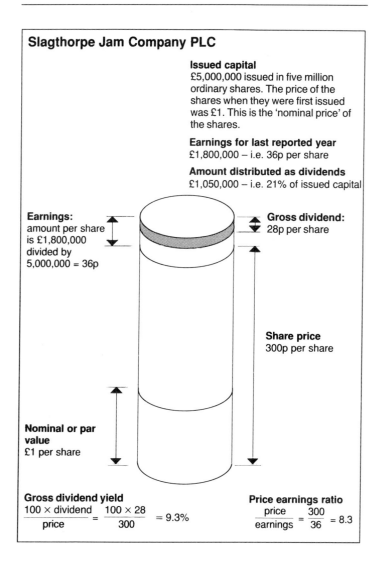

Slagthorpe Jam Company PLC

Issued capital
£5,000,000 issued in five million ordinary shares. The price of the shares when they were first issued was £1. This is the 'nominal price' of the shares.

Earnings for last reported year
£1,800,000 – i.e. 36p per share

Amount distributed as dividends
£1,050,000 – i.e. 21% of issued capital

Earnings:
amount per share is £1,800,000 divided by 5,000,000 = 36p

Gross dividend:
28p per share

Share price
300p per share

Nominal or par value
£1 per share

Gross dividend yield
$$\frac{100 \times \text{dividend}}{\text{price}} = \frac{100 \times 28}{300} = 9.3\%$$

Price earnings ratio
$$\frac{\text{price}}{\text{earnings}} = \frac{300}{36} = 8.3$$

Scrip (or bonus) issue

As a company grows, its share price may increase so much that it becomes too unwieldy to trade easily. So the company may make an extra issue of free shares to its existing shareholders. This is called a scrip or bonus issue. If, for example, you have 500 shares in Slagthorpe Jam and the share price is 300p each, your shareholding is worth £1,500. If the company makes a one-for-one scrip issue, you will get another 500 shares, making 1,000 in total. But the share price will instantly fall to 150p each, so your shareholding is still worth £1,500. After a time, the share price will go ex-scrip, marked 'xc'. This works in much the same way as ex-dividend – see p. 255.

Rights issue

Occasionally, a company may decide it needs to raise more money from its shareholders, perhaps to finance some new investment. It usually makes a rights issue to its existing shareholders. This means the company offers the right to invest more money in exchange for new shares.

You will know about this rights issue because the company will send you a document, telling you what it is raising money for and enclosing a form so that you can apply to take up some new shares. Do not ignore this document, it is valuable. If you don't understand what it is, ask a professional adviser.

There are four choices facing you as shareholder:
- you can do nothing
- you can pay up
- you can sell your rights to the new shares on the Stock Exchange
- you can sell part of your rights and take up part, so keeping your investment in the company at the same level.

What you do depends on whether you have the cash available and whether you want to increase your investment in the company.

Suppose, for example, you have 500 shares in Battendown Foods, the share price is 400p each and the company makes a one-for-one rights issue at 200p each. If the company has three million shares already issued, it is raising £6 million by the rights issue (issuing another three million shares for 200p each). The market value of the company before the rights issue is £12 million; afterwards it is £18 million. The share price after the rights issue will be:

$$£18 \text{ million} \div 6 \text{ million} = £3 \text{ each}$$

If you do nothing, your 500 shares are now worth only £1,500, so on the face of it you might have lost £500. However, all UK companies will sell rights which haven't been taken up and send you the proceeds. If you take up your rights, your investment is now worth £3,000, but you've had to hand over another £1,000 to the company. Alternatively, you can sell your rights to the new shares on the Stock Exchange – in theory, for £500. This is worked out by taking the new share price from the old one, i.e. £4 − £3 = £1 per share.

Your fourth choice is to sell part of your rights and use the proceeds to buy the rest of the new shares.

After a while, the share price will go ex-rights (marked 'xr'). This works in much the same way as ex-dividend – see p. 255.

Mergers and takeovers

One company may decide it would like to acquire another company and it therefore offers to buy the shares from the company's shareholders. For example, suppose Battendown Foods decides to take over Slagthorpe Jam. Battendown will send you a document offering to buy your shares. This document will contain a lot of information, including:

- what Battendown will pay for your shares. It may offer you cash, or some of its own shares in exchange, or a mixture of loan stock and shares and possibly cash
- why Battendown wants to buy Slagthorpe
- a profit forecast for Battendown
- the date on which its offer closes.

If Slagthorpe decides it doesn't want to be taken over, it will also send you a document telling you why you shouldn't accept Battendown's offer, probably giving a profit forecast for Slagthorpe, and so on.

Things can get very complicated after this, if, for example, a second company decides it would like to acquire Slagthorpe, or Battendown decides its first offer will not be accepted by the majority of shareholders and so increases its offer. You might end up with quite a few documents. Don't ignore them. You have to decide which is better – sticking with Slagthorpe or accepting one of the offers. If you have a professional adviser, ask his or her advice.

Other ways of investing in companies

Companies can raise money by issuing *company loan stock* or *debentures*. They work like British Government stocks – they normally pay a fixed rate of interest and the loan will be repaid some time in the future. Because they are riskier than British Government stocks, you can expect the return to be higher. And if the company is in financial difficulties, the return – and the risk you have to take – may be very high indeed.

A variation on this is a *convertible loan stock*. This starts out as a loan when the company first gets the money. But the person holding the loan stock has the right to convert it or part of it into an agreed number of shares on a fixed date (or between certain dates). If the share price of the company rises, this may make the price of a convertible loan stock rise substantially too. If the share price falls, then it may not be worth converting the loan.

Some companies have *preference* shareholders, though these are becoming less common. A fixed rate of dividend is usually paid on preference shares. There are different types of these shares, but this is a highly specialised market not usually cut out for the average investor.

There are some very risky types of investments you can buy and sell on the stockmarket – *warrants, options* and *traded options*. A warrant is issued by the company, and is often tacked on to a loan stock – it can be detached and sold by the loan stockholder if he or she wants. A warrant gives you the right to buy shares in the company, usually during a fixed period and at a fixed price. If the shares of the company never reach that price, the warrant is worthless. But if the share price does rise, the price of a warrant will rise substantially.

An option is similar but is not issued by the company. Instead you pay a market-maker (see p. 250) for the right to buy or sell shares in a company at a fixed price within a three-month period. Once you've got the option you can't sell it. You can buy and sell only the shares of the company.

A traded option is slightly different and can itself be bought and sold. It lasts for a period of up to nine months and you can use it to buy or sell shares at predetermined prices.

Other ways of investing in shares

Employee share schemes

Some employers encourage their employees to invest in the company that they work for through employee share schemes. There are three types:

■ **approved profit-sharing schemes** – open to all employees who have been with the company at least five years. The company sets aside some of its profits to buy shares which are then allocated to employees. Not everybody gets the same amount; it depends on things like age, seniority and length of service. The maximum one employee can get is shares with an initial value of £3,000 (or 10 per cent of earnings if higher), with an overall limit of £8,000 worth of shares. There is no tax to pay when the shares are allocated. You have to keep the shares for two years. If you keep them for five years, there is no income tax to pay on the money you make from selling them. However, you will have to pay income tax on dividends and any profit you make on the sale could be liable to capital gains tax.

■ **SAYE share option schemes** – again, open to all employees who have been with the company five years or more. The employee agrees to pay a fixed monthly sum between £10 and £250 into a building society or National Savings Save-As-You-Earn (SAYE) plan, for five (or sometimes seven) years. At the end of the period there is a bonus. You can use the money in your plan to buy shares in your company at a discount, but you don't have to. There's no income tax to pay, but you could be liable for capital gains tax when you sell any shares you've bought.

■ **approved share option schemes** – such a scheme doesn't have to be offered to all employees. You are given the option to buy shares in your company. If you use your option between three and ten years after it is granted, and only at three-yearly intervals, you pay no income tax. Again though, you may be liable to capital gains tax.

Verdict

Share option schemes can be a very good deal indeed, but don't be tempted to buy shares in your company if, for example, it's in difficulties. Some companies offer share option schemes as an alternative to a portion of your salary. If so, make sure that the extra risk is really what you want.

The Business Expansion Scheme

The Business Expansion Scheme (BES) was set up to encourage investment in new companies. The Scheme is due to end in December 1993. When you buy shares in a company that qualifies under the BES rules, you get tax relief at your highest rate of tax on the money you invest. To qualify, your shares must be in a UK company. It must not:

■ be quoted on the Stock Exchange or the Unlisted Securities Market

■ deal in land or shares (except for some companies specialising in certain types of residential lettings), provide

financial or legal services, or hold collectable goods (e.g. antiques, wines) for investment.
■ be a company owned by you, or one in which you (or your family or business partners) own more than 30 per cent of the business
■ be a company of which you are a paid director or employee.

How to invest in BES
You have a choice. You can invest either directly in companies or through a fund. If you opt for the direct route, the minimum investment is £500 per company. You should take advice before investing directly, from a stockbroker or accountant, for example.

A novice investor would probably do better to invest through a fund. Your money is pooled with that of other investors and spread around several BES companies, which helps to reduce the risk. The minimum investment through a fund is usually £2,000 and there's likely to be an initial fee of, say, 7 per cent of your investment.

Tax
You can get tax relief at your top rate on up to £40,000 invested in BES in one tax year. You have to hold the shares for at least five years. If you sell before then, or the company ceases to qualify within three years (e.g. by changing business), you can lose some or all of the tax relief.

Higher-rate taxpayers will benefit most from BES, but should only invest if they're prepared to take the risks. Basic-rate taxpayers have less to gain from BES. Non-taxpayers obviously won't benefit from BES tax relief at all.

Shares in BES companies issued after 18 March 1986 are free of capital gains tax on their first disposal.

Verdict
Because BES companies tend to be new and small, they're likely to be risky (though some of the companies special-ising in residential lettings may be less risky). You shouldn't invest in a BES unless you're prepared for the chance that you might lose the lot.

Personal Equity Plans (PEPs)

The attraction of Personal Equity Plans are that the income from the shares, unit trusts or investment trusts you buy is free of income tax, any capital gain when you sell is free of capital gains tax, and someone else takes care of the day-to-day detail of share-ownership – buying and selling and dealing with paperwork. You can have only one PEP each tax year. You no longer have to hold a PEP for a minimum period to get your tax relief, but can cash it in at any time. Some PEPs, though not all, have high charges; you need to be careful when choosing a scheme.

How to invest in a PEP
You can invest up to £6,000 a year (in the 1992–3 tax year) in shares in UK companies or in certain EC shares. You can also invest any part of your £6,000 in qualifying unit trusts or investment trusts. These must have up to 50 per cent of their investments in UK or qualifying EC shares. Alternatively you can invest £1,500 in a unit or investment trust which does not qualify, and the rest of your £6,000 directly into UK or certain EC shares.

You can also invest a further £3,000 in a single company PEP, which can only hold the shares of one company. You can transfer shares from an approved profit-sharing scheme or an SAYE share option scheme into a single company PEP without paying any capital gains tax. You must invest through a *plan manager* – a bank, building society or other investment adviser. The plan manager deals with all the administration – buying the shares, registering your name with the company, collecting dividends and reclaiming tax. In general, your investment in a PEP must be in the form of cash, i.e. you can't normally transfer shares you already own. But if the plan manager agrees, you can transfer new issues of shares (including privatisations) if you decide to do so within a set time of the share allocation being announced. The value of the new issue shares at the offer price counts towards the £6,000 a year maximum you're allowed to invest. You are allowed to accumulate cash in your PEP, so you don't have to invest in shares straight away, but can choose what seems best to you at the right time. But income on this cash may not be tax-free – see under *Tax* overleaf. You have a choice of schemes:
■ **discretionary PEPs** – your money is pooled with that of other investors. The plan manager chooses investments for you
■ **non-discretionary PEPs** – you choose your investment yourself and tell the plan manager to buy and sell on your behalf. An advantage of this method is that you can plan your share-buying over a period of time, and by concentrating on the shares of only one or two companies each year build up a reasonable spread of shares, yet have share-

holdings that are large enough to avoid over-the-odds commission when the time comes to sell.

Of course, you have to pay for the services of a plan manager. Costs vary, but on an investment of, say, £3,000 in a PEP, you could find yourself paying anything from £30 to £100 in the first year.

Tax

Dividends from shares in a PEP, and distributions from unit trusts, are free of income tax. This applies whether the income is paid to you directly, or reinvested in the PEP; and it is the job of the plan manager to reclaim tax on your behalf. But any interest you withdraw on cash in a PEP, e.g. money awaiting investment, is subject to tax if it is more than £180 a year.

Verdict

If you're a taxpayer (especially if you're a higher-rate taxpayer, or if you tend to use up your annual capital gains tax exemption of £5,800) a well-chosen PEP with low charges is a best buy for long-term investment in the shares of UK companies, whether directly or via unit trusts or investment trust companies.

15

UNIT TRUSTS

Unit trusts have traditionally been a way of investing in shares. However, some unit trusts invest in British Government stock and other loans, and a few invest in other unit trusts. They can also be used to invest in deposits and short-term loans, property, futures, options and commodities or a mixture of all these investments.

For many investors, investing in a unit trust is less risky and more convenient than investing directly in shares, for example. If you invested directly, and put all your money in one company, say, you'd lose it all if that company went bust. But a unit trust invests in the shares of a lot of companies (around 60 or 70, say – though it varies widely), so if one company goes bust you lose only a bit of your money. Of course, you can invest directly in many companies' shares, but this involves more money and more work. For more details on different ways of investing in shares, see Chapter 14.

The return you get back from a unit trust comes in two parts:
■ **income** – this is made up of dividends from the shares in which the unit trust invests. It can normally be paid out to you
■ **capital growth** – the hope is that the prices of shares which the unit trust has invested in will rise.

In practice, you can always reinvest your income to give more capital growth or cash in part of your investment to use capital growth as income – see p. 281.

This chapter looks at the points to consider before investing in unit trusts and the choices open to you if you decide to invest. Then, on p. 277, it moves on to look at the nitty-gritty of unit trust investment, including how prices are calculated, how to buy and sell, and what charges you can expect to pay.

Timing your investment

Investing in unit trusts is riskier than many types of investment, e.g. building society accounts. But although there is a chance of you losing money with a unit trust, the hope is that you get a better return. You can see from the diagrams in this chapter that investors in unit trusts have had a bumpy ride over the years, doing very well in some periods, very badly in others. So the success of an investment depends very much on when you invest and when you cash your investment. If you'd invested in a typical general unit trust (see diagram on p. 268) in the middle of 1987 and cashed in a year later, you'd have lost about 20 per cent of your money. But over a longer period you'd have done well – an investment in this unit trust of £1,000 in 1982 would have been worth more than four times as much in 1992.

Sadly, there's no foolproof way of forecasting *when* share prices are going to rise or fall, or *which* unit trusts you should invest in.

For the long-term or short-term?

There are two schools of thought about how long you should invest in a unit trust. Either:
■ you invest for a long time (at least seven years or so) and stick pretty well to the same trust (or trusts),
or
■ you invest for a shorter time and move your money in and out of unit trusts or from trust to trust as the prospects alter.

For most small investors, the former is most probably the better strategy. Switching your money in, out or between trusts, could be expensive in charges (see p. 278) and unless you're lucky or very knowledgeable you might time it badly. Unless you're prepared to do the work and take the chance of getting the timing wrong, you should think of unit trusts as a long-term investment.

Size of investment

The minimum you can invest varies, but with most unit trusts it's in the £250 to £1,500 range, or, for regular saving, often £20 to £50 a month. Regular saving means less worry about timing your investment – see p. 281.

Different types of unit trust

The diagram on p. 269 shows how the outcome of an investment in unit trusts could have varied depending on the trust you'd chosen. It shows what has happened to an investment of £1,000 in three different unit trusts made in 1982. The middle line is an investment in a typical general unit trust, the others are typical specialist unit trusts in one of the best-performing and one of the worst-performing sectors (for an explanation of a specialist unit trust, see p. 270).

There's no magic formula to tell you which trust will do best – we've tested several theories from p. 272 onwards. And you can't automatically expect that an investment adviser or newspaper will pick a trust which is going to perform well. But the step-by-step guide on p. 275 should help you narrow down the choices.

Different investment strategies

Unit trusts vary in their aims and the kind of shares in which they invest. One way of grouping them is as follows:
- general funds
- income funds
- capital growth funds
- international funds
- specialist sector funds (e.g. commodities, energy)
- specialist regional funds (e.g. Japan, USA)
- managed funds (which invest in other unit trusts).

General funds (or balanced funds)

The longest-running unit trust of most unit trust groups is likely to be a general fund. The aim of the fund, as described in company literature, might be something like:

The fund's objective is to produce steady growth of both income and capital.

Most general funds invest mainly in the UK, but in several different industries. You should expect the value of your investment to go up and down as the UK stock market goes up and down.

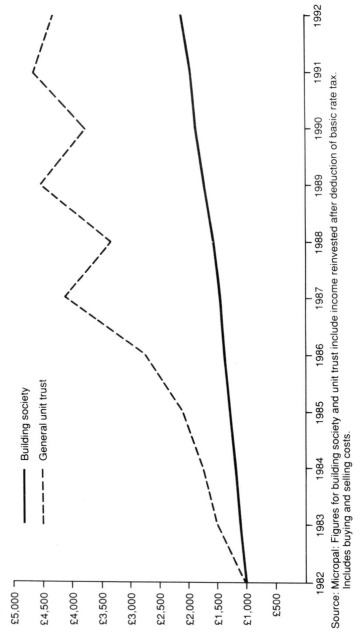

A general unit trust compared with a building society investment

Building society
General unit trust

Source: Micropal: Figures for building society and unit trust include income reinvested after deduction of basic rate tax.
Includes buying and selling costs.

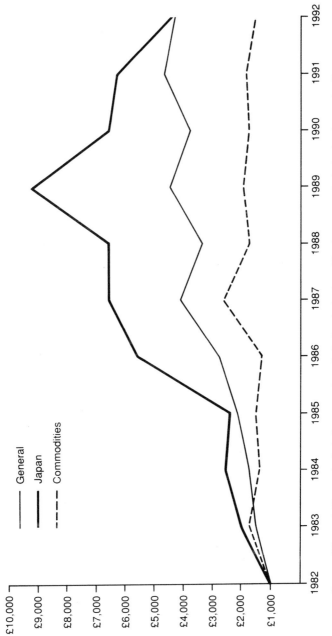

A general unit trust compared with two specialist trusts

General
Japan
Commodities

£10,000
£9,000
£8,000
£7,000
£6,000
£5,000
£4,000
£3,000
£2,000
£1,000

1982 1983 1984 1985 1986 1987 1988 1989 1990 1991 1992

Source: Micropal: Figures include income reinvested after deduction of basic rate tax. Includes buying and selling costs.

Income funds

These funds are often called *High Yield, Extra Income* and the like. The objective of the fund might be described by the company as:

> *Designed for investors whose primary requirement is an above average and increasing income. The fund's objective is to provide a return about 60 per cent higher than that of the FT-Actuaries All-Share Index.*

Funds with this sort of name do tend to pay out a higher-than-average income. Many of these income funds invest in British Government stocks, preference shares or loan stocks as well as shares giving a high income.

Capital growth funds

The aim of these funds is to concentrate on getting increases in the unit price, rather than to pay out a high income. Many funds with names like *Capital Growth, Special Situations* or *Smaller Companies* come into this category. The aim of this type of fund might be described in company literature as:

> *The investment aim is maximum capital growth through the active management of a small portfolio of shares. Yield (i.e. income) is not normally taken into account.*

With *active management* the shares in the fund may be changed more frequently than with other types of funds, thereby incurring a higher level of costs, because of buying and selling shares.

International funds

Some general funds (often called *international funds*) invest in several different stock markets around the world, so the fortune of your investment is not so tightly tied to the fortune of the UK stock market. However, international funds are subject to an additional risk: currencies can fluctuate as well as share prices.

Specialist sector funds

These funds invest in particular industries, e.g. financial or energy. The aim of a specialist fund might be described as:

> *The fund's main objective is long-term capital growth, but there may be wider than average day-to-day price fluctuations.*

In other words, the managers are warning you that you could be in for a bumpy ride, because if a unit trust invests its money in one UK industry and that industry does particularly badly or well the unit trust will perform likewise.

Specialist regional funds

These unit trusts invest in certain overseas stock markets. A typical fund might have an objective like:

> *This fund aims to achieve growth of capital through investment in the Far East in countries such as Japan, Hong Kong, Australia and Singapore.*

These funds concentrate mainly on getting increases in unit prices rather than income. Typically there are funds specialising in Europe, Japan, the USA, the Far East and Australia.

You should not expect specialist funds to move in line with the UK stock market. This is why specialist regional funds and commodity funds often appear at the top and the bottom of tables showing unit trust performance.

Note that funds which invest overseas are also affected by the caprices of the currency market – the unit price of an overseas trust will tend to rise if the exchange rate of the £ goes down, fall if the exchange rate of the £ goes up.

Managed funds

The idea behind managed funds is that one unit trust invests in other unit trusts, with the aim of providing a managed investment for more cautious investors. These unit trusts are also known as 'funds of funds'. There are rules about how such unit trusts can be invested. For example, they cannot invest in another managed fund and must invest in at least five unit trusts. Limits are also put on what management charges can be made. A managed fund cannot make an initial charge, but you will still have to pay this when it invests in other unit trusts. However, the managers of managed funds are allowed to make a yearly charge.

As such a fund is designed for investors wanting lower risk, the return is also likely to be a bit pedestrian.

Verdict: which type of fund?

If you want to invest in a unit trust and hang on to it for a while, it's probably best to choose a general or income unit trust. If you have enough money, spread it between two or more unit trusts, perhaps one general and one other; the other could be a growth or specialist fund. If you want to invest with the idea of shifting from fund to fund, you can choose from the full range, according to your educated guess.

Best and worst performing unit trusts

1990
TOP 5

Schroder Japan Smllr Cos	+15.5%
Whittingdale City Reserve	+15.2%
Abbey Capital Reserve	+11.7%
Fidelity Cash	+11.2%
Framlington Gilt Gth Inc	+10.7%

BOTTOM 5

Windsor Smaller Cos	−58.8%
Waverley Australian Gold	−51.2%
MIM Brit Smaller Cos	−47.8%
Brown Shipley Smaller Cos	−46.5%
Thornton Golden Opps	−46.2%

1991
TOP 5

Hill Samuel US Smaller Cos	+115.2%
Framlington Health Fund	+111.2%
Framlington Amer Smllr Cos	+101.1%
Fidelity Amer Special Sits	+96.6%
Cannon North American	+90.5%

BOTTOM 5

MGM Special Situation Gth	−29.7%
Gartmore Euroventures	−18.9%
Hambros Japan & Far East	−14.6%
Thornton European Opps	−10.6%
Hambro-Generali Prop Share	−10.5%

Note: year to 1 December; includes net income reinvested; valued on an offer to bid basis
Source: Money Management

How to choose a unit trust

There is no magic recipe for choosing a unit trust. Below, we look at some well-known systems for picking a winner and put them to the test. Note that our verdicts on the theories are general: there are always exceptions to a rule.

None of the systems below would prove to be an ideal strategy to pick winners. There may be slight evidence to support one or other of the theories, but any advantage is for a limited period, and any limited gain could be cancelled out by buying and selling costs.

'Small funds do best'

It's argued that the managers of small funds can buy and sell investments more easily and so get the best return.

We looked at how all UK trusts had performed over four-year and nine-year periods. The results showed that you could rely on neither large funds nor small funds to be consistently good performers; but small funds tended to move more in line with UK stock markets than larger funds.

Verdict: size is not a particularly useful criterion for picking a unit trust.

'Go for last year's winners'

This theory claims that trusts which have done well in the past will do well in the future.

We looked at the performance of all UK trusts over five 12-month periods from 1985 to 1989. There was no evidence that trusts would do well in the future just because they had done well in the past.

Verdict: past performance is not a good guide for picking a unit trust.

'Go for last year's losers'

Is it true that last year's winners are likely to be this year's losers, and vice versa? That if things are bad they can only get better? We looked at what would have happened if we had invested in 1980 in the bottom five trusts for the previous year, sold them at the end of the year, and reinvested in the bottom five for that year (repeating the exercise until 1989). There tended to be more of a pattern here: consistently re-investing in last year's losers could be a good way to lose money. On the other hand, had we invested in the bottom five at the beginning of 1980 and *stuck* with our investment until the end of 1989, we would have been on to a winner, compared with other unit trust investment strategies we tested.

Verdict: not a good guide for picking a unit trust.

'New is best'

Because the managers will be giving a new unit trust a lot of expert attention, it's claimed they'll do better than with old unit trusts.

We looked at new trusts launched each year over a five-year period in each unit trust sector and compared them with other trusts in the particular sector. There was an initial benefit, but it didn't last for very long.

Verdict: a newly launched trust may have some initial benefit compared with others in its sector, but it's not guaranteed (and it may not compare well with unit trusts in other sectors).

'Pick a management company'

It's claimed that some management companies do better than others.

We looked at trusts managed by companies with at least five trusts, and measured their performance over one, five and seventeen years. We couldn't find any evidence that good performance in one period would mean good performance in the next.

Verdict: there was little evidence that choosing by management company was a good way to pick a unit trust, though, of course, unit trust performance could have changed because of a change of managers. But if you do believe in going for the 'best' managers, you'll have to keep a very close eye on developments in a way which may not, in fact, be practicable.

'Look for investments in small companies'

There is a theory that the shares of small companies are likely to produce better results than those of larger companies. Some evidence from studying the UK and US stock markets supports this view. However, we looked at trusts whose names suggested that they specialised in this sort of investment. Only over the longest period at which we looked (17 years) was there the possibility that investing in smaller companies improved the performance of these trusts compared with all other trusts investing in similar (though not necessarily small) companies.

Verdict: there's just a little evidence to back up this theory, but only over the very long term.

For a more detailed look at our survey results, see *Which?*, July 1990, p. 384.

A step-by-step guide to choosing a unit trust

Although there's no certain way of choosing the unit trusts which will perform best, you can narrow down your choice among the bewildering number available following the steps below. But be warned – it's a long job. You could ask advisers to do it for you – see p. 276.

Step 1 Make sure a unit trust really is a suitable investment for you – see Chapters 1 and 2. Don't feel that you have to invest *now* just because you've got the cash available; bear in mind that the success of your investment will depend very much on when you buy and when you sell.

Step 2 Decide how many trusts in which to invest. If you have enough £££ (minimum investment is usually in the £250 to £1,500 range), invest in more than one unit trust.

Step 3 Decide which types of fund to go for – see p. 267.

Step 4 Do you want to invest a lump sum or a regular amount each month? If you want to save a certain amount each month, look for a unit trust which offers a savings plan. You could consider investing via a life insurance policy instead – see Chapter 20.

Step 5 Find out when you can deal. With a few unit trusts you can't deal daily, and this may be inconvenient.

Step 6 Still left with lots of unit trusts to choose from? Look at the investements the fund holds, whether they've been changed much (which can be costly) and so on. Ask the company to send you the manager's reports and the scheme particulars (see below).

Step 7 Finally, choosing between these unit trusts will have to be based on your own hunches.

Getting information

From the company

If you want information about a unit trust, ask to see the latest *manager's report* and the *scheme particulars*. What goes in each of these documents is laid down by the Securities and Investments Board (SIB) – see Chapter 5. The scheme particulars have to be revised once a year, or more frequently if a major change occurs in the unit trust. The managers of the unit trust have to produce a report every six months. From these two documents you should be able to find out most of what you want to know about the unit trust.

The manager's report should, among other things, tell you what the objectives of the fund are, how the fund has done over the last six months, how much income will be paid out, what changes have occurred in the investments and information about the highest buying and lowest selling prices for the last 10 years (or since the fund began, if less).

The scheme particulars will give the name and address of the manager, the trustee, the investment adviser for the fund (if there is one), the auditor and the registrar (if there is one). There should be a statement saying what the investment policy of the fund will be and giving details about its valuation, the charges and expenses of the fund.

From newspapers and magazines

Details of most unit trusts are listed in several newspapers. An entry might look like this:

Westover income 494.8   523.2   470.2 − 0.3   3.83.

This tells you the name of the unit trust and (in the order above) the price you could sell your units for yesterday, the price at which you could buy them yesterday, the cancellation price (the lowest *bid* price worked out using the laid-down formula – see opposite), how much the price has changed since the previous day, and the yield – see p. 280. Once a week the initial charge will be shown as a percentage of price.

Magazines, such as *Money Management* and *Planned Savings* give other details, e.g. what £1,000 invested five years ago would be worth now.

The *Unit Trust Year Book* (published by FTBI) gives a lot of information about each unit trust and each management group – try your library.

From investment advisers

In Chapter 6 we looked at the various sources of professional advice, many of which will help in choosing unit trusts. But remember that it's up to *you* to evaluate their advice.

Both independent advisers and unit trust company representatives can sell you unit trusts, and will generally get a commission on the value of unit trusts they buy for you.

If you buy from one of these groups as a result of an unsolicited sales call (see p. 77), in certain circumstances you have the right to cancel the investment within 14 days of receiving a notice of your rights. What you will get back will be the price you would have paid if you had bought on the day you decided to cancel.

Investing in unit trusts

Units

When you invest in a unit trust you buy units in the trust from the management company. When you cash your investments, you sell units back to the management company (it *has* to buy them from you). The management company puts the cash you pay for units into the fund and it's used to buy investments, such as shares.

Prices

A unit has two prices. These prices are based on the value of the investments in the trust fund. The higher price (the *offer* price) is what you pay to buy units. The lower price (the *bid* price) is what you get if you sell units. You usually buy or sell at the price worked out when the fund is next valued (called the *forward* price), which means that, as with shares, you won't know the exact price until the deal is done. But some funds deal at the price which was worked out when the fund was last valued (the *historic* price). Generally speaking, the fund is valued once a day, but a few are valued less frequently.

The prices are worked out using a method originally laid down by the Department of Trade and Industry (DTI). To arrive at the offer price, the company finds out the lowest price it would have to pay to buy the investments currently in the unit trust fund. It then adds various costs to this, e.g. management charges. The value it has after doing this sum is divided by the number of units the company has issued, and this gives the maximum offer price the company can charge you to buy units.

The lowest bid price, i.e. the price the company has to pay you for your units, is worked out in a similar way. But this time the company has to find out what is the highest price it could get if it sold the investments currently in the unit trust fund.

The difference between these two prices is called the *spread*. The average spread quoted in the newspapers is around 7 per cent. If you want to sell a large number of units (£15,000 plus), the management company does not necessarily have to buy at the bid price it is quoting other sellers of units. Instead, it could offer to buy your units at a price nearer or equal to the minimum bid price, or make you wait until it has worked out what the price will be at the next valuation.

In fact, it's possible for the unit price for any size purchase to rise or fall without the share prices of the investments in the unit trust rising or falling. This is because the spread the management company quotes is usually less than the spread it could quote under the DTI rules. So, for example, if many unit-holders are selling, the management company can shift the unit prices downwards to discourage selling and attract buyers. However, if it wants to alter where its prices are in the permitted range, the company cannot do so and carry on using the price from the last valuation. It can only let you deal at the price worked out at the next valuation.

Buying and selling

You can buy or sell in several ways, e.g over the telephone, by letter or through a company representative or independent adviser. Note that an order over the telephone is just as binding as one made in writing. If the fund is dealing only at the prices worked out at the next valuation, you can, of course, set a limit on the price you're prepared to pay for units or accept if you sell them, e.g. only sell at £2 or more. In this way, you should get no surprises.

Once the unit trust manager has received your unit trust certificate, if you are selling, you should get the money in five days.

Charges

There are two different sorts of charges. These are:
- **initial charge** – often 5 per cent and included in the spread between the bid and offer prices, although some companies have now cut their initial charge to as little as 1 per cent
- **regular charge** – often in the range 1 per cent to 1½ per cent a year (plus VAT), but can be higher, especially if the initial charge is low. This charge is usually taken from the income of the fund. The trust deeds allow some funds to raise charges to 2 per cent or 2½ per cent after giving the required notice.

Management of the unit trust

There may be three groups of people involved. Firstly, a management company, which does the administration and advertising. Secondly, there is an investment adviser, usually the same company as the management company, although some have advisers such as stockbrokers deciding how the fund should be invested. Thirdly, there is the trustee (see below).

Under the Financial Services Act (see Chapter 5), there is a procedure for handling complaints about unit trusts. Contact the unit trust company first, and they will tell you which of these three groups will deal with an unresolved complaint. If this doesn't work, contact LAUTRO, if your complaint is about marketing, IMRO if your complaint is about the management of your investment, or if you have a complaint about an independent financial adviser who sold you the unit trust, the organisation which regulates them, probably FIMBRA – see p. 80.

Trustee

There are over a dozen companies, mainly banks, acting as trustees to hundreds of different unit trusts. Trustees have several jobs. Firstly, the trustee keeps all the cash and investments of the fund in its name.

Secondly, the trustee makes sure that the managers stick to the terms of the trust deed and the scheme particulars – see p. 275. The trust deed will have the following information among other things:

- name of the fund and its investment aim
- the currency of the fund
- when income of the fund will be paid out.

Thirdly, the trustee checks that the unit price calculation has been done correctly and cancels and issues units.

Exactly how much the trustee does can vary, depending on how the trustee interprets the trust deed.

Income

The investments which are held in the unit trust fund get income in the form of share dividends, interest from British Government stocks and so on. The management company takes its regular charge from the income and will usually pay out what's left to unit-holders in the form of *distributions*. There are usually two distributions a year, but some trusts, which concentrate on producing income, pay out distributions once a quarter.

As the income comes into the fund, the unit prices rises to take account of this, until it finally includes the whole of the distribution. On a certain day, the price will be marked *xd* (i.e *ex distribution*) and will fall by the amount of the distribution. After that time, if you buy units, you will not get the next distribution to be paid; if you sell units, you still get the next distribution.

There are four different types of trust:
- accumulation trusts
- distribution trusts
- trusts with both accumulation and distribution units
- trusts where you can automatically reinvest income.

With accumulation trusts, the income of the unit trust fund is not paid to you in £££. Instead, the unit price is simply increased to reflect the income.

With distribution trusts, the income of the unit trust fund must be paid out in £££ to each investor.

With many unit trusts, you can buy either accumulation units (where the income of the fund is used to increase the unit price) or distribution units (where the income of the fund is paid out to you).

With the rest of the funds, you can choose to have the income automatically reinvested (rather than paid out). This means the income is used to buy more units – you have to pay an initial charge on these.

Tax

Distributions from a unit trust come with a *tax credit*. The effect of this is that if you're a basic-rate taxpayer there's no income tax to pay on the distribution. If you pay tax at the higher rate, you'll have to pay more tax. If you're a non-taxpayer, or pay tax only at the lower rate, you'll be able to claim tax back. For more details, see p. 102.

The normal capital gains tax rules apply to unit trust investments. See p. 107 for details.

Size of income

If you are buying a unit trust as a way of getting an income, look at the *yield* of the fund. The higher the yield, the higher the income is compared to the £££ you invest.

To get the yield, the amount of the distribution per unit is divided by the unit price. This is then multipled by 100 to give a percentage. For example, if the distribution per unit is 3p and the unit price is 60p, the yield is $3 \div 60 \times 100 = 5$ per cent.

Of course, if you were to buy units when the price was lower, say 50p, the yield on your investment would be $3 \div 50 \times 100 = 6$ per cent.

Note that the yield usually quoted is the gross yield, i.e. based on the distribution *plus* tax credit – see above.

Another way of getting an income from unit trusts

The disadvantage of using the distribution from a unit trust to provide you with an income is that it can go up and down, because the dividends paid by shares held by the unit trust fund can also go up and down. It alters also because managers of the fund will buy and sell the investments of the fund. Some unit trust companies have *withdrawal schemes* which allow you to have as your income either:

■ a percentage, say 5 per cent, of the original amount of £££ you invest, so you can be certain you get the same income each year, or
■ a percentage, say 5 per cent, of the current value of your investment. In this case, the income would still go up and down each year.

If the distributions of the unit trust are not high enough to meet this amount of income, then some of your units are sold. But more units will have to be sold to make up your income when unit prices are low than when they are high – the opposite of what you want. And selling units can lead to you using up your capital increasingly quickly – the more units you sell, the lower your income from distributions in the future, so that more units will have to be sold in the future.

If you decide a withdrawal scheme could be useful, you'll need to check the minimum investment the company will take; it varies, but can be as high as £15,000.

Some unit trust groups organise regular income schemes, where you invest in three or more unit trusts, each with a different month for paying income. In this way, you can get a regular, if varying, monthly income.

Size of investment

For lump sum investments, all unit trusts ask for a minimum investment when you first invest, e.g. £250 or £1,500. If you want to increase your investment you can usually do so by smaller amounts.

Some unit trust companies will let you invest a regular amount, e.g. £25 a month. This is known as a *savings plan*. For an explanation of how this can be linked to a life insurance policy, see p. 335.

One advantage of a savings plan is that you don't have to worry as much about when you should invest as you would with a lump sum. *Pound-cost averaging* is sometimes cited as being one advantage of a regular savings plan. What this seems to show is that you can get a bargain by investing regularly. This is because, if the unit price goes up and down, the average cost of your units will be less than the average of unit prices – when the unit price is low your fixed sum of money buys more units than when it is high. But there's nothing magic about this, it just shows the advantage of not having to worry about timing your investment correctly. Don't let this sort of advertising for savings plans persuade you that you are getting a bargain. You still have to worry about when you should cash in your investment.

If you already hold shares, you could swap these for units, through a *share exchange scheme*. The unit trust company will usually do one of two things with your shares:

■ put them in one of its funds, if the fund already holds that company's shares. In this case, in exchange for the shares, the company will often give you units equal in value to the price that it would have to pay to buy them through the Stock Exchange. As this is more than you could get by selling the shares yourself through the Stock Exchange, this seems to be a good saving

■ sell them for you if the company does not want to put them in a fund. In this case, the company often pays the selling costs, e.g. stockbroker's commission.

Most unit trust companies have a share exchange scheme. The details about minimum value of shares, number of shares and so on vary from company to company.

But don't let quite small savings push you into poor investment decisions.

Cost of switching

With the growth of more and more specialist funds and specialist advisers, there has been an increase in the number of companies which will let you switch your investment from one of their unit trusts to another for a lower-than-normal initial charge. Most unit trust companies will normally give you a discount of between 1 per cent and 4 per cent off the price of units in the trust to which you are switching.

16

INVESTMENT TRUSTS

Investment trusts, like unit trusts, are a way of investing in shares, Government stock and property throughout the world. An investment trust can hold a number of different types of investment, in a range of different industries and countries. The funds are managed by professional investment managers. However, unlike a unit trust, you cannot put money into the fund, nor can you take money out again. All you can do is buy shares in the fund.

Investment trusts are limited companies floated on the Stock Exchange. When an investment trust is created its shares are sold on the stock market, just like any other company. But the money raised is then re-invested in shares, loans and property. The trust deeds (the documents that legally establish the trust) will specify what investments the trust can invest in and what sort of return the trust aims to make.

You can invest in investment trusts either for income, capital growth or both. Holders of the investment trust shares receive income distributions from the fund, and as the value of the fund rises the value of the shares should also rise.

Investment trusts are like unit trusts or shares in that the value of your investment can fall as well as rise. If you buy shares in an investment trust, you cannot be sure of getting back the amount you invested at any particular time; and the income you receive from the fund can fluctuate. So you should not invest money in an investment trust unless you are certain you won't need it in the near future.

Investment trusts versus unit trusts

When it comes to choosing between unit trusts (see Chapter 15) and investment trusts there are a number of differences to consider. Investment trusts are *closed end* funds. This means that once an investment trust is created, the number of shares is fixed and cannot be altered (except in the case of a rights or scrip issue – see p. 257). The money raised forms the trust's capital, and investors cannot add to or take money from the trust's capital. Shares in the trust cease to be under the control of the managers of the trust after it is launched and are traded on the Stock Exchange.

This is very different from a unit trust, whose managers create units when you want to buy them and buy units back from you when they want to sell them.

Pricing

The difference between unit trusts and investment trusts has important consequences for the way the trusts are priced. Unit trusts are priced according to the value of the assets they hold. The managers create as many units as people want to buy at that price. The price of investment trust shares is determined by supply and demand for them on the stock market. If nobody wants to buy shares in a particular investment trust, their price will be low, regardless of how valuable the assets held by the trust are.

Occasionally, the shares of very popular investment trusts sell for more than the value of the assets held by the trust (or the *net asset value*, as it is called). This price is *at a premium*. But most investment trust shares tend to sell at a price below the net asset value of the trust. This is known as *discount to net asset value*. The discount for most investment trusts tends to be from 10 per cent to 20 per cent of the net asset value.

This can be bad news for the managers of trusts since it encourages large institutions to buy up investment trusts and then sell off their assets at a profit. But for the investor it is good news. If you buy shares in an investment trust at a discount, you will benefit from the income produced by a correspondingly larger investment.

Discounts are not as good for the investor if the discount arises or increases during the time you hold the shares. If, for example, you buy shares in an investment trust at the launch (when there will be no discount) you may find, when you come to sell your shares, that they are trading at a discount, thus preventing you from realising the full capital gain of the underlying assets.

The Association of Investment Trust Companies (see p. 290 for their address) publishes information about the net asset value and discounts of most investment trusts.

Selling assets

Another important difference between unit trusts and investment trusts may be seen when stock markets values are falling rapidly. If unit trust investors rush to cash in their investments, the managers have to sell off assets to pay back the investors. Unfortunately, if the stock market is spiralling downwards, managers may have to sell the best shares first, since no one wants the worst shares. As a result, the value of units can accelerate downwards as unit trusts sell off their best holdings.

Investment trust managers, in the same circumstances, may be under less pressure to sell their investments and can take a more strategic view of the falling markets.

Borrowing money

Because investment trusts are companies they can borrow money on behalf of their investors. Unit trusts are not allowed to do this. When an investment trust borrows money and invests it, the result is known as *gearing*. Gearing increases the volatility of the share price. When the market is rising, gearing will make an investment trust's shares rise even quicker than the market. But when the market is falling, a geared investment trust will fall in value that much quicker than the market.

Gearing is a double-edged sword. If the investments bought with the borrowed money produce a greater return than the interest payments, the additional return will make the value of the shares rise more quickly than they would otherwise. However, if the interest on the loan comes to more than the return on the investment, then the shares will be worth less than they would be otherwise. If share prices generally start falling, a heavily geared trust, i.e. one which has borrowed large amounts of money, can fall in value very quickly.

Most investments trusts involve some degree of gearing. The amount an investment trust has borrowed can be seen in the trust's annual report. The Association of Investment Trust Companies publishes information on the level of gearing for most investment trusts.

Costs

The costs of investing in a unit trust are fixed by the trust managers and usually consist of an initial charge of, say, 5 per cent plus an annual charge of between 1 and 1.5 per cent. The costs of investing in an investment trust vary according to where you buy. Firstly, there will be the cost of commission to whichever stockbroker or savings scheme you buy from – see p. 290. This cost alone will almost certainly be less than the charges made by a unit trust.

However, to make a fair comparison you also need to take into account the cost of the *spread* between *bid* and *offer* prices quoted by dealers in the shares. Share dealers make their money by buying at one price (bid) and selling at another higher price (offer). The spread between them represents a cost to the person investing in the shares. The spread between bid and offer prices is different for different investment trusts and can change from day to day.

This means that it is impossible to say whether investment trusts are cheaper or more expensive than unit trusts to buy. If you bought a popular investment trust, i.e. one which is traded often, through a savings scheme (see p. 290) it would almost certainly be cheaper than a unit trust. But for investment trust shares which are less often traded, the bid/offer spread can be over 10 per cent.

Reinvesting income

Unit trusts usually have a facility to allow you to reinvest your income from your investment directly back into the unit trust. This is very useful if you are investing solely for capital growth. Investment trusts do not have this facility.

Specialisation

Unit trusts can be set up at little cost and without too much risk. They are also allowed to advertise themselves much more easily than investment trusts. As a result there are hundreds of small specialisied unit trusts, set up to take advantage of particular opportunities, which invest in specific markets, e.g. Japanese Warrant funds or American Smaller Companies.

Investment trusts are more difficult to establish, requiring a full stock market flotation. As a result there are fewer of them and they tend to be more general in their investment objectives.

Different types of investment trusts

Investment trusts, like unit trusts, break down into different categories:
- **international** with less than 80 per cent of assets in any one geographical area. International trusts break down into three varieties: *general*, which aims to produce balanced income and growth; *income growth*, which aims to maximise the level of income produced; and *capital growth* which concentrates on increasing capital.
- **UK** with at least 80 per cent of assets in the UK. Like the international trusts they are divided into *general, income growth* and *capital growth*
- **high income** with 80 per cent of assets in shares and aiming to produce a yield at least 10 per cent higher than the yield of the FT-Actuaries All-Share Index.
- **North America** with at least 80 per cent of assets in North America
- **Far East (including Japan)** with 80 per cent of assets in the Far East including a Japanese content
- **Far East (excluding Japan)** with 80 per cent of assets in the Far East and no Japanese assets
- **Japan** with 80 per cent of assets in Japan
- **Europe** investing either in Europe generally or in specific European countries
- **emerging markets** with at least 80 per cent of assets in emerging markets like Mexico
- **financial and property** with up to 80 per cent of assets in property or the financial sector, e.g. banks
- **commodity and energy** with at least 80 per cent of assets in commodities and energy
- **technology** with at least 80 per cent of assets in technology. Unlike a unit trust, an investment trust can buy up patents in new technology. These trusts do this as well as investing in technology-based companies
- **smaller companies** concentrating on investing in smaller companies in the hope that they are going to be the large companies of tomorrow
- **venture and development capital** concentrating on small and growing companies. As well as investing in shares, they will provide capital for buy-outs and new companies, something which unit trusts are not allowed to do. The risks of such investments are greater, but so are the possible rewards.

Split-capital investment trusts

Split-capital investment trusts are a relatively new form of investment trust. The first was launched in 1987. In a split-capital investment trust there are different kinds of shares which give different kinds of returns. The most basic division is between *income* shares and *capital* shares. People with income shares will receive all the income from the fund and people with capital shares will receive all the capital growth from the fund. Both will receive more income or capital growth than they would have received otherwise since the income or capital growth that would normally have been distributed among all shares will only go to those shares designated income or capital.

So that investors in the capital shares can be certain of realising the full value of their investment, split-capital trusts are given a fixed life and are wound up at the end of that time; otherwise the price of capital shares might be constantly at a discount preventing investors from getting back their return.

Income shares will produce a higher income than other shares. And if the fund grows, the income produced will also grow so that over a number of years the income produced can become very high indeed. This may also result in the price of the shares rising, giving investors some capital growth. However, at the end of the term the trust will pay back only the initial capital investment. Even being paid back the initial investment may not be guaranteed but may depend on how well the fund has performed.

Capital shares will behave very much like heavily geared investments. When the market is rising they will rise much quicker than other investments. However, when the market is falling they will fall much quicker. This makes them a risky investment over the short term. But if you have money which you will not need in the short term and which you want to invest for capital growth, capital shares in an investment trust could be worth considering.

Who should invest in investment trusts?

Whether they are the right investment for you depends on how much you have to invest, over what time period you are investing, what kind of return you hope to get from your investment, and how much risk you are prepared to tolerate. Ultimately, your choice of investment will also depend on how you think different investments and markets are going to perform in the future.

How long are you investing the money for?

Investment trusts are medium- to long-term investments. There may be no point in putting your money into an investment trust for less than two or three years as you may well get back less than you put in. The chances of not making a reasonable return get less the longer you leave your money in the trust.

What are your investment objectives?

If you are looking solely for *capital growth*, over the medium- to long-term an investment trust or a unit trust would be a suitable investment. If you are looking for capital growth over a period of 10 years or more, then investment in capital shares from a split-capital investment trust could be worth considering.

If you are looking for a *moderate income* (say a yield of 4 to 6 per cent) and want some capital growth, e.g. to compensate for inflation, then an investment in a general investment trust might be the answer.

If you are looking to *maximise income*, investment trusts are not the obvious choice of investment. However, if you are prepared to risk your capital and feel that shares are likely to perform very well in the future, you might consider investing in the income shares of a split-capital investment trust.

How much risk are you prepared to accept?

If you need to be certain of being able to draw out your capital at any moment, then investment trusts are not for you. However, if you are prepared to see the value of your investments rise and fall, investment trusts could be a suitable long-term investment. Some investment trusts are riskier than others. Technology and venture capital trusts are relatively high risk. They can perform spectacularly well but they can also perform extremely badly. The more general a trust, the less risk involved. A general international trust which spreads your investments world-wide may be less risky than a trust which invests in only a few countries.

Buying investment trust shares

There ar two ways to buy investment trust shares. You can buy them through a stockbroker or other intermediary, like any other share, or you can buy shares in many investment trusts from the management company through an investment trust savings scheme.

Stockbroker

The cost of buying and selling shares from a stockbroker means that it is impractical to buy shares worth less than say, £1,000 to £1,500. Most stockbrokers will charge commission and have a minimum charge – see p. 250.

Savings schemes

Many investment trust managers run savings schemes for their investment trusts, set up to encourage private investors to invest in them. Companies are not allowed to advertise their own shares but investment trusts can advertise their savings schemes. An advantage for private investors is that the investment trust company pays the brokerage costs for you. The cost of buying investment trust shares through a savings scheme is much less than buying from a stockbroker. Most savings schemes charge less than 1 per cent of your investment in commission. Investment trust savings schemes have minimum investment levels which vary, but most are either £25 per month or £250 as a lump sum.

Information about savings schemes is available from the Association of Investment Trust Companies. Many of them are advertised in the national weekend newspapers.

Further information
The best place to get information is either from the companies themselves or from the Association of Investment Trust Companies, Park House (6th Floor), 16 Finsbury Circus, London EC2M 7JJ, tel: 071-588 5347.

Tax

The shares of investment trusts are taxed in the same way as other shares. The dividends are subject to income tax (see p. 102) and any growth in the value of the shares could lead to a capital gains tax bill (see p. 107).

17

BRITISH GOVERNMENT STOCKS

The government issues British Government stocks as a way of borrowing money. There is a very large market in them and Government stocks can prove to be good investments; but they can also turn out to be poor investments, e.g. when interest rates and inflation rise.

British Government stocks could suit four quite different categories of people:

■ those who want a regular (normally fixed) income and who are confident that they won't want their money back in hurry

■ those who want to invest for a specific time period and want a fixed return over that period, and may not be too bothered how much of that return comes as income or how much as capital gain

■ those who want to gamble that interest rates, in general, will fall (stock prices are then likely to rise, leading to a capital gain)

■ those who want to protect some of their money against inflation – they could choose index-linked British Government stocks.

Below, we describe how *conventional* stocks works. For more details on *index-linked* stocks, and on their pros and cons, see p. 299.

How conventional stocks work

Most British Government stocks (commonly called *gilt-edged securities* or just *gilts*) pay a fixed amount of income each year (though there have also been a few issues of stocks whose income could vary).

With stocks which are *dated*, the government also promises to pay the holder of the stock a fixed number of

£££ in a lump sum at the time the stock comes to an end. With *undated* stocks, no final date is specified, so the government need never pay off its debt.

Like shares, stocks are bought and sold on the Stock Exchange. And, as with shares, the prices of stocks fluctuate, so once you've bought some stock, the value of your investment can vary widely.

The diagram opposite shows what has happened to the price of an undated stock since 1975. You can see, for example, that if you'd bought in August 1979 and sold two years later you'd have done badly. You'd have got a before-tax income of 10.5 per cent a year on your original investment, but when you sold you would have got back only three-quarters of the money you originally invested – an overall loss of around 4.5 per cent a year for a basic-rate taxpayer.

If, on the other hand, you'd been lucky (or shrewd) enough to invest in October 1981 and sell four and a half years after that, you'd have done very much better. You'd have got a before-tax income of 14.2 per cent a year on your original investment and your investment would have increased in value by 66 per cent by the time you sold – an overall return to a basic-rate taxpayer of around 19.7 per cent a year.

So when you buy and when you sell is crucial to the success or failure of your investment. Of course, if you buy a dated stock and hold it until it comes to an end, you'll know from the outset what you'll get, both in income and capital gain (or loss).

Getting to know the different stocks

Nominal value

British Government stocks are bought and sold in amounts which have a nominal value (or *face* value) of so many £££ and pence. For each £100 nominal of stock you hold, the government promises to pay you £100 in cash at an agreed time in the future – see *Redemption date*, p. 294.

But you don't have to buy stocks in multiples of £100 nominal. You could, for example, invest £260 in a stock costing £80 for each £100 nominal. You would then get: £100 × 260 ÷ 80 = £325 nominal of stock.

Name

Each stock has a name, like Exchequer, Treasury or War Loan. This is of no particular significance to investors but helps to distinguish one stock from another.

How the price of undated stock [1] has changed

£ for each nominal £100 of stock

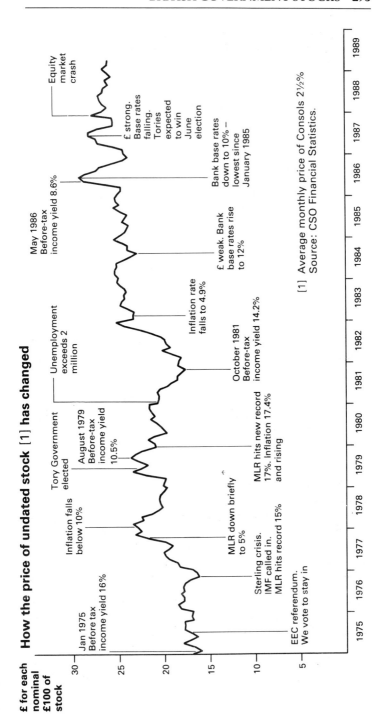

Jan 1975 Before tax income yield 16%

Inflation falls below 10%

Tory Government elected

August 1979 Before-tax income yield 10.5%

Unemployment exceeds 2 million

May 1986 Before-tax income yield 8.6%

Equity market crash

£ strong. Base rates falling. Tories expected to win June election

EEC referendum. We vote to stay in

Sterling crisis. IMF called in. MLR hits record 15%

MLR down briefly to 5%

MLR hits new record 17%. Inflation 17.4% and rising

October 1981 Before-tax income yield 14.2%

Inflation rate falls to 4.9%

£ weak. Bank base rates rise to 12%

Bank base rates down to 10% – lowest since January 1985

[1] Average monthly price of Consols 2½%
Source: CSO Financial Statistics.

Coupon

The percentage immediately after the name of each stock, e.g. 10 per cent, in Treasury 10 per cent 1994, is called the *coupon*. It tells you the before-tax income the stock pays out each year, expressed as a percentage of the nominal value; in the case of Treasury 10 per cent 1994, the stock pays out £10 for every £100 nominal. Interest on nearly all stocks is paid twice yearly in two equal instalments.

Redemption date

Following the name and the coupon is a year – 1994 in the example above. The date on which the government has promised to redeem the stock, i.e to pay out the nominal value of the stock, falls in this year.

The date may be a range of years, e.g. 1995–8. In this case, the government (but not the investor) can choose in which year out of this range to redeem the stock.

With a few stocks, the coupon is followed by a year and the words *or after*, e.g. 1923 *or after*. This means that the government can choose 1923 or any later year which suits it in which to redeem the stock. These, and a few other stocks which have no year quoted at all, are called *undated* and need never be redeemed, e.g War Loan 3½ per cent.

The life of a stock

Stocks are generally split into four groups according to the length of their remaining life, i.e. the time left until redemption. The precise splits vary somewhat depending on their use, but these are what the groups are called:
- **short-dated** if the stocks must be redeemed in the next five (or sometimes seven) years
- **medium-dated** if their latest redemption date is more than five (or seven), but not more than fifteen years away
- **long-dated** if over fifteen years
- **undated** if no latest redemption date is given.

What makes stock prices change?

In general, it is changes in interest rates in the economy as a whole. If interest rates rise, the price of stocks is likely to fall. If interest rates fall, stock prices are likely to rise. Why is this?

Suppose you invest £100 in an undated British Government stock which pays out an income of £10 a year. The yearly return is then roughly 10 per cent. But suppose interest rate in the economy as a whole were expected to rise. New investors could then get a higher return on their money by investing elsewhere, so they'll hold off buying British Government stock. This means that the price of Government stock is likely to fall until the yearly return it offers is comparable to the return investors could get elsewhere. For example, if interest rates double, the price of the undated stock which pays out £10 a year may have to halve to £50, so that the yearly return it then offers is roughly 20 per cent.

Similarly, if interest rates as a whole fall, the price of British Government stock is likely to rise.

Dated stocks, however, pose more problems because there are other factors at work, the most important of which are:

■ **how long there is to go until the stock comes to an end** In general, the shorter the period left to run, the smaller the fluctuations in price. Take the example above of an undated stock paying interest of £10 a year and halving in price from £100 to £50. Suppose this stock was due to end in a year's time when the government would pay the holder £100. If the price was £50, someone buying it now would get back £100 in a year's time plus £10 in income in the meantime, which gives a return of around 120 per cent a year. The price needs to fall from £100 to only £90 or so to give a return of around 20 per cent.

■ **the stock's coupon** (see opposite). In general, the higher the coupon, the smaller the fluctuations in price. Take a stock with a coupon of 10 per cent, for example, and five years to go before it comes to an end. If it is currently selling for its nominal value (see p. 292) of £100, the yearly return will be 10 per cent. For the return (taking account of both income and capital growth over the next five years) to rise to 20 per cent, the price of the stock would have to fall by about 28 per cent to £72. But if the coupon was only 2 per cent, the stock would have to be selling for around £71 to give a yearly return of 10 per cent. For this return to rise to 20 per cent the price would have to fall by around 32 per cent to £48 or so.

What makes interest rates change?
There are a whole host of reasons. For example, the government may increase interest rates to discourage people from borrowing, or to attract investors' money from abroad (a key reason for the high interest rates during the first 9 months of 1992). An important influence will be the gap, if any, between the government's income and its spending, which will determine how much the government needs to borrow (by issuing Government stocks and by other methods).

The price you pay

The price of British Government stocks is quoted as the price for each £100 nominal of stock. Prices are normally quoted in £££ and fractions of a £, and shown to the nearest £1/32 (just over 3p) for short-dated stocks, and to the nearest £1/16 (just over 6p) for others.

Buyers pay more than the quoted price, sellers get less. For example, buyers might pay £1/8 more and sellers get £1/8 less. The difference between these two prices – the *spread* – will vary according to the size of your transaction and how actively the particular stock is traded. Spreads will tend to be larger with inactive stocks and small deals.

The price at which you buy or sell will be adjusted for something called *accrued interest* (see below).

Cum-dividend and ex-dividend

Most of the time, when you buy a stock, you buy it *cum-dividend*. This means that you are entitled to a full half-year's interest when it next becomes due, even if you haven't held the stock for that long. The price will be shown as say, £98 1/8 + 23 days accrued interest; this means you have paid for 23 days of interest which will be included in the next dividend.

However, some five weeks before the interest is due to be paid, the stock is declared *ex-dividend*. If you buy a stock ex-dividend, you are not entitled to the next interest payment and therefore have a longer-than-normal wait for your first interest payment. The quoted price for an ex-dividend stock has *xd* written after it.

For stocks with more than five years to go before redemption, except War Loan 3½ per cent, there's an additional period of three weeks before the stock is declared ex-dividend, during which you can choose to buy or sell the stock either cum-dividend or ex-dividend; during this time, the ex-dividend version is called *special ex-dividend*. Because the cum-dividend version of the stock entitles you to the next interest payment, it costs more than the ex-dividend version. You'll find only the cum-dividend price quoted in the newspapers during this three-week period.

Accrued interest

This is the interest that a cum-dividend buyer gets for the period when he or she didn't own the stock, or which an ex-dividend buyer forfeits by getting his or her first interest payment late.

The quoted prices for all stocks do not include the

accrued interest. This means that you have to pay a bit more than the quoted price when you buy cum-dividend, a bit less when you buy ex-dividend. Similarly, when you sell you'll receive a bit more or less than the quoted price.

Working out accrued interest

Since the quoted price of a stock does not include the accrued interest, you'll need to work out the amount of interest accrued so far in order to find out the total price you'll have to pay.

Accrued interest should be worked out in a way that takes each day's interest into account. But you won't go far wrong if you do the sums in terms of weeks.

For a cum-dividend stock, count the number of weeks between the last date interest was paid and the date for which you want the accrued interest. For an ex-dividend stock, count the number of weeks still to go before the next interest date. Ignore odd days. The approximate accrued interest in pence is then:

coupon × weeks just counted × 2.

For a cum-dividend stock, you need to *add* the answer you get to the quoted price to give you the total price you'll pay. For an ex-dividend stock, you need to *subtract* the answer from the quoted price to get the total price you'll pay.

Accrued Interest

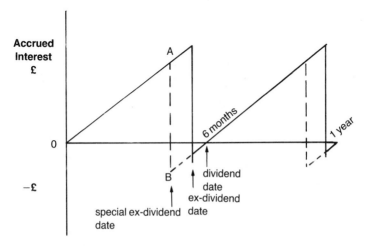

When the stock is special ex-dividend you can choose to buy or sell the stock cum-dividend (A) or special ex-dividend (B).

The return you get

In income

A stock's coupon (see p. 294) tells you the before-tax income paid on each £100 nominal of stock. But it won't tell you how much income you'll get as a percentage of the amount invested, because you are unlikely to pay £100 for each £100 nominal of stock. To work out the percentage income you'll get, do this sum:

coupon × 100 ÷ quoted price for each £100 nominal of stock.

This is known as the income yield (or interest yield).

Capital gain (or loss)

If you hold the stock until it comes to an end, you know you'll be paid its nominal value, so you can work out the capital gain (or loss) you'll make. But with undated stocks or stocks sold before they come to an end, you don't know in advance what price you'll get, so you can't be sure of what capital gain (or loss) you'll make.

The total return

With a dated stock, you can get some idea of the average yearly return on the stock if you hold it until it is redeemed by looking at what's known as the redemption yield. This takes account of both income paid out and the capital gain (or loss) you make in redemption. But it doesn't normally take account of buying and selling costs, and it assumes that the income paid out is reinvested at a rate of return equal to the redemption yield (for higher coupon stocks this overstates the return you're likely to get in practice). Before-tax redemption yields are printed daily in the newspapers mentioned on p. 303.

Working out the after-tax redemption yields for any stock is not easy. It depends not only on the rate of tax you pay, but also on how much of the return comes as taxable income and how much as tax-free capital gain.

In general:
- stocks vary widely in redemption yields
- for stocks with about the same period of time left to run, people who pay the higher rate of tax tend to get the best after-tax redemption yields from relatively low coupon stocks. By contrast, people who pay no tax tend to get the best redemption yields from high coupon stocks
- when it is possible to buy the same stock in the special ex-dividend period, taxpayers normally get better redemption yields if they buy ex-dividend.

Index-linked stocks

How they work

When the life of an index-linked stock comes to an end, the person then owning it will be paid the nominal value (see p. 292) of the stock increased in line with inflation over the lifetime of the stock. So, for example, someone owning £1,000 nominal of 1996 stock, issued in 1981, would get however many £££ are needed in 1996 in order to have the same buying-power as £1,000 back in 1981. This might be £2,000, £3,000, or more, depending on the rate of inflation between 1981 and 1996.

All the stocks also pay out a small income; their coupon (see p. 294) is 2 per cent or 2½ per cent depending on the stock. The income is guaranteed to increase each year in line with inflation.

For technical reasons, inflation is measured by the twelve-month change in the Retail Prices Index (RPI) recorded eight months before the dividend dates.

What happens to the buying and selling prices of the stocks?

Over the long term, the prices of the stocks will tend to rise roughly in line with inflation. If the price is £100 and the RPI goes up by 5 per cent a year, the price after a year might well be £105. But the price will also be affected by people's views on the future rate of inflation and interest rates, and by the return they can get on other investments.

The price of stocks with a longer life may well fluctuate more than the price of those with a short life.

Will your investment keep pace with inflation?

This depends entirely on the price at which you buy (or sell) the stock and whether or not you hold the stock until redemption. If you bought £100 nominal value of stock for £100 when the stock was issued, and if you then kept it throughout the lifetime of the stock, the increase in capital would exactly match the increase in inflation.

But suppose you had bought your £100 nominal value of stock for £90. As it's the £100 nominal value which is index-linked, your capital gain at the end of the stock's lifetime would be more than the rate of inflation. If you'd bought at £110, your capital gain would be less.

If you want to buy stocks some time after they are first

issued, you should compare the current market price with the nominal value adjusted for the increase in the RPI between the issue date and the time at which you want to buy. If the RPI has increased by 10 per cent, say, you should compare the market price with £110. If the price is higher, then your capital gain if you hold the stock to redemption will be less than inflation; if the price is lower, your capital gain will be more than inflation.

If you can't hold on to the stock until redemption, your gain will depend on the price you can sell at – see p. 294.

How do they compare with other British Government stocks?

■ **pro:** If you buy at the right price (see above) and hold them until redemption, you're guaranteed that the money you invest will at least keep pace with inflation.
■ **con:** The coupon for all index-linked stocks is low. And it could be costly to sell small amounts of stock to boost the income. So if you're after income, a high coupon stock may suit you better.

Are they worth buying?

If you're a higher-rate taxpayer not looking for a large increase in income, you should consider putting some of your money into these stocks. And they're definitely worth considering for anyone who wants to keep a nest-egg on ice for a fairly long time.

If you need to sell stocks, the price should roughly match inflation over the time you've owned it, though fluctuations in price may work against you.

New issues of stocks

In the more distant past, stocks were usually issued for sale at a fixed price, but this method was replaced with issues *by tender*. With a tender issue, it's usual for only a minimum price to be quoted. You can offer to buy stock at whatever price you like at or above the minimum.

If the whole issue (of, say, £800 million) is able to be sold at or above the minimum price, the issue is closed. But you don't need to worry about bidding too high, as everyone who bids pays the price paid by the lowest successful bidder, rather than the price they themselves bid. And issues don't normally sell out on the first day, so everyone who applies usually gets stock at the minimum price. After the initial offer, the stock that's left over is sold on the Stock Exchange by the Gilt-Edged Division of the Bank of England over a period of time, and not necessarily at the issue price.

During this period, the stock is commonly called a tap stock (because the supply of the stock is turned on and off like a tap, depending on the demand for it). When all this extra stock is sold, the tap is said to be exhausted. New short-dated stocks are called short taps; new medium-dated stocks, medium taps; and so on.

More recently, another method has become the preferred way of issuing stocks – the *bid price auction*. In an auction, you also choose the price at which you bid for stock. The main difference between a tender and an auction is that at auction all the stock is usually sold and the bidders pay the price they bid – so bidding too high could turn out to be costly. However, 'small' investors do not have to join the main auction. They can put in non-competitive bids, in which case they will be sure of getting stock at the *average* price of the issue.

Buying stock direct from the Bank of England when first issued has the advantage that you don't have to pay any stockbroker's commission (and there's no price spread – see p. 296). Most newly-issued stocks can eventually be registered on the National Savings Stock Register (see p. 303), which may keep your eventual selling costs down too.

New issues of stock may be partly-paid. This means that you don't have to pay the full cost of the stock when you first buy it, e.g. you may have to pay 15 per cent with your application and the remainder a month later.

How stocks are taxed

Government stocks are completely free of capital gains tax. You have to pay income tax on the income you get from the stocks at your highest rate of tax – see p. 100.

If you buy stocks on the National Savings Stock Register (see p. 303), income is paid without any tax deducted, though if you're a taxpayer you will have to pay the tax eventually – see p. 100 for details. If you buy through a stockbroker or an advertisement, your interest is normally paid after deduction of basic-rate tax. However, if your interest payment is £5 or less, or if you buy War Loan 3½ per cent, tax won't be deducted, regardless of how you bought the stock. And, if you are resident abroad, there are a few stocks on the Bank of England register (see opposite) that can have income paid without the deduction of tax.

The price you pay for, or get from, stocks equals the quoted price with accrued interest either added or deducted – see p. 296. The amount of this accrued interest used to be treated as part of your capital gains or loss and was subject to the capital gains tax rules, which often meant no tax to pay at all. But since 28 February 1986, accrued interest has been treated as income and is subject to income tax rules. There are a few exceptions: the main one for private investors is that, if the total nominal value of *all* the stocks you hold is no more than £5,000, the accrued income scheme does not apply; in this case, there is no income tax on accrued interest.

The contract note you get when you buy or sell stock will show how much accrued interest is involved in the deal. How it is treated for income tax depends on whether you are a buyer or a seller:
- if you sell cum-dividend, you are taxed on the accrued interest included in the price you get
- if you sell ex-dividend, you get tax relief on the accrued interest that has been deducted from the quoted price
- if you buy cum-dividend, you get tax relief on the accrued interest included in the price you pay
- if you buy ex-dividend, you are taxed on the accrued interest which has been deducted from the quoted price.

For more details about how accrued interest is taxed, see Inland Revenue leaflet *IR68* (available from tax offices and Tax Enquiry Centres).

Choosing a stock

Which stock to choose depends on what you want from your investment.

A high fixed income?
Go for a high coupon stock. But beware of choosing a stock which has a long time to go before it has to be redeemed. If you're forced to sell before then, you may lose heavily if the price of the stock has fallen in the meantime.

A known total return over a fixed period?
Go for a stock which lasts for the period you're interested
in. If there's a choice, choose one which gives the best
after-tax redemption yield (see p. 298) for someone in your
tax position. In general, a higher-rate taxpayer should go for
a low coupon stock, a non-taxpayer for a high coupon
stock.

Want to gamble on interest rates falling?
Go for a stock with a long time to run, or for an undated
stock. And choose one with a low coupon. But bear in mind
that if interest rates rise, you may end up losing heavily.

Protection against inflation?
Index-linked stocks might suit you. But bear in mind that
you have to buy stock at the right price and hold it until
redemption to be sure that the full index-linking will
apply; the extent to which your investment will be
protected against inflation will depend on the price at
which you buy.

Where to get information and advice

Several newspapers give information each day about
British Government stock prices; the most comprehensive
information is given in the *Financial Times* and *The
Times*.

 To find the after-tax redemption yield for someone
paying tax at the rate you pay it, and to get advice on which
stock would best suit your needs, contact a stockbroker,
bank or one of the increasing number of other organisations
offering a similar service.

How to buy and sell

You can buy and sell British Government stocks through
a stockbroker, high street bank (many now have their own
stockbroking arm rather than just acting as agents for other
stockbrokers), or through some building societies and
solicitors or accountants, say, who act as an agent for a
stockbroker. Most financial advisers will buy or sell stock
for you on the Bank of England register unless you
specifically ask otherwise. Around two-thirds of the stocks
are also listed on the National Savings Stock Register (you

get forms for buying and selling these at post offices). There are important differences between buying and selling on the Bank of England Register and via the National Savings Stock Register. In particular, buying through the National Savings Stock Register is much cheaper, except for large amounts of stock. If you own stock on the National Savings Register you cannot sell it in the stockmarket and vice versa, so it's important if you decide to sell your stock to be clear about where the stock is registered.

Investing via a unit trust

There is now a wide choice of unit trusts specialising in British Government stocks and other fixed income investments.

Investing via a unit trust is generally more expensive than investing in stocks direct. The difference between the buying and selling prices of units can be as high as 5 per cent, and there's a yearly charge.

From the income tax point of view, there's not a lot of difference between investing in a unit trust or investing direct. There is a difference with capital gains tax. British Government stocks are not liable for capital gains tax, but gains on trusts are, though the first £5,800 of gains made by selling assets (in the 1992–3 tax year) is exempt. Nor can you get an *indexation allowance* to reduce your capital gain – see p. 110.

Another problem with unit trust investment is that you have to accept the spread of stocks in which the trust chooses to invest. By investing directly, you can choose the particular stock which is best for your particular tax rate and investment needs.

18

LOCAL AUTHORITY INVESTMENTS

At the time of going to press, there are virtually no local authority investments being offered to the private investor and no immediate prospect that local authorities will return in force to this method of raising money. But the following information may be useful to you if you already hold local authority investments.

There have been two main ways in which you could invest in local authorities:
■ by lending money direct to a local authority for a fixed period, usually a year or more. We call this type a *local authority loan*
■ by buying *local authority yearling bonds* or *local authority stocks* on the Stock Exchange.

Money lent to local authorities is not guaranteed by the government, and therefore the returns from local authority investment have usually been higher than British Government stocks to reflect the slightly higher risk. But the government has laid down rules which strictly control how much a local authority can borrow, and what it can use the money for, so the money lent to a local authority is pretty secure.

Local authority loans

You have to agree to lend your money for a fixed period, usually between one and ten years. In general these loans are not designed to be cashed in early. If you want to do this you may have to convince the local authority that your circumstances have changed, e.g. if you've lost your job, and can't afford to live off the income you're now getting. If the authority agrees to your request, it may make a charge. You can transfer your loan to someone else but it may be hard to find a buyer, and these loans are not quoted on the Stock Exchange.

The rate of interest you get will tend to move in line with the general movements in interest rates in the economy, so will depend on when you invest. It will also depend on which local authority you choose, how much you invest (you may get a higher rate of interest if you invest £2,000, say, than if you invested only £500) and how long you invest for. Once you've invested your money, the interest rate is fixed for the period of the loan.

Local authority bonds and stocks

There are two main types of local authority investments which you can buy and sell on the Stock Exchange: *Local authority negotiable bonds* which are normally called *yearling bonds* (because they commonly last for a year or so), and *local authority stocks* (often called *corporation loans* or *stocks*) which are generally issued for fixed periods of six or more years. In both cases, they work very like British Government stock. However, very few new stocks have been issued in recent years, and there are no new issues currently available.

Yearling bonds

Most yearling bonds have been issued for a fixed period of a year and six days. On the day they are issued, all bonds lasting the same length of time pay the same rate of return. There is no difference between the rate paid by different local authorities, and once issued, the rate of return is fixed for as long as the bond lasts. There is a minimum investment of £1,000 and you have to invest in multiples of £1,000, although in practice it can be hard to buy amounts less than about £10,000. Normally half the income is paid after six months and the remaining half when the bond is redeemed.

Local authority stocks

There are only a very few stocks currently available and no new ones were being issued when this book went to press. It is possible that by the end of March 1993 all issues will have been redeemed and this type of investment will no longer be available.

Local authority stocks behave very like British Government stocks, there is no fixed minimum amount you can buy (but the stockbroker charges make investments of, say, less than £1,000 not worthwhile). The rate of return you get from your investment is a mixture of the income you get each year and the capital gain (or loss) you make when you sell the stock (or when it is redeemed).

Both local authority yearlings and local authority stocks are bought and sold on the Stock Exchange, but because there are so few issues it may be difficult to deal at all.

19

WITH-PROFITS ENDOWMENT POLICIES

An endowment policy is basically a long-term investment with life insurance tacked on. It's a way of investing in a mixture of shares, British Government stocks, company loans, property and so on; but you invest via a life insurance company.

How an endowment policy works

You agree to save for a certain period, which must normally be for 10 years or more. With a *with-profits endowment policy* you are guaranteed at the outset that if you save until the end of the period you will get a guaranteed lump sum in return. But you hope that you will get much more than the guaranteed sum when your policy comes to an end. In the past, with-profits policies have paid out perhaps three to six times as much as the sum you have been guaranteed at the outset, but in the past couple of years insurance companies have tended to become more conservative in the amounts they pay out.

What happens is that the guaranteed sum grows over the years as the life insurance company adds *bonuses* to it – see p. 312. If you had started saving 10 years ago in a 10-year with-profits endowment policy you would find that when the policy pays out you would be getting an average return of around 13 per cent, without allowing for any tax relief you might have got on the premiums. With one of the best-performing companies, the return for a 10-year policy ending now would be up to 15½ per cent, say; for a 20-year policy the return is slightly less, around 14½ per cent for one of the best performing ones (both of these figures ignore tax relief that you could have got at that time).

How endowment policies work [1]

start here

You agree to pay a premium of, say, £20 a month to the life insurance company

£20

When you first take out a policy you decide how long you want it to last (25 years, say)

The life insurance company puts the £20 into its long-term fund

Insurance company's long-term fund
£200 million, say

Your money is invested in ordinary shares, British Government stocks, loans, property and so on

[1] Example is for a premium of £20 a month. What you might get back is based on what has happened in the past

Expenses
Each year, the insurance company deducts money to pay for office expenses, sales reps' commission, cost of life insurance and so on

With-profits policy
Provided you carry on paying the premiums, the insurance company guarantees to pay you at least £5,000, say, at the end of the 25 years. If you die before 25 years are up, the policy comes to an end and your heirs get at least £5,000. But read on to see how this guaranteed sum may increase over the years

Each year, the company announces reversionary bonuses for with-profits policy holders (based on the 'profits' made by its long-term fund). The sum guaranteed by your policy goes up by the amount of this bonus – so if the bonus is 5 per cent each year, for example, you'd get the amounts shown, right

At end of YEAR 1
guaranteed sum is
£5,000 + bonus = £5,250

At end of YEAR 2
guaranteed sum is
£5,250 + bonus = £5,512

At end of YEAR 3
guaranteed sum is
£5,512 + bonus = £5,788

UNTIL

At the end of the policy the company may add a terminal bonus

At end of YEAR 25 you may get back much more than the amount guaranteed at start of policy. Reversionary bonuses could give you another £15,000, say. And a terminal bonus might add a further £10–15,000. Total amount might be £30–35,000

Bonuses

There are two sorts of bonuses – *regular* and *terminal*. *Regular* bonuses (usually called *annual* or *reversionary* bonuses by the insurance companies) are added to your with-profits policy. Once a reversionary bonus has been added to your policy, this new figure becomes your new guaranteed sum; it cannot be taken away once it has been added. For how bonuses are decided, see p. 314.

If the company announces a compound bonus of 4 per cent, say, it works out what this would be on the guaranteed sum. If, for example, your original guaranteed sum is £6,000, the amount of the bonus at the end of the first year would be £240, and the new guaranteed sum would be £6,240. At the end of the second year, the bonus would be 4 per cent of £6,240, which is £250, and the new guaranteed sum would become £6,490.

Some companies add different rates to the original guaranteed sum and to the reversionary bonuses already added to the policy. For example, a bonus of 4 per cent might be added to the original guaranteed sum and a bonus of 6 per cent to the reversionary bonuses already announced.

It's important to realise that there's no guarantee a bonus will be added each year. In the past, it has been rare for a company to reduce its rate of bonus, let alone not pay one. But in 1992 many companies reduced their reversionary bonus rates.

Life insurance companies usually also pay a *terminal* bonus as well as reversionary bonuses. This is a one-off bonus added at the end of the policy, either the end of the savings period or on earlier death. So, for example, in a 25-year policy, it is added at the end of the 25 years when your policy matures (or if the policy pays out on death). If you cash in your policy early (see p. 316), you normally get no share of the terminal bonus.

These terminal bonuses can vary widely from one company to another, depending on the current market value of the insurance company's investments, e.g the shares it owns, and on the insurance company's policy: for example, as much as 60 per cent of some top performing companies' payouts may be made up of terminal bonuses. The amount of the bonus can fluctuate each year. For example, after the fall in share prices at the end of 1987, some companies cut their terminal bonuses and this happened again in 1992.

Comparing bonus rates with other rates of return

You can't compare them directly. First, you have to work out what a given bonus rate means in terms of the cash you get back at the end of the policy. Then you have to work out what rate of return this represents on the amount you save each month. Only then can you compare the rate of return you might get on a with-profits endowment policy with the rate currently offered by, say, a building society.

Is a with-profits endowment policy life insurance or investment?

It's an investment. If what you want is life cover to protect your family from financial hardship in the event of your early death, you should take out *term insurance*. With this sort of insurance, you insure for an agreed period. If you die within that period, the insurance pays out. If you survive, the policy pays nothing.

For a given amount of cover, term insurance is very much cheaper than other types of life insurance. You can also take out term insurance policies which pay out a tax-free income (instead of a lump sum) if you die within the term. These are known as *family income benefit policies*.

Whole-life insurance is also worth considering if you think your family will need very long-term protection, or if you want the policy to pay off a possible inheritance tax bill on your death.

What sort of return do you get from a with-profits endowment policy?

The returns you get depend on your age, your sex and your health. A younger person, therefore, would get a slightly better return than an older person, a woman a slightly better return than a man and a healthy person a better return than someone in poor health. This is because there is life insurance tacked on to the investment and the life insurance company deducts some money from what you invest to pay for the life insurance.

The returns you could have got in the past vary widely from company to company. For example, the best-performing company could be paying out almost twice as much as the worst-performing company for the same amount of savings. Sadly, you can't be sure in advance which is going to be the best-performing policy.

Where your money is invested

Your money goes into the life insurance company's long-term fund. The long-term fund is invested in a spread of different types of investment. For example, a company might have:

- 50 per cent of its long-term fund in ordinary shares
- 15 per cent in property
- 30 per cent in British and foreign government stocks, company loan stocks, mortgages, etc.
- 5 per cent in cash or other investments.

The idea of spreading the money around in this way is that it reduces the risk of the fund doing very badly. If all the money were invested in shares, for example, the value of the fund would plummet if shares as a whole plummeted. At the same time, of course, spreading the money around reduces the chances of the fund doing extraordinarily well.

How reversionary bonuses are worked out

By law, an insurance company has to keep the money concerned with its *long-term business* in a *long-term fund*, separate from the rest of its other business. Long-term business includes life insurance, permanent health insurance, annuities and pension schemes. The company has to value the assets and liabilities of its long-term business at least once a year. The government lays down rules about the valuation of the assets.

Assets

Some examples of the maximum values that can be given to assets are:

- land and property – its market value, estimated by a professional surveyor or valuer not more than three years before
- debts due to be collected in more than a year's time – what the company could expect to get if it sold the right to collect the debt
- ordinary shares, debentures, British Government stock and other investments quoted on a stock exchange – the closing middle market price.

In addition, there are rules which limit the value that can be put on one particular investment, e.g. shares in one particular company. This is to prevent the fund becoming too dependent on that investment.

Liabilities

The liabilities are the benefits that the insurance company will have to pay out in the future, e.g. when policyholders die or their policies come to an end. The company's actuary estimates how much the insurance fund will have to pay out in each of the next 35 years, or more.

But the actuary also has to take account of the fact that £1 which has to be paid out next year is of more immediate concern to the company than £1 to be paid out in 10 years' time, say. This is because the company can earn interest on the assets of its long-term fund, so that less than £1 needs to be set aside now, to meet the debt in 10 years' time.

The value the actuary puts on future liabilities depends on the assumptions made about the future return on the assets. In practice, the actuary tends to assume a much lower rate of return than the one currently being earned.

The actuary then values the premiums the company is going to receive in the same sort of way, allowing for office expenses, commission and so on. By taking away the value of the premiums from the liabilities, the actuary arrives at a figure for net liabilities.

Surplus (or excess)

This is simply the amount by which the assets of the long-term fund exceed the net liabilities. Having worked out the surplus, the actuary recommends how much of it should be paid out to the company's shareholders, and what rate of bonus should be paid on each type of with-profits policy, e.g. endowment and whole life.

When returns from all sorts of investments are generally good, large surpluses aren't particularly relevant, since all companies should be able to pay competitive bonuses. Even those with high margins may not pay out all their spare cash to investors. But when times are leaner, as at present, lower surpluses can reduce companies' freedom to manoeuvre.

Note that once a bonus has been announced, it becomes part of the liabilities of the company, and cannot be taken away from the value of your policy (unless you cash the policy in early).

Does the company have to pay a bonus?

The Department of Trade and Industry has considerable powers to intervene in an insurance company's affairs if, for example, the policyholders' *reasonable* expectations won't be met. If a company wasn't going to pay a bonus, it would probably be in a poor state of health and would be closely supervised by the Department of Trade and Industry, who might try to get another company to take it over.

In practice, companies do add bonuses to with-profits policies each year, although it is generally accepted that bonuses are unlikely to be as high in the next few years as they were in the 1980s.

How endowment policies are taxed

There's normally no tax to pay on the money you get back from an endowment policy provided you don't cash it in (or made it *paid-up* – see opposite) within its first 10 years or within the first three-quarters of the period you insured for, if this is shorter. But if you do cash it in before this time, and you pay tax at the higher rate or would do if the gain on your policy is added to your income, there may be some tax to pay. The amount of the gain is normally the amount you get less the total of the premiums paid. There is no basic-rate tax to pay on the gain, because the life insurance fund has already paid tax.

Any gain on cashing a policy counts as part of your 'total income', which is used to work out age-related allowances you can get. So, if you are 65 or over during the tax year, be careful about cashing in an endowment policy before the end of the agreed saving period. It may mean a reduction in your allowances and more tax to pay.

Before 14 March 1984, when you took out an endowment policy you also got tax relief (really a premium subsidy) on what you paid for the policy. You can carry on getting the premium subsidy on a policy which you took out before that date, as long as you have not changed the policy to give you more benefits, e.g. by extending its term or increasing its cover. The amount of the subsidy is currently 12.5 per cent. For more information on tax, see Chapter 7.

Ending a policy early

To get the best return on a with-profits endowment policy, you have to keep it going for the period you originally agreed, often 10, 15 or 25 years. But your financial life could be drastically altered during this time (through marriage, divorce, having children, moving home, being made redundant or starting your own business, for example).

So you may find yourself wanting to end the policy early.

There's no doubt that a substantial number of endowment policies are cashed in early (or simply allowed to lapse). In 1990, 18 per cent of policy holders cashed in their policies in the first year alone, losing around £165 million in the process. If you need your savings back early, or can no longer afford the premiums, what are the alternatives?

Cashing in your policy

The cash-in value (also called the *surrender value*) of an endowment policy is usually decided entirely at the discretion of the insurance company.

Cashing in a policy early can reduce considerably the return on your investment. With a few companies you get nothing back if you cash your policy within its first two years, and even after five years you will be lucky to get back as much as you have paid in.

Making the policy paid-up

You stop paying the premiums and the insurance company reduces the guaranteed sum for which you are insured. This new guaranteed sum, called the *paid-up value*, is paid out at the end of the period you originally insured for (or when you die, if this is earlier). Most insurance companies continue to add bonuses to the paid-up value of a with-profits policy.

Getting a loan on it

Many insurance companies will consider lending you money, using your policy as security for the loan. Generally, the maximum loan is between 80 per cent and 90 per cent of the cash-in value. Some companies will not make a loan of less than a certain amount, say £100 to £250. If you are considering a loan, check the current rate of interest and compare it with what's available from other sources.

What should you do?

If you need the cash, you'll have to choose between cashing in your policy and getting a loan on it. If you don't need the cash, but can no longer afford the premiums, you could also consider making your policy paid-up.

Which is the best choice for you will depend on your

particular circumstances. The first thing to do is to ask the insurance company for:

■ the policy's cash-in value
■ details of any loan you can use your policy to get (e.g. rate of interest charged and how much you can borrow)
■ the current sum guaranteed by the policy
■ the current rate of bonus and, if you don't need the cash,
■ the paid-up value and whether bonuses will continue to be added to this value.

Then you'll have to work out for yourself what the best course of action is. The example below will give you an idea of how to do this.

Example: deciding what to do

Simon Smart has a 25-year with-profits endowment policy, for which he has been paying premiums of £30 a month for the last 15 years. (He actually pays less than this because he is getting the premium subsidy not now available for new policies, see p. 316). In September 1992 he finds he can't afford to carry on paying his premiums. He writes to his insurance company and finds:

■ the cash-in value is £11,409
■ he can borrow up to £10,268 on his policy. The rate of interest would be 13 per cent at present, but could vary
■ the current sum guaranteed by the policy is £20,959 (the original £7,946 plus £13,013 in bonuses)
■ the current rate of bonus is 5 per cent compound plus 2 per cent extra on the bonuses
■ the paid-up value is £16,684, and bonuses will continue to be added.

Cashing in
Simon doesn't need the cash. So if he cashed his policy in, he'd invest the £11,409. He finds that if he invested the money in a 10-year British Government stock, for example, he might get a return of around 9 per cent a year before tax. He'd get a total of around £27,000 in 10 years' time (assuming he could reinvest the interest at 9 per cent too, which, of course, may not be possible).

Making the policy paid-up
The paid-up value is £16,684. The company would add bonuses to this amount for the remaining 10 years of the policy. So, if the current 5 per cent bonus rate plus 2 per cent extra on bonuses continues, Simon would get back around £31,811 in 10 years' time. The company may add a terminal bonus to this, say £8,000. This would make a total of £39,811.

Selling your policy

Unless you took on the policy very recently, you may be able to get more than its cash-in value by selling it in an auction or in some other way.

What happens is that whoever buys the policy carries on paying the premiums and collects the money paid out when the policy comes to an end.

The name and address of one firm that auctions policies is, H.E. Foster & Cranfield, 20 Britton Street, London EC1M 5NQ, tel: 071-608 1941. If the policy is sold, it currently charges a fee of £50 plus a commission of one-third of the difference between what the policy sells for and its cash-in value. (You don't have to sell the policy if the highest bid is below the cash-in value or whatever you set as a reserve price.)

Another firm acts as agent for you in selling a policy. They are: Policy Network, 25a Kensington High Street, London W8 6SH, tel: 071-938 3626. Four other firms (Policy Portfolio, tel: 081-203 7221; Beale Dobie, tel: 0621 851133; Policy Plus, tel: 0225 753643; and Policy Register Ltd., tel: 061-763 1919) all value your policy and then buy it from you themselves.

Getting a loan

Though Simon doesn't need the cash at the moment, it might still make sense for him to get a loan on his policy and use this to help pay his premiums.

The amount his policy is likely to pay out if he continues to pay the premiums, and if the current rate of bonus continues, is £39,030 (i.e. the current guaranteed sum plus bonuses of 5 per cent compound a year and 2 per cent extra on the bonuses). And the company may add a terminal bonus to this of, say, £9,760, making a total of £48,790. As he took out the policy before 14 March 1984, Simon gets the premium subsidy of 12.5 per cent and his £30 a month premium actually costs him £26.25. So he'd need to borrow around £3,150 over the 10 years.

When his policy came to an end he could expect to get back £48,790 less the £3,150 loan, i.e. £45,640.

Of course, he'd also have to pay interest on the loan. This could be kept to a minimum if he borrowed the money in instalments, rather than borrowing the full £3,150 straight away. In this case, the interest might work out at about £3,400 over the 10 years, rather than the £7,500 or so if he borrowed the full £3,150 now.

Deducting £3,400 interest from the £45,640 he'd get back from the policy, leaves a net amount of £42,240.

What Simon decides to do

Simon sees that, in his particular case, the best thing to do would be to get a loan from the company to pay his premiums. If he can, he'll get a loan each year; if not, he'll get a loan now to pay all the premiums, and invest the money in a building society until it's needed.

The worst thing he could do at the moment is to cash in the policy. He realises, however, that he can only make an estimate of the outcome. Things could alter in the next 10 years – interest rates could go up and bonus rates could go down, for example.

Other types of policy

There are a number of variations and similar policies. These are:

■ **non-profit** endowment policies. These were common 10 or 20 years ago, but are rare today. With a non-profit policy you agree to save for a certain period, which must be 10 years or more. The policy gives a poor, but guaranteed, return. You get the amount guaranteed if you save to the end of the agreed period; your heirs get the same amount if you die within the period. You get no bonuses on the guaranteed amount

■ **low cost** endowment policies. These are sold linked to mortgages for the purpose of buying a home, and are a special type of insurance package. The package is a combination of a with-profits endowment policy (which has bonuses added on over the years) and term insurance: the endowment policy is for less than the mortgage to keep premiums affordable. Whether or not there will be enough to pay off the mortgage will depend on how well the policy does

■ **unitised with-profits** endowment policies. These are similar to a unit-linked policy – see Chapter 20. With a unitised with-profits policy, what you pay buys units in a fund, but each year bonuses are declared. Once a bonus has been announced, it cannot be taken away

■ **with-profits bonds.** You pay a single premium, which is invested in a unitised with-profits fund. These bonds were heavily sold in 1991, to such an extent that the regulators LAUTRO became concerned about mis-selling and ordered some companies to write to all customers who'd bought them, to make sure they understood the policy conditions. The policy terms vary considerably from company to

company, and there may be hefty penalties if you cash them in or take early withdrawals: tread carefully
- **whole life** policies. With these, you agree to pay premiums for the rest of your life or up to a certain age, 65 or 85, say. The policy pays out only when you die, not at the end of the premium-paying period. The insurance company agrees to pay out a fixed sum (plus bonuses if the policy is a with-profits one). You can cash in your policy at any time, but in the first few years the cash-in value is likely to be little or nothing. Even after a very long time, the cash-in value is likely to be fairly low.

In general, if you want protection for your dependants, it would be better to go for *term insurance* (see p. 313) which is cheaper, unless you are getting on in years. If you're looking for an investment, you may get a better return elsewhere, without being tied to such a long savings period.

But a whole life policy may be useful if you're sure you want lifelong protection, for example to pay an inheritance tax bill on your death – see p. 118. The policy should be made out so the proceeds go to your heirs, not to you (otherwise the proceeds could form part of your estate and become liable for inheritance tax). You can do this by having the policy 'written in trust': the insurance company can arrange this for you. If you go for a whole life policy, don't take out a non-profit one (see opposite), which will give a poor return.

Is an endowment policy suitable for you?

With-profits endowment policies with their wide mix of investments (shares, property and fixed-interest investments), provide a safer home for your money than, say, unit trusts alone. The way that endowment policies work means that the ups and downs in performance which can be experienced from year to year are smoothed out by the actuary, and so there will not be a huge difference between the payment for a policy maturing in one year and the payment for another policy maturing in the next year. In return for this lower risk, you have to expect that you may experience a lower return than you would from other investments.

Of course, it is possible for you to spread your own savings among a number of different types of investments and to avoid cashing your investment all at the same time. If you do it yourself, you do not incur the expenses of the life insurance company, which are mainly its costs of marketing and selling policies. However, you may not want to undertake it yourself, prefer saving regularly or simply not have enough money to get a reasonable spread of investments. If so, you could consider a with-profits endowment policy as a relatively safe home for part of your savings.

You should, however, think carefully before committing yourself to such a long-term savings plan, as cashing in a policy before the agreed saving period is up means a lower return, and, in the first five years or so, not even getting your money back.

How to choose a company

If you're taking out a with-profits policy, you'll be planning to pay money to a company for at least 10 years. It makes sense, therefore, to choose the company carefully. In the past, you have been able to get almost twice the return with the best-performing company compared to the worst-performing company.

The return from a with-profits policy depends on factors such as how successfully the management invests the long-term fund, how much of your premium goes in commission and expenses, whether the company has any shareholders to share in the surplus made by the long-term fund, and what proportion of its total business is with-profits policies, which are entitled to receive the surplus.

Success at investing money (which is unpredictable) is only one of the important factors. A company's past performance may give some guide to the future, although there are a number of reasons why it might not. Actuaries, for example, can move jobs or fall under a bus just like ordinary mortals. A change in actuary can mean a change in policy and hence in the trend in adding bonuses to a policy. Actuaries are also subject to changes in company policy, e.g. different marketing strategies, which can mean more emphasis being put on one product rather than another (and so influencing the amount of bonuses added).

The other factors which affect return are the amount of expenses (including representatives' and independent sales people's commission) and the amount of the reserves put aside over the years in the long-term fund. Information on these factors is shown in the 'with-profits guides' available from companies on request.

Buying a policy

Under the investor protection rules (see Chapter 5), if anyone tries to sell you a with-profits endowment policy, the person should either be a company representative or an independent financial adviser. They are normally paid by commission on the policies they sell.

Independent financial advisers have to tell you if they are being paid by commission, but they don't at present have to tell you the amount there and then (unless you specifically ask for it). You will be told when you receive the cancellation notice (or before) what the commission is, as a percentage of your premiums. Company representatives don't have to tell you at all about the amount of commission they receive, but the 'product particulars' you get after you buy will give details of the expenses the company incurs: the bigger the expenses, the smaller the amount of your money that is actually invested.

There are a number of rules about how endowment policies can be sold to you by representatives and intermediaries – see p. 75.

Company safety

Insurance companies are closely supervised by the Department of Trade and Industry, which can intervene in the affairs of an insurance company if it's getting into difficulties, e.g. by preventing it taking on any new business. Friendly societies are supervised in much the same way, but by the Chief Registrar of Friendly Societies (the head of a different government department).

Insurance companies, but not friendly societies, are covered by the Policyholders' Protection Act. If your company fails, the Policyholders' Protection Board has to try to get another company to take over the policy. In this case, provided you carry on paying your premiums, the Act guarantees that at the end of the policy you'll get at least 90 per cent of the sum guaranteed at the time your company went bust, unless the Board considers this amount to be *excessive*. You get no guarantee of what bonuses the new company will add.

You may, therefore, lose out on quite a lot of money if your company goes bust, so it makes sense to be cautious when choosing a company. It would be prudent to avoid relatively new or small companies.

A dispute with a life insurance company?

Take it up with the insurance company first. If the complaint is unresolved by the end of three months, the company must tell you what the complaints procedure is (which may be to contact the Life Assurance and Unit Trust Regulatory Organisation or the Insurance Ombudsman Bureau). For more details and addresses, see pp. 80 and 91.

20

UNIT-LINKED LIFE INSURANCE

In the past, unit-linked insurance was attractive mainly because of the favourable tax rules – in particular, tax relief on the premiums you paid. Over the years, the tax rules have become less favourable, and a more attractive competitor has emerged, in the form of Personal Equity Plans (PEPs) – see p. 262.

If you want to invest in shares (directly or via unit trusts), whether regularly month by month, or in a lump sum, a PEP has clear advantages over unit-linked insurance, since the money you invest is totally free of tax, and charges can be lower. But if you want to invest more than the upper limits for a PEP (in the 1992–3 tax year, £6,000 in shares, unit trusts or investment trusts plus £3,000 in a 'single-company' PEP), or if you don't want the investment restrictions which apply to PEPs, unit-linked insurance could still be worth considering.

To invest, you buy either a single-premium bond, e.g. an equity, property or managed bond, or a unit-linked regular premium plan. Both are technically life insurance policies, though the amount of life cover you get may be small.

In general, when you invest your money buys you units in a fund of investments run by the insurance company, less a deduction for charges. The price of each unit you buy is, approximately, the value of the investments in the fund divided by the number of units issued. The unit price goes up and down as the value of the investment in the fund, e.g. property, shares and so on, fluctuates.

When you sell your units, what you get back depends on the price of the units at the time. If the fund has been performing badly, you could make a loss. On the other hand, you stand the chance of making a profit if the fund is doing well when you sell.

The first part of this chapter deals with things which apply in general, whether you've got a lump sum to invest

or want to save something each month. The second part of
the chapter looks at particular types of policy. Information
about single-premium bonds starts on p. 328, and about
unit-linked regular premium plans on p. 335.

How unit-linking works

Where your money is invested

Your money goes into a fund of investments, usually run
by the insurance company. Most insurance companies run
a number of funds. The main types are:
- property funds, which are invested in office blocks,
factories, shops and so on
- UK equity funds, which are invested in shares of British
companies
- fixed-interest funds, which are invested in things which
pay out a fixed income, e.g. British Government stocks and
company loan stocks
- managed funds, which are invested in a mixture of
things such as property, shares and fixed-interest investments
- cash or money funds, which are invested in bank deposit
accounts, short-term loans to local authorities and other
investments which pay out rates of return which vary
along with interest rates in general.
   There are also more specialist funds, such as:
- international equity funds, which are invested in a
mixture of shares all over the world
- North American funds, which are invested in North
American securities
- Far East funds, which are invested in the stock markets
of countries such as Japan, Hong Kong, Australia and South
Korea
- European funds, which are invested in European shares
- index-linked funds, which are invested in British Government stocks increasing in value with the Retail Prices
Index
- unitised with-profits funds (for regular premium plans
only), where you buy units in the normal way, but the
value of the units is worked out by allocating *bonuses*, in
the same way as for with-profits policies – see Chapter 19.
This means that the value of the units can't fall, unless you
cash in early when a market value adjustment may be
deducted. See p. 320 for more on with-profits bonds.

A number of equity funds are invested through a unit trust, and managed funds may be invested in a selection of unit trusts. On p. 329 we help you decide whether unit trusts or unit-linked insurance funds are the best type of investment for you.

What should you expect if you invest?

Funds investing in property and shares all aim at long-term growth. Traditionally, property and shares have been seen as more suitable long-term investments than those investments which pay interest, like building society and bank accounts.

Investing on a regular basis, instead of putting a lump sum into a bond, removes the danger of investing all your money at the wrong time. On the other hand, it also removes the chance of doing extremely well by investing all your money when unit prices are low. And the success of your investment, whichever way you choose, will still depend very much on the price of your units at the time you cash them.

Reducing the risks

Unit values can go down as well as up and the unit values of funds in different geographical or industrial sectors can rise and fall at different times. In general, the more specialised a fund is, the more you should avoid putting all or most of your money into it.

A fund specialising in Japanese stocks, for example, may show spectacular returns for a period, but may then slow down and be overtaken by another sector. To minimise the risk of having your money in the wrong sector at the wrong time and to maximise your chances of being ready to take advantage of a rising sector, you should spread your money across different types of investment.

The easiest way to do this is by investing in a managed fund. Alternatively, try to invest in two or more different types of fund, if you have a large sum to invest.

If stock markets crash

Towards the end of 1987, share prices suddenly fell very sharply all over the world. At a time such as this, the best thing to do if you have a lump sum invested is to sit tight and wait for prices to go up again, rather than take a loss.

If you are paying regular premiums and prices have

dropped, you at least get the consolation of picking up more units for your money than when prices are high. This is known as *pound cost averaging*. Of course, pound cost averaging won't leave you better off, unless the price recovers before you sell your units.

If your regular premium policy reaches maturity just after share prices have fallen, your policy proceeds may be disappointing. You are still likely to get back far more than you put in. But this is a disadvantage of unit-linked as compared to with-profits insurance (see Chapter 19), where gains, once made, cannot be taken away. You can reduce the risk by moving your money to a more conservative fund as maturity approaches.

Keeping track of your investment

You can follow the fortunes of your investment by looking up the unit price in a newspaper (the *Financial Times* lists most companies' unit prices – look under the section headed *Insurances* in the FT *Managed Funds Service* section).

Buying and selling

You can buy or sell your units at any time at the going price. Buying and selling units in a unit-linked insurance fund is the same as buying and selling units in a unit trust.

Each unit normally has two prices. What you pay for the units (the *offer* price) is usually between 5 and 6 per cent more than what you can sell your units for (the *bid* price). Details of buying and selling units are given on p. 278.

Single-premium bonds

With these policies, you hand over a lump sum to the insurance company. The company takes part of the money to cover its expenses and to provide you with a little life insurance. The rest of the money buys units in whichever fund you choose.

Who should consider investing in these bonds?

You should not invest in bonds if:
■ you are likely to want your money back at short notice (because the property or share market may be in a slump when you find you need to cash your bond)

- you object to the value of your investment fluctuating.

However, even if neither of the points above apply to you, a single-premium bond may still not be the most suitable investment for you unless you're in one of two groups of investors. The tax rules give them some advantage for higher-rate taxpayers who've used up their capital gains tax allowance, though a PEP, which is totally free of tax, would be a better choice. In theory, bonds are also suitable for people who will want to switch from one type of fund to another from time to time, in the hope of putting their money where it will increase in value quickest, though the chances of doing this successfully are not great.

If you aren't in one of these groups, but still want an investment where you lock a lump sum away for several years in the hope that it will increase in value in the long-term, a unit trust is an alternative worth considering.

Bonds or unit trusts?

Investing in a single-premium bond is very similar to investing a lump sum in a unit trust. In fact, many insurance funds are invested in unit trusts. The advantages or disadvantages of either investment depend largely on taxation and how the charges compare.

Life insurance companies and unit trust companies pay income tax on the dividends they receive on shares in their portfolios. If you are a non-taxpayer, you can reclaim this tax from the Inland Revenue for a unit trust investment, but not for a bond investment.

When shares in an insurance fund are sold at a profit, insurance funds have to pay capital gains tax. Insurance companies set aside an amount to meet this tax which is passed on to the policyholder indirectly, through lower unit values.

Unit trust investors pay capital gains tax according to their own personal liability when they cash in their units. Since you are allowed to make a certain amount of gains (£5,800 in the 1992–3 tax year) before having to pay capital gains tax, you should invest in a unit trust if you are not likely to use up this allowance.

If you want to withdraw money from a unit trust to provide an income, you could face a capital gains tax bill. But special rules let you take some income from a bond without paying tax, or you can put off paying tax on your income until a further date. See *Taking an income* over the page for details. When the bond is finally cashed in, only higher-rate taxpayers have to pay income tax on the gains they have made and only at the higher rate. This is explained in greater detail in Chapter 7.

Single-premium bonds are more suitable for investors who want a spread of investments and like to change from fund to fund. You pay higher charges for taking your money out of one unit trust and putting it into another and you will either use up some of your capital gains tax allowance or face a capital gains tax liability every time you do this. See *Switching* on p. 332.

Taking an income

With most insurance company funds, you don't get an income in the conventional sense of having interest paid to you. This is because you don't directly own the things the fund invests in. The income earned by the fund's investments is generally put back into the fund to buy more shares, property or whatever.

Instead, you can normally arrange to cash in part of your investment from time to time, on either a regular basis (under a withdrawal scheme) or an irregular basis. If you're a higher-rate taxpayer, cashing in part of your bond could possibly lead to a bill for income tax (see p. 104), but in general paying tax on the gain you make at the time can be avoided if you withdraw no more than 5 per cent (or one-twentieth) of your original investment in any one year. The diagram opposite shows how this works.

To make getting an income easier, bonds are often sold as a cluster or series of identical mini-policies so that you can cash in a whole policy, or several policies at a time, according to your needs. The tax rules are simpler, too, if you cash in a whole policy rather than part of one. Of course, cashing units to get an income will start eating into the value of your investment if the unit price is increasing at a lower rate than the rate at which you are cashing units.

You can normally choose for the income to be either:
- a percentage of the number of units you hold (in which case your income will go up and down with the price of units)

or
- a percentage of the amount of your original investment (in which case your income in £££ will be fixed, but the number of units cashed in will go up when the unit price falls, down when the unit prices rises)

or
- the income the fund earns can be paid straight to you (in proportion to your unit-holding), rather than being reinvested in the fund.

Taking an income from your bond

Special rules mean that you can take an income from your bond but put off paying any tax until you eventually cash in the bond. Then there's only higher-rate tax to pay – no basic-rate tax – and only at the rates that apply at the time you cash in the bond.

The maximum income you can take under these rules is one-twentieth of your original investment (i.e. ignoring any growth) for each year, up to a maximum of 20 years, e.g. if you invest £1,000, you can withdraw up to £50 a year.

Original investment
each year you can take as income $\frac{1}{20}$ of original investment

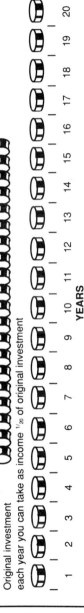

YEARS

If you take less than one-twentieth any year, you can carry the unused portion forward indefinitely to add to the amount you can withdraw in future years, e.g. if you invest £1,000 and take nothing for the first two years, you could withdraw up to £150 in year three, and so on. If you take more income than the rules allow in any year, you may have to pay higher-rate tax at that time.

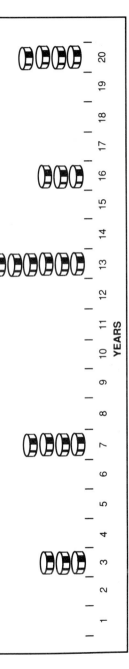

YEARS

Charges

The insurance companies normally make:
- an initial charge of around 5 per cent of the amount you invest. This is usually included in the spread between the buying and selling prices
- a regular charge. The insurance company deducts a charge from the fund at regular intervals to cover the costs of managing the fund. This charge might add up to between ½ and 1½ per cent of the value of the fund each year. Brokers charge between ¾ per cent and 1 per cent on top of these charges for investment in a broker managed fund.

Not all companies spell out in their policy documents the maximum charges they can make, so check up on charges before investing.

Switching

The majority of insurance companies allow you to switch your money from one fund to another, e.g. from the equity fund to the property fund, without paying their initial charge again. This could prove to be a useful facility for investors who want to move their money around between different types of investment from time to time in the hope of keeping it in the type of investment which will increase in value quickest. If you're tempted to use the switching facility, bear in mind that if you time your switches wrongly, you could end up doing very badly.

Switching your investment between funds doesn't count as cashing in your bond for tax purposes, so does not affect your tax position at all.

Most companies make some charge when you switch, typically £15 each time you move. But some companies allow you one free switch a year. The minimum amount you can switch is usually £500 or £1,000.

Policy wording

The policy document is the contract between you and the insurance company, so it makes sense to see a copy before you invest. Check that most of the following points are spelled out:
- how the fund is valued. For example, it might show that stocks and shares are valued at the market prices quoted on the Stock Exchange
- that property in the fund is valued by an independent valuer, such as a surveyor

- the maximum period between valuations
- how unit prices are worked out
- the charges the company makes, and the other costs it can deduct from the fund
- that you won't be double-charged if your fund invests in other funds run by the company
- what happens to the fund's income. See *Choosing a company* on p. 335.

Tax

When you cash your bond, the gain you make is added to your investment income for the tax year. The gain is the amount you get (including any amounts you got earlier on which weren't taxed at the time) less the amount you paid for the bond in the first place. You don't pay basic-rate tax on the gain (the insurance company has already paid tax on the income and capital gains of the fund), but you do have to pay any higher-rate tax that is due, though your tax bill may be reduced by *top-slicing relief*. The tax rules are complicated (especially if you cash in only part of your bond), but can be used to your advantage, if you are careful over when you cash your units in – see p. 105.

How to invest in single-premium bonds

Minimum investment

All the companies set a minimum amount you can invest, usually £1,000. Note that if you invest a substantial amount in one go, over £25,000, say, or invest in a newly launched fund, some companies give you extra units, e.g. 1 per cent more.

Age limits

Many insurance companies set minimum age limits for bondholders, 18, say. And a few set maximum age limits for new bondholders, 80, say.

Life insurance

Single-premium bonds normally pay out only slightly more than the value of the investment if the investor dies, say 101 per cent of the value of the units. For a young man under 30, however, the death benefit could be 2½ times the value of the bond. The death benefits are limited to reduce the costs. A large amount of life cover would be expensive for an older person. If what you want is greater protection for your dependants, see p. 313.

Adding to your investment

As the term implies, a single-premium bond is bought with one lump sum payment. With an *additional premium facility* you have the option of buying more units at any one time by paying an additional premium. (This is subject to a minimum amount which varies from £250 to £1,000 depending on the company.) These units are added to the original policy you took out. The advantage in doing this is that if you are liable to tax on the gain when you cash the policy in, top-slicing relief relating to the additional premium can be spread over all the years since you originally invested, and not just from the date you paid the additional premium. This could reduce your tax bill.

Cashing in part of your investment

Most companies allow you to cash, i.e. sell, part of your bond. But you often have to cash a minimum amount, and leave a minimum amount. The minimum amouint you can cash is usually £50 or £100, and the minimum amount you must leave varies between £100 and £1,000. There may be a maximum on the amount you can cash in, say 10 per cent of the value of your investment.

If you already have shares

Most companies are prepared to give you units in their funds in exchange for your holdings of stocks and shares through their *share exchange schemes*, though different companies have different rules about the size of the holdings they'll accept and the value they'll place on them.

Usually, if the company is happy to put your shares into one of its funds, it will value them at the price it would have to pay to buy them on the open market. This benefits you because if you sold them, you'd normally get a somewhat lower price and would have to pay commission to a stockbroker.

If the company doesn't want to put your holdings of stocks and shares in a fund, it will usually sell them for you (and with many companies, you pay no commission on the sale).

Note that exchanging your shareholding counts as a disposal for capital gains tax purposes, i.e. you may have to pay capital gains tax on any gain you've made. But there are ways in which the tax can be kept to a minimum, so get professional advice, particularly if you are exchanging substantial shareholdings.

Where to buy bonds

Bonds are sold in a variety of ways: through newspaper advertisements, by insurance brokers, by company sales-people, and by agents such as accountants and solicitors. Brokers, agents and so on normally get commission from the insurance company for selling bonds; the rate varies between 3 and 6 per cent or so of what you pay for the bond.

Some brokers offer their own *broker managed bonds*. An insurance company provides the life cover while the broker chooses from that company's range of funds to make up what he or she thinks is the best mix in his or her own fund. Many broker bond funds are listed in the *Financial Times* under the insurance company's funds.

Choosing a company

For details about the insurance companies and their funds, the following magazines do regular surveys (including details of past performance): *Planned Savings* and *Money Management*. Remember, though, that past performance is not a guide to the future. Try asking a financial adviser (or perhaps several) for advice, but make sure he or she knows what it is you expect to get from your investment, At the end of this chapter is a list of things to check when deciding which company to choose.

Unit-linked regular premium plans

With a unit-linked regular premium plan you agree to pay premiums at regular intervals (monthly, quarterly, half-yearly or annually). In return, the insurance company uses some of your money to pay for life cover and expenses. The rest is invested in the funds of your choice – see p. 326.

You can select a plan which lasts for between 10 years and the rest of your life (a few plans last for less than 10 years, but they're not common). You can choose, within certain limits, the amount you think your dependants would need were you to die before the end of the policy.

Types of plan

Unit-linked plans fall into three main categories:
■ maximum investment plans – for minimum life cover and high investment

- endowment plans – for higher life cover and longer term investment
- flexible cover plans – designed to adapt to your changing circumstances throughout your life.

Look at the table below for how three typical plans might compare.

How typical plans might compare

For a 29-year-old man (non-smoker) paying premiums of £50 per month

	maximum investment plan	endowment plan	flexible cover plan
length of plan	10 years	between 10 and 25 years	whole life
amount of life cover	£4,500 for 10 years	£10,000 to £60,000 for 20 years	£100,000 (but you can choose more or less) for whole life
minimum monthly premium	£15 to £100	£15 to £50	£15 to £25

If you die

If you die during the period of your plan, the life insurance company guarantees to pay out a set amount of life cover or death benefit. But your dependants would receive the full value of your units if this is more than the death benefit.

The amount of death benefit payable under your policy depends on the length of your plan and the premiums you pay as well as your age and state of health when you take out your plan.

The end of your plan

When your plan comes to an end you should be entitled to a lump sum on which you do not have to pay tax. This is because most unit-linked policies are set up as *qualifying policies* under the Inland Revenue rules – see p. 104. However, although the lump sum is tax-free in your hands, the insurance company will already have paid tax on the money in its funds. With some plans, a *capital gains tax deduction* is shown on the statement you get when the plan matures. This is tax on the company's gains, not yours; you can't claim it back, even if it is below your annual capital gains tax-free slice.

Insurance companies will give you an illustration of what a plan will provide, based on a standard growth rate laid down by the regulators, LAUTRO. Remember, though, that the final payout is not guaranteed and neither are these growth rates. Only the death benefit is guaranteed.

At the end of some plans you may have the option of continuing your plan, normally with a higher proportion of future premiums being invested for you.

How the plans work

Maximum investment plans

These plans may be known as high investment plans or capital accumulation plans. They usually last for 10 years and the minimum premium can be as little as £10 per month or as much as £100 per month. There is no maximum investment.

These plans usually provide the minimum life cover under the 'qualifying' rules. A low level of life cover means that the maximum amount of your premiums can be invested.

Unit-linked endowment plans

Endowment plans, often called savings plans, can last for up to 25, or even 30 years, and provide a higher level of life cover. Minimum premiums for these policics vary from £20 per month to £50 per month.

These plans have become accepted by many lenders as a way of repaying a mortgage. You pay only the interest on your mortgage every month, and your endowment plan should provide enough to repay the amount you have borrowed when your mortgage ends (though there is no guarantee of this), perhaps leaving you with something over. The death benefit with an endowment mortgage plan is equal to the amount you have borrowed. When you move you can usually take your policy with you. If you increase your mortgage you may also be able to increase your level of cover without giving proof of your state of health. However, when choosing an endowment mortgage, you should bear in mind that the bonuses allocated to a with-profits policy cannot be taken away once they have been allocated, while the value of a unit-linked plan may fluctuate.

Flexible cover plans

Sometimes called flexible whole life plans, these plans last throughout your life or until a given age, 85, say. Given the size of the premium and your age and state of health at the start of the plan, you can choose the amount of cover you want.

You can alter the level of cover and premiums to suit your needs during the various stages of your life. Some plans include a variety of benefits and insurance you can add on to the plan as and when you need them. These are sometimes called *universal* plans.

Monitoring your investment

With longer term policies, life insurance companies keep an eye on your investment to make sure its value will be sufficient to provide the expected payouts. This is done by reviewing your policy, usually after ten years and then every five years.

During the last five years your policy may be reviewed once a year. Some companies suggest you invest in a cash fund during the last five years so as not to lose any of the money you have made if share prices fall suddenly near the end of your plan.

If the growth of your investments has fallen below the expected rate, you will probably have to pay higher premiums or accept reduced benefits.

On the other hand, if the growth of your investment is greater than the expected rate, you may be able to reduce your premiums or build up a larger sum. If you have an endowment mortgage, you may be able to repay your mortgage early (with the lender's agreement).

If you stop your plan early

You should look on most unit-linked life insurance plans as a long-term commitment. The way that most companies arrange their charges means that their expenses, such as administration and commission to brokers or salespeople as well as life cover, are deducted from the premiums in the first few years.

If you cashed in your policy (often called *surrendering* it) in the first two years, say, you may not get anything back and you would be most unlikely to get back as much as you had paid in. The amount you would get varies from company to company, depending on how they calculate the cash-in value.

If you don't need to cash in your plan but want to stop investing, you could make your plan *paid up*. This means you stop paying your premiums but the money you've

How a unit-linked regular premium plan works

You take out a policy running for a set length of time – 10 years in this example – and agree to pay premiums of £300 a year, say. The insurance company takes a cut to cover the cost of life insurance and other expenses – in this example, 40 per cent in the first year and 3.3 per cent thereafter (charges vary considerably from company to company). What's left is used to buy units in a fund. The number you can buy depends on the offer price of the units when the money is invested – so the same amount buys different numbers of units from year to year.

The number of units you have increases month by month. But their value depends on what the insurance company will buy them back at (the bid price) – normally around 5 to 6 per cent lower than the offer price.

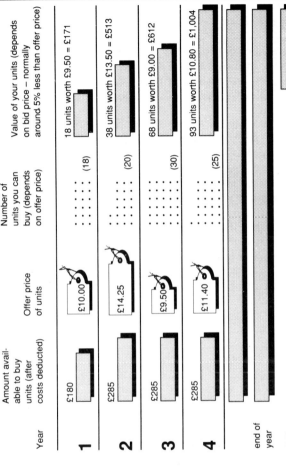

Year	Amount available to buy units (after costs deducted)	Offer price of units	Number of units you can buy (depends on offer price)	Value of your units (depends on bid price – normally around 5% less than offer price)
1	£180	£10.00	(18)	18 units worth £9.50 = £171
2	£285	£14.25	(20)	38 units worth £13.50 = £513
3	£285	£9.50	(30)	68 units worth £9.00 = £612
4	£285	£11.40	(25)	93 units worth £10.80 = £1,004
end of year 10				You now have 200 units worth, say, £23.75 = £4,750

already paid in is invested in the fund. Even so, you may only be allocated the number of units which you could buy with the money you'd get if you actually cashed in your plan.

Alternatively, go for a plan which is broken up into a series of mini-policies. Then, if your circumstances change later, you have the option of cashing just some of your units, keeping your plan going and paying a reduced premium.

Provided you've kept the policy going for 10 years, or three-quarters of the premium-paying term if less, you shouldn't have to pay tax on any gains from cashing in your policy.

You may also be able to get cash from your policy by taking out a *policy loan*, which you could then use to pay the premiums. Normally you can borrow up to 90 per cent of the cash-in value of your plan, and the interest rate will often be lower than that for other forms of borrowing. The loan repayments and interest payments are usually paid annually in addition to your normal premiums. See p. 316 for guidance on working out the best way of stopping your plan early.

Charges

As we've already said, the costs of administration and life insurance are met by deductions from your premiums in the first few years. Some companies make these deductions by investing your premiums in what are called *capital* or *initial* units. These are not worth as much as the ordinary units and they hide the amount of charges. Other companies use a more straightforward system of unit allocations so you can see exactly how much you are paying.

For example, with an endowment plan you might get a unit allocation of 55 per cent in the first year. In other words, just under half of your premiums are going towards administration costs and life cover in the first year. Your unit allocations depend on the length of your plan, the amount of life cover and the premiums you pay.

Don't forget that there is also a difference between the price at which you buy and the price at which you sell units, usually 5 to 6 per cent. Also, a management fee is deducted from the fund, usually between ½ and 1½ per cent a year. Companies now have to tell you how their current charges reduce the value of your policy, assuming you keep it for the whole term. You get this information after you have bought, shown as the 'Reduction in Yield'

Life insurance or unit trusts?

	Unit-linked regular premium plan	Unit trust savings plan
Income tax	Paid by the life insurance company and *cannot* be claimed back by non-taxpayers	Paid by the unit trust company and *can* be claimed back by non-taxpayers
Capital gains tax	Paid by the insurance company and reflected in lower unit values	Not paid by the unit trust company
At the end of a plan	No tax is payable on qualifying policies (tax has already been paid on the insurance company's funds)	Capital gains tax is charged according to personal liability – you get a tax-free allowance (£5,800 in the 1992–3 tax year)
Cashing in a plan early	If policy has been going less than 10 years or ¾ of the policy term, whichever is less, higher-rate taxpayers may pay the difference between the higher and lower rate of income tax on any gains	

(RIY). The smaller the RIY the better, but charges can go up or down during the life of the plan, and are much higher if you cash in early.

Should you invest?

Keeping insurance and investment separate

Unit-linked life insurance policies can lock away your money for a long time. It is best to keep your insurance and your investment separate – you might want your money back early but still need protection for your dependants.

If all you want is life cover to protect your dependants from financial hardship, term insurance is the cheapest way to buy life cover – see p. 313. It may be possible to convert it into an investment-type policy during its term without having to give proof of continued good health.

If you are considering a unit-linked insurance plan, compare the costs and the benefits with a separate term insurance policy and a savings plan suited to your tax position, e.g. a unit trust savings plan. In particular, consider a PEP, which produces income and capital gains totally free of tax. Chapter 8 gives a bird's-eye view of the main investments available.

Provided none of the points above apply to you, a unit-linked regular premium plan may be suitable if you are higher-rate taxpayer and already have the maximum PEP allowed (£6,000 a year, plus a further £3,000 a year in a single-company PEP in the 1992–3 tax year).

If you want to invest in a fund, the main differences between the taxation of unit trust savings plans and unit-linked insurance plans are set out in the table on p. 341.

Special features to look out for

Endowment plans and flexible cover plans may offer some of these features:

■ **waiver of premium option** – you stop paying premiums but the plan continues if you become ill or disabled over a long period (more than six months, say) and can't continue with your normal job. Some companies will continue the plan for you if you have a joint policy and either partner is ill or disabled

■ **total disability cover** – some companies will pay out the death benefit if an accident or illness leaves you unable to work again

■ **accidental death benefit** – if you die as the result of an accident, the plan pays out an extra lump sum

■ **inflation linking** – you can take out further plans or increase your cover (or premium) in line with changes in the Retail Prices Index

■ **special event cover** – a further plan can be taken out, or your cover can be increased, on marriage or the birth (or adoption) of a child without you having to prove you are still in good health

■ **family income benefit** – if you die, the plan pays out a regular tax-free income for a given number of years rather than a lump sum

■ **low-start option** – for the first year of your plan, premiums are reduced to, say, half the normal amount. Then they will increase by, say, 20 per cent a year for 5 years or 10 per cent a year for 10 years, and be level for the rest of your plan. This option usually costs more in the long run

■ **stop-start option** – if you are made redundant or suffer financial hardship, you may be allowed to stop paying premiums for a limited period (up to two years, say) and keep your policy going. You will have to make up for these missed premiums at a later date though

■ **increasing or extending options** – you may be able to

increase your cover or extend the term of the policy
without having to prove that you are still in good health
■ **term insurance** – if you die within a given period, the
plan pays out an extra lump sum. Check, though, that it
isn't cheaper to take a separate term insurance policy.

If you already have a unit-linked policy

Over the years, unit-linked policies have changed a great
deal. If you already have a unit-linked policy, you may find
it is different from the types of policies now available and
described in this chapter. It would be unwise to cash in an
old-style policy in favour of a new one without considering
the surrender value and the cost of setting up a new policy.
What is more, your life cover will be more expensive now
that you are older than when you took out your policy.

The government still subsidises the premiums on policies
taken out before the Budget in March 1984 – see p. 316.

Choosing a company

Sadly, there is no foolproof way of picking a company
whose policies are going to perform better than those of
other companies. In particular, just because a company's
funds have done well in the past it doesn't mean that they
will do as well in the future. But, when choosing a
company, there are a number of things to watch out for:
■ what the company's charges are
■ whether the company makes any charge for cashing in
the whole or part of your bond or policy, what you get if
you cash your plan in early and how cash-in values are
calculated
■ whether the company offers a *withdrawal scheme*, i.e.
partial cash-in, for single premium bonds and whether
income withdrawals have to be on a regular basis or can be
on an irregular basis to suit your circumstances. Check if
the policy or bond is split into a series of policies to allow
simple and tax-efficient cashing-in
■ whether the company offers an *additional premium
facility* so that you can add to your investment without
having to take out a new policy each time (see p. 334),
should you want to increase your investment
■ whether the company has a good choice of funds and, if
you want to switch between funds, includes a cash fund
(which can be a useful temporary home for your money

when prospects for shares, property and fixed-interest investments look bleak)
- what the company's switching charge is (one 'free' switch a year is fairly common), and whether you can switch just some of your units
- the size of the funds and how they are split between different types of shares or property. Funds range in size from less than £1 million to over £1 billion (£1,000 million); you may feel happier going for a larger fund. Also check that a property fund is not too heavily invested in just one locality, or too dependent on one huge office block, say. (Some companies provide reports which list the properties in the fund)
- with a managed fund, the size of fund (see above), and how the investments are split between different sectors, though this, of course, may well change.

If things go wrong

It's important to realise that although the performance of your bond or policy depends upon the performance of a fund of investments, investors do not own the investments.

However, insurance companies, but not friendly societies (to which different legislation applies), are covered by the Policyholders' Protection Act. This effectively says that, if your company goes bust, you'll get back 90 per cent of what you were owed when the company failed. If your policy has benefits, such as guaranteed cash-in values, which are considered excessive, you may get back less than 90 per cent of what you were owed.

These plans are also covered by the Financial Services Act allowing you to take up complaints with the relevant *Self-Regulating Organisation*. See Chapter 5 for details of these and other useful organisations.

21

GUARANTEED INCOME AND GROWTH BONDS

These are investments issued by insurance companies, which are suitable for lump sums. You have to invest your money for a fixed period (usually four or five years, but it can vary between one and ten years). In return, you normally get a fixed rate of return for that period.

With an *income bond*, the return is paid out as a regular income (usually yearly, but some companies will pay monthly). With a *growth bond*, it is left to accumulate, and paid out when the bond comes to an end.

If you die before the bond comes to an end, the insurance company normally pays out the amount you originally invested plus, with growth bonds, the return accumulated to date.

The insurance company normally arranges for the return from an income or growth bond to be free of income tax at the basic rate. If you pay tax at no more than the basic rate (even after adding what you make on the bond to the rest of your income) you should get the return quoted in the advertisements. But if you or your husband or wife are 65 or over (or approaching 65), see *Warning* on p. 347.

If you've got a lump sum to invest, and you don't mind locking your money away for a time, and you want a fixed return for this period, an income or growth bond may be suitable for you. But remember, inflation will reduce the value of the fixed return. Alternatives to consider include National Savings Certificates or Income Bonds and bank and building society high interest accounts. Don't invest in a bond if you may need to cash it in early. Some insurance companies don't allow you to do this, while others may give you back less than you originally invested.

If you don't pay tax, or pay more than basic-rate tax

If you don't pay tax at all, you'll get more than the quoted return with some types of bond. But if you pay tax at the higher rate, the return is likely to be lower than the rate quoted in the advertisements. To find out how you'd be affected, see *How to choose a bond* below.

How bonds work

Bonds are set up in different ways, often using one or more life insurance policies with or without one or more annuities. The mechanics needn't concern you, though your age or tax position will usually make certain types of bond a better buy for you than others. For devotees, *Types of bond*, opposite, gives brief details of how the different types of bond work. But note that bonds are normally available for only limited periods of time, and the mechanics of newly issued bonds change from time to time.

How to choose a bond

For a list of which companies issue which types of bond, get a copy of the most recent issue of *Planned Savings* or *Money Management* magazine. But because bonds may be available for a short period only, the returns listed in such a magazine may soon be out of date.

Telephone the companies offering the best returns on suitable bonds and ask for details of their latest bonds. If you're not a basic-rate taxpayer, ask them what someone in your tax position would get from their bond (after tax). Then choose the bond which gives the best return for the period for which you want to invest. You could ask a couple of independent financial advisers to do this for you.

In general:
- if you don't pay tax or you are liable for less tax than the insurance company deducts, a guaranteed income or growth bond is unlikely to be suitable for you – see p. 34 for alternatives
- if you pay tax at the basic rate you will probably find the endowment type of bonds the most attractive investment
- if you pay tax at the higher rate, a series of single-premium endowments may well give you the best returns or, if you can arrange for the bond to end in a year when you pay only basic-rate tax (after you've retired, perhaps), one single-premium endowment bond.

Warning: if you cash in all (or part) of a bond based on an endowment policy, your 'total income' (see p. 96) is increased. For most people, this has no significance at all. But if you get age-related tax allowances, for people who are 65 or over during the tax year, you could find that your tax bill rises – see p. 53 for details.

Types of bond

Single-premium endowment bonds

Your investment buys a single-premium endowment policy with guaranteed bonuses. You can choose whether to have bonuses paid out as income or reinvested for growth (or you may be able to have part paid out, part reinvested). At the end of the term, you get back your original investment plus bonuses that you haven't cashed in.

Series of single premium endowment bonds

Your bond is divided up into a series of single premium policies, one to provide an income for each year of the term and one to return the original lump sum at the end of the investment term.

Tax

There is no tax to pay on either the income or the final payout for basic-rate taxpayers, because this has already been paid by the insurance company. Non-taxpayers can't claim this tax back, though.

With a single endowment bond, you can take income of up to 5 per cent of the investment each year until the end of the bond's term without paying any tax. If income of more than 5 per cent is taken, a higher-rate taxpayer may have to pay some tax, but see pp. 331 and 333.

With a series of endowments, an endowment policy is cashed in every year to provide the income. This income is effectively tax-free.

At the end of the term the proceeds from an endowment bond are free of tax unless you are a higher-rate taxpayer, but you may get *top-slicing relief* – see p. 105 for details.

22

ANNUITIES

You may come across annuities either in connection with pensions, or as a form of investment you buy yourself. In this chapter, we concentrate on annuities you buy yourself, separately from a pension: for more on annuities tied to pensions, see Chapter 13.

An annuity you buy yourself is probably only worth considering if you've reached your 70s. You hand over a lump sum to an insurance company in return for a guaranteed income for the rest of your life. The older you are when the annuity begins, the larger the income it gives you. For example, in return for £10,000, a 72-year-old man who paid tax at 25 per cent could (in September 1992) have got an after-tax income of around £1,400 for life.

The insurance company will make a large loss on people

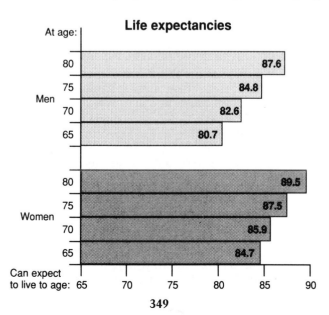

who live for years and years, but will make a handsome profit on those who die early, because with most types of annuity, however soon you die after buying it, you get none of your lump sum back. The diagram on p. 349 shows what age you can expect to live to, if you're 65, 70, 75 or 80. You'll see that someone who has already reached 80 can be expected to live to a greater age than a 70-year-old.

People who buy annuities tend to be healthier than those who don't, and the insurance companies allow for this in the income they offer. In this chapter we look at the various different types of annuity that are available, and assess their pros and cons. Starting on p. 355 you'll find details of home income schemes – where you borrow money to buy an annuity and use your home as security.

Types of annuity

This chapter deals with *immediate* annuities. With these, the company starts paying you the income 'immediately'. There are also *deferred* annuities, where you pay a lump sum now and arrange for the income to start in the future (in five years' time, say). Deferred annuities form the basis of many personal pension plans.

The most common type of immediate annuity is a *level* annuity, where the income is the same each year. For a given outlay, this type gives you the largest income to start with, though, of course, inflation will erode its buying-power over the years. Another type is an *increasing* annuity, where the income increases at regular intervals by an amount you decide on when buying the annuity. *Unit-linked* annuities are offered by a few companies. With these, your income is linked to the value of the fund (e.g. of property) and so goes up and down in amount. *Inflation-linked* annuities (also offered by a few companies) give an income which is linked to the Retail Prices Index; but this type usually provides the lowest starting income.

The basic type of annuity stops when the person buying it dies: a *single life* annuity. But you can also get annuities which carry on until both the person buying the annuity and someone else, usually a wife or husband, are dead. These are called *joint life, last survivor* annuities.

Variations

Companies normally quote their annuity rates on the basis that the income will be paid to you half-yearly, starting six months after you buy the annuity. These terms may not suit you, e.g. you might want to be paid monthly; you can usually get any of the variations listed below, although some are fairly costly in terms of a reduced yearly income.

■ Payments to be made more frequently than half-yearly, i.e. quarterly or monthly. The same outlay gives a smaller yearly income than an annuity paid half-yearly – the more frequent the payments, the smaller the income.

■ First payment to be made at the time you buy the annuity. The same outlay gives rather less income than an annuity paid half-yearly, starting six months after you buy it.

■ First payment to be made a year after you buy the annuity, then at yearly intervals. The same outlay gives a higher yearly income than an annuity paid half-yearly.

■ An extra, proportionate, payment (made after you die) for the period between the date you receive the last half-yearly payment and the date you die. This will give less income than the normal version.

■ Some of the payments to be *guaranteed*, i.e. paid out by the company for a minimum number of years even if you die early. The same outlay gives you less income than the normal version – how much less depends on your age and the length of the guaranteed period (usually, five or ten years).

■ A payment (made after you die) of the difference between your outlay and the income paid out so far by the company. You get less income than the normal version.

■ With a joint life, last survivor annuity, less income to be paid after the first person dies, often half or two-thirds of the amount paid while both are alive. The starting income will be higher than normal.

The income you get

This depends on a number of factors, in particular your age when you buy the annuity, the type of annuity you go for and the level of interest rates in general at the time you take the annuity out. A woman gets a lower income than a man of the same age (women, on average, live longer than men). Joint life, last survivor annuities pay lower amounts overall.

Insurance companies tend to vary their annuity rates frequently and at short notice, but what you get stays at the rate that applied when you bought the annuity.

Basic-rate tax will normally have been deducted from the annuity income before you get it. The income you get from an annuity consists partly of interest and partly of a return of the capital you invested, and each part is treated differently for tax purposes – see p. 354.

Inflation

When deciding whether to buy an annuity you should consider the effect that rising prices will have on the buying-power of your income. For example, a women of 70 who buys an annuity could expect to live for about another 16 years. If prices rise at around five per cent a year, each £100 of income she gets at the start will be worth only £46 or so in 16 years' time. Of course, no one knows what inflation will be over the next 16 years: it could be less than five per cent a year, or more. To see how rising prices might reduce the buying-power of an annuity, look at the diagram opposite.

To protect the buying-power of your capital you could consider investing in index-linked National Savings Certificates (see p. 173) – cashing them in if you need income – or index-linked British Government stocks (see p. 299).

An annuity would then be worth considering for part of your remaining money if you're over 70 or so.

Why an annuity is a gamble

Whether or not an annuity proves to be a good buy in the long run depends on:
■ how long you live. Obviously an annuity will be a better buy if you live for years and years after buying it, than if you die soon after investing your money. If you are in poor health, you'd be wise to steer clear of annuities, and invest your money elsewhere
■ what happens to interest rates after you have bought your annuity. The annuity income offered by an insurance company is related to the general level of interest rates at the time you buy. If, later on, interest rates go up, companies are likely to offer better annuities, but you'll be stuck with your relatively poor-value-for-money annuity. On the other hand, if interest rates go down, companies will offer poorer annuities, and you'll be sitting pretty
■ the extent to which inflation will erode the buying-power of your income.

But you don't know how long you're going to live, and you don't know what's going to happen to interest rates or to inflation, so you can't know if an annuity will turn out to be a good buy or not.

**Fall in buying-power of
income from an annuity
(annuity bought for £10,000
by 72-year-old-man)**

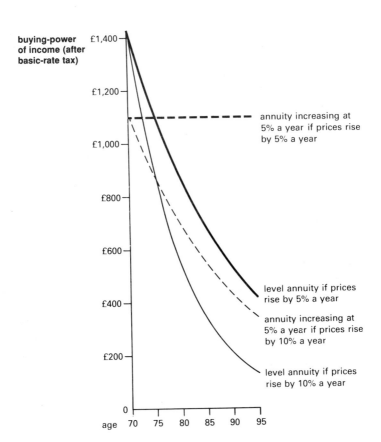

**buying-power
of income (after
basic-rate tax)**

annuity increasing at
5% a year if prices rise
by 5% a year

level annuity if prices
rise by 5% a year

annuity increasing at
5% a year if prices rise
by 10% a year

level annuity if prices
rise by 10% a year

age

Should you buy an annuity?

Once you have bought an annuity, and handed over your
money, you can't go back on the arrangement, so you
shouldn't buy one without pausing for thought. You
should first make sure your dependants would have
enough to live on when you die. Then consider how much
you want to leave your family (or favourite charity), how
much you want to put by for a rainy day, and how much
you want to leave available for holidays, replacing your car,
colour television and so on. You could consider spending
part of what is left on an annuity – *provided* the extra

income you get, compared with what you'd get from another type of investment, is large enough to compensate you for handing over part of your savings for good.

Which type?

A unit-linked annuity, where your income is linked to investment performance, is unlikely to suit most people. The income will vary from year to year, and might be very low in some years.

Your choice, therefore, lies among the remaining types. A level annuity pays the highest starting income, but gives you no protection against inflation. An increasing annuity, where, for example, each year's income is 5 per cent higher than the year before, gives protection against lowish rates of inflation. An inflation-linked (index-linked) annuity is the type which provides the best protection against inflation, but pays the lowest starting income. The tax-free part of the income (see below) is fixed with level and inflation-linked annuities, but rises with increasing annuities (in step with the increases in the annuity). This treats index-linked annuities unfairly, because the whole of any increases are fully taxed: so even this type cannot protect you fully against inflation. Increasing and inflation-linked annuities, which start at a relatively low level, work out best if you live a long time.

All in all, unless you sincerely believe that inflation will stay at a low level, an increasing or inflation-linked annuity is probably the most sensible choice.

Tax treatment

Part of the income is treated as your initial outlay being returned to you, and is tax-free. The remainder counts as interest, and is added to your income.

The amount of the tax-free part is worked out according to Inland Revenue rules. It is fixed in terms of £££, not as a proportion of the income from the annuity. For each type of annuity the tax-free amount is based on your age when you buy the annuity, the amount you pay for it, and how often the income is paid. The older you are when you take out the annuity the higher the capital part of the income you get, and the higher the total amount of income. This is because the older you are the shorter the period for which the insurance company expects to have to pay the income.

With increasing annuities, the tax-free amount normally increases at the same rate as the income from the annuity increases. With unit-linked and inflation-linked annuities the tax-free amount stays fixed.

An annuity is treated in this special way only if you buy it voluntarily with your own money, e.g. if you use a lump sum from your employer's pension scheme.

The insurance company normally deducts tax at the basic rate from the taxable part of your annuity income before paying you. If you are liable for less tax than the insurance company deducts, you can claim tax back from your tax office. If you pay tax at higher rates, you'll have to pay extra tax.

If your income from all sources, including the taxable part of the annuity, is below certain limits, you can apply through the insurance company to have your annuity income paid without deduction of tax.

From which company?

Companies can change their annuity rates frequently. To choose a company yourself, get an up-to-date copy of *Money Management* which regularly compares companies' immediate annuity rates.

Get quotations from companies which do well for your age (or one close to it). The rates, however, may well have changed since the magazine went to press, so it might be as well to consult an independent insurance adviser. Some advisers subscribe to computer systems which list annuity income from different companies.

Company safety

The Policyholders' Protection Act (see p. 323) gives you partial protection should your insurance company go bust. However, you'd still be faced with a lot of anxiety while it was happening. To avoid this, you may do as well to avoid very new or very small insurance companies. Get an independent insurance adviser to check for you.

Home income schemes

If you're elderly and own your home outright, you may be able to boost your income with a home income scheme.

How the schemes work

You get a loan based on the security of your home. The loan is used to buy an annuity from an insurance company. While you live, you get the income from the annuity from which basic-rate tax and interest on the loan has been deducted. When you die, the loan is repaid out of your estate (possibly by the sale of the home) before inheritance tax is worked out. (Note that with some schemes, called *reversions*, you sell all or part of your house to the company. Any increase in the value of the part you have sold then goes to the company, not to you.)

Everyone aged over 65, taxpayer and non-taxpayer, gets tax relief on the full amount of the loan interest (provided the loan is not more than £30,000). This means that basic-rate taxpayers and non-taxpayers have their interest payments reduced by 25p in each £ (in the 1992–3 tax year).

The nuts and bolts

The schemes are available for freehold houses, and for leasehold property with a substantial part of the lease still to run (50 to 80 years, depending on the company). When you apply for a scheme, your home will be valued by an independent valuer – you pay the fee, but it may be returned if you take out the scheme. The most you can usually borrow is a percentage (65 to 75 per cent) of the market value of your home.

The interest rate is normally fixed at the time you take the loan, and so is the income from the annuity. This means that the income you get from the scheme won't change as time passes. However, there are schemes where the interest rate varies – we don't recommend them, because if interest rates rise, your income would drop. And you should be wary of rolled-up interest schemes, where the payments on the loan are 'rolled-up' and added to the amount you owe; the size of your loan will increase at an alarming rate. With this type, you may have to pay interest (or even sell your home) if the total you owe gets close to the home's value.

You may be able to take part of the loan in cash in return, although at least 90 per cent of the loan must be used to buy an annuity in order to qualify for tax relief. There's often a minimum loan, usually £15,000 or so.

If the house is occupied by two people (husband and wife, or brother and sister, say) the annuity is arranged so that it continues for as long as either person is alive. You generally have to be at least 70 to be eligible for a home income plan (somewhat older if you're a couple applying).

Pros and cons

If the value of your home goes up after you've taken out the loan, you may be able to use the increase in value to get a further loan (up to the maximum £30,000 on which you can get tax relief) and buy another annuity. In this way you might be able to increase your income to keep up with inflation.

And while inflation still reduces the buying power of your fixed income, it correspondingly reduces the value of your debt to the insurance company. So rising prices don't wholly work against you.

On the other hand, you'd be almost certain to get a better after-tax increase in your income by paying cash for an annuity (if you could do so) rather than mortgaging your home. And if it's likely you'll have to sell your home (to move in with relatives or into an old people's home, say) think twice before going for a home income plan. If you do move later on, you'll have to repay the loan, and may get left with a rather low fixed-income annuity.

If you get state benefits, such as income support or housing benefit, a home income plan could mean that you'll lose some or all of that benefit. So get advice from an independent solicitor (your Citizens Advice Bureau can suggest one) before signing on the dotted line.

Suitable for you?

A home income scheme is worth considering if you need the extra income, provided you're at least 70 (or preferably older). But you'd almost certainly get a better after-tax increase in your income by paying cash for an annuity (if you could do so) rather than mortgaging your home. Be sure you understand the scheme and always check the details with a solicitor before going ahead: in recent years some types of scheme have caused considerable problems. Steer clear of variable interest rate schemes and rolled-up interest schemes. And remember that you can't cancel an annuity and get your money back.

23

COMMODITIES

You might think that investing in commodities is a way of investing your long-term savings so that they stand a chance of keeping pace with inflation. Investing in commodities can, however, give you a very bumpy ride. Chapter 25 tells you about investing in things like stamps, antiques and wine. Here we deal with a different group of commodities: raw materials which are bought and sold in large quantities on organised markets based in the City of London. The main raw materials which come into this category fall into two groups: *metals*, such as copper, lead, silver and zinc; and *soft* commodities such as cocoa, coffee, rubber, sugar and gas oil.

Investment in commodities is high risk, which means that while you might make large gains, you might instead make large losses. So it's suitable only for investors who understand what they are doing, and who have the resources to withstand the possible losses. Indeed, under the *know your customer* provisions of the Financial Services Act (see p. 75), commodity brokers are required to be careful about who they accept as a private investor.

How commodity markets work

Commodities are bought and sold in two main ways:
■ for delivery straight away, but in the main, it's end-users of the commodity who buy in this way
■ for delivery at an agreed date in the future. This is the market in which investors (often called speculators) are more likely to be interested.

For delivery straight away

You can buy or sell copper, for example, which has already been mined, and is being stored in a warehouse. In the trade, this is known as buying or selling *physicals* or *actuals*; and the price you pay is known as a *spot price*. You have to pay (in full) for the commodity at the time you buy it. And you have to buy at least a minimum amount, e.g. 25 metric tons of copper.

The commodity will be kept in a warehouse, and you'll have to pay charges for storing and insuring it.

If you buy a commodity for delivery straight away, you are hoping that the price of the commodity will go up and you'll eventually be able to sell it at a profit (after taking account of buying and selling costs, and storage and insurance charges).

For delivery on an agreed date in the future

This is the usual way in which investors buy and sell commodities. You agree *now* to buy or sell a fixed amount of, for example, copper at a fixed price for delivery on some agreed date in the future. In the trade, this is known as dealing in *futures* and your agreement is known as a *futures contract*. There are rules about how far in advance you can arrange to buy or sell each commodity, e.g. up to three months with copper, and up to seventeen months or so with cocoa. If you agree to buy or sell cocoa in December 1993, say, you are said to be dealing in *December 1993 cocoa*.

If you buy a commodity for delivery in the future, you are hoping that its price will rise about the price you've agreed to buy it at, and that you'll be able to sell it at a profit before it is due to be delivered.

But you can also make a profit if you expect the price of a commodity to fall. You can agree to *sell* rather than buy, December 1993 cocoa, for example, at a fixed price. You then have to buy, before December 1993 arrives, the cocoa you've agreed to sell. If the price of December 1993 cocoa does indeed fall below the price you've agreed to sell at, you will be able to make a profit on the deal. But if it goes up in price, you'll end up having to buy your cocoa at a higher price than the one you've agreed to sell at, and so make a loss on the deal.

You don't have to pay out the full cost of the futures contract you are dealing in, only a deposit (of perhaps 10 per cent of its value). But this doesn't mean that it's only your deposit you can lose. You'll indeed lose a 10 per cent deposit if the value of a futures contract you've bought goes down by 10 per cent by the time you sell it. But if the price goes down by 50 per cent before you sell, you'll lose five times that amount. In practice, if the price falls, your broker (see p. 367) will ask you for more money (this is known as a *margin call*). If you don't hand over this extra money, the broker is likely to insist that you sell your futures contract straight away and accept the loss you've already made.

Trading in futures is not a long-term investment

If you're an investor (often called a speculator) who deals in commodity futures, you are not making a long-term investment. You are gambling on what will happen to the price of a commodity over a relatively short period. If you buy December 1993 cocoa, for example, it's what happens to cocoa prices before December 1993 that decides whether you profit or lose on your trade.

You may believe – quite correctly, perhaps – that cocoa prices will double over the next five years. But you can't buy a futures contract which lasts that long. Buying December 1993 cocoa doesn't make sense unless you believe that cocoa prices are going to go up more than expected over the period before then.

Commodity options

A commodity *option* gives you the right to buy or sell a commodity futures contract at its current price at any time up to an agreed date. The amount you have to pay to buy an option varies widely, depending on what is expected to happen to the price of the particular futures contract in which you are interested.

The advantage of taking out an option to buy a futures contract is that it gives you the chance of making a profit if the price of the commodity goes up, while at the same time limiting the amount of money you can lose if the price of the commodity falls, to the amount you paid for the option. The main disadvantage is that the price of the futures contract has to go up by at least the amount you paid for the option before you start making a profit.

Why futures markets exist

Futures markets enable people who trade in commodities, e.g raw material producers (such as mine owners and farmers), manufacturers (such as chocolate firms) and wholesalers, to reduce the risk they face of losing money because of changes in the prices of commodities. Futures markets allow the raw material producers to get a guaranteed price for raw materials they haven't yet produced. And they allow manufacturers to know exactly how much they'll have to pay for their raw materials in some months' time.

The investor (or speculator), who has no intention of producing or using commodities, is one of the people who take on the risk that the producers and manufacturers want to avoid. You, the investor, are the person who loses if, say, you have bought December 1993 cocoa and the price falls before you can sell it. But you are the person who gains if the price goes up before you sell it.

How commodity prices vary

Commodity prices in general

The chart opposite shows how the *Financial Times* index of commodity prices changed between July 1952, when the index was started, and October 1985, when it was suspended following the collapse in the tin market – see p. 367. We've adjusted the index to take account of inflation, so the chart shows what's happened to commodity prices compared with UK prices in general. Note that when the index started, commodity prices were almost as high as they had ever been, due mainly to shortages caused by the Korean War.

The chart shows two main things:
- compared with prices in general, the commodity price index fell fairly steadily between 1952 and 1972
- prices tend to go up and down quite quickly. A change of 5 per cent in a month is common.

Prices of individual commodities

The charts on pp. 364 and 365 show the average monthly prices (not adjusted for the fall in the buying power of the £) of three commodities – sugar, coffee and cocoa – from 1985 to 1992. You can see that all three commodities fluctuated in price during this period.

Looking at past performance, commodities would seem to offer the investor a rough passage: their price may well double or halve in a year or two. You can, of course, make a profit on commodities even when their price is falling, if

Commodity prices 1952–1985

**Index of
commodity prices**

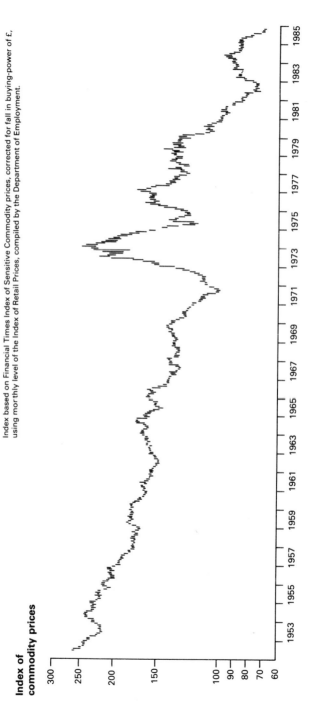

Index based on Financial Times Index of Sensitive Commodity prices, corrected for fall in buying-power of £, using monthly level of the Index of Retail Prices, compiled by the Department of Employment.

Raw sugar – average weekly price

Source: Datastream International

Coffee – average weekly price

Source: Datastream International

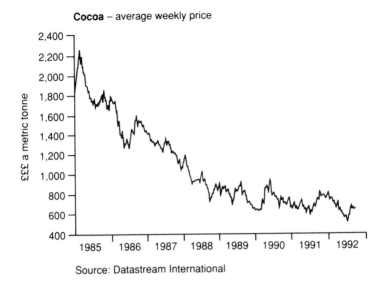

Cocoa – average weekly price

Source: Datastream International

you are successful in your use of futures or options contracts (see pp. 360 and 361), but you should never underestimate your possible losses.

What commodity prices depend on

The prices of most commodities depend on supply and demand. In the end, the demand for a commodity comes from us, the consumers. To make the things which we want to buy, firms have to buy raw materials, e.g. copper for making electrical wire and copper pipes, cocoa for making chocolate.

If firms want to buy more of a commodity than is available, its price will rise. This may persuade producers that it will be profitable to produce more, e.g start another copper mine, or plant more cocoa trees. But it may take some years before any more copper or cocoa is actually produced. The production of some other commodities, e.g. sugar, can be increased within a year or so of producers deciding to produce more (weather permitting).

Prices in the long-term

There's no way of predicting what will happen to commodity prices over the long-term, the next 20 or 50 years, say.

You might think that if the world economy grows, and the total amount of goods and services produced in the world goes up, the price of raw materials would tend to rise in response to increased demand. But if new and better ways of producing raw materials are found, if new producers come into the market, or if cheaper synthetic alternatives to some raw materials are developed, commodity prices *may* go down over the long-term.

Prices in the short-term

Commodity prices have fluctuated a lot from one year to another, and even from one month to another. These fluctuations can be the result of a number of factors, in particular:

■ **natural disasters** Droughts, floods, hurricanes, disease and so on, may damage crops, and so lead to higher prices for commodities such as sugar, coffee and cocoa. Conversely, good harvests may lead to lower prices. Natural disasters can also damage mining areas, causing reduced production and high prices for a commodity such as copper

■ **booms and recessions** In the past, most economies have had periods of boom (with low unemployment and a high rate of growth of the amount of goods and services produced) followed by periods of recession (high unemployment and little, if any, growth in the amount of goods and services produced). In a boom, firms need to buy more raw materials in order to increase the amounts they produce, so raw material prices tend to rise. In a recession, firms cut back on the amounts they produce and the amount of raw materials they buy, so raw material prices tend to fall. In the early 1990s, much of the developed world is in recession

■ **political problems** If a war breaks out, or a political revolution takes place, in an area of the world where a large proportion of the world's supply of a particular commodity is produced, the price of that commodity is likely to rise because of fears that supplies of the commodity will be reduced. For example, the invasion of Kuwait by Iraq in the summer of 1990 led to dramatic increases in the price of oil

■ **the exchange rate of the £** Most of the world supply of commodities is bought by foreign firms who naturally work out their cost in foreign currencies, such as US dollars and German marks. If they continue to pay the same price for their commodities, and if the exchange rate of the £ (i.e. the number of US dollars, German marks, and so on, you can get for a £) goes down, the price of commodities in terms of £££ will go up. Conversely, if the exchange rate of the £ goes up, the price of commodities in terms of £££ will go down.

Commodity price agreements

With some commodities, the main producing and consuming countries have got together to try to reduce price fluctuations. Most of these efforts haven't been very successful as there's always been the chance that some country will break an agreement by exporting more of a commodity than it is supposed to. And not all producing countries may join an agreement in the first place.

The best known commodity price agreement is probably the one for oil, run by OPEC (the Organisation of Petroleum Exporting Countries), but this depends on the co-operation of producing countries only. The UK is not a member of OPEC.

In October 1985, The International Tin Council, which controlled the price and supply of 52 per cent of tin production, defaulted on huge debts. The London Metal Exchange suspended tin trading and the price of tin collapsed from around £9,000 per tonne to around £3,500 per tonne. It was not until June 1989 that tin trading was restarted.

How you can invest in commodities

You can invest directly in commodities in two ways:
■ by buying and selling commodities through a commodity broker
■ by putting money into a fund which has been set up specially to invest in commodities.

Buying and selling through a broker

Investing in physical commodities isn't a practical idea for most people. The minimum quantities you can buy are very large, and so is the corresponding cost of the investment. And with many commodities, such as cocoa and coffee, you run the risk of your commodity deteriorating in quality before you sell it.

If you deal in futures, you don't have to pay out such large sums of money, and you don't have to worry about the quality of your commodity. You have to put down only a deposit, perhaps 10 per cent of the value of what you're buying or selling. But the risk of losing a large sum of money is still there. Suppose, for example, you bought the minimum possible quantity of cocoa for delivery in a year's time. You might have to put down an £800 deposit at the time you arranged the deal. But then, if the price of cocoa fell, you'd have to hand over more money to the broker. And if the price fell by 50 per cent before you decided it was time to get rid of your cocoa, you would have lost around £4,000 (half of the £8,000 the cocoa was worth when you arranged the deal).

You may be able to join a syndicate of people who pool their money and invest in commodities. Some commodity brokers run such syndicates. And, in some cases, there's a guarantee that you can't lose more than the amount of your original investment. But you might face problems about getting your money out when you want to. And there's still a fairly high chance of losing a lot of money.

Offshore commodity funds

Putting money into a fund which has been set up specially to invest in commodities has three main advantages. Firstly, it allows you to invest in commodities even if you can afford to lose only a more modest amount (£3,000 perhaps, though £5,000 or £10,000 may be a more common minimum investment). Secondly, you can choose a fund which guarantees you won't lose more than the amount you put into the fund. Thirdly, most of the funds invest your money in a lot of different commodities, something you couldn't do yourself without investing a good deal of money. This means that if one commodity does very badly, it won't have a disastrous effect on the value of your investment.

For legal and tax reasons, the commodity funds currently available to the public are based outside the UK, often in the Isle of Man, or the Channel Islands. This means that investors do not have the protection provided by the Financial Services Act and have to be particularly careful. Offshore investments such as these are not allowed to send their booklets, prospectuses and so on, direct to members of the public. So if you want these, you'll have to ask for them to be sent via a professional adviser, such as a bank manager or stockbroker.

How the funds work

Commodity funds work in much the same way as unit trusts. The fund is divided into a number of units, and your stake in the fund is represented by the number of units you own. The value of a unit is roughly the value of the fund dividied by the total number of units.

Most of the commodity funds can invest in both commodity futures and physical commodities. But a few invest only in physical stocks of just one commodity, e.g. copper or silver.

The performance of the funds which deal in just one commodity depends, on the whole, on what happens to the price of that commodity. But how your investment fares if you invest in a fund which deals in futures depends, to a large extent, on the skill of the fund managers. Since these funds started there have been some vast differences in performance. For example, assuming all income had been reinvested in the fund, if you'd invested £1,000 in 1983, it would have been worth over £2,837 five years later if you'd chosen the best performing fund. If you'd chosen the worst, £1,000 would have dwindled to £908 or so (worth only around £711 in terms of buying-power).

All the funds have minimum investments – £5,000 perhaps. And all make charges – perhaps an initial charge of 5 per cent of the amount you invest, a yearly charge of 2 per cent of the value of the fund and, in some cases, a 'performance' fee of, say, 10 per cent of any increase in the price of units. Some of the funds pay out an income, but some don't. And the funds vary in how often the unit price is calculated and, therefore, how long you may have to wait to buy or sell units; with some this happens daily, with others you may have to wait a week or possibly even longer. Some of the funds, but not all, have independent trustees or custodians who look after the fund's cash and the bits of paper which say what assets the fund owns.

Is commodity investment for you?

Buying physical commodities and storing them in the hope that their value will rise isn't a practical idea for most people. And with commodities such as cocoa and coffee you run the risk of the stocks deteriorating in quality before you sell them. Also, there's no guarantee that commodity prices will, in the long run, rise as quickly as prices in general.

Buying and selling commodity futures is a way of gambling on what's going to happen to the price of a commodity over a relatively short period – two years at the most. It could be a way of making, or losing, a lot of money in a short period. One large firm of commodity brokers estimated that 95 per cent of commodity speculators who take their own investment decisions lose money.

If you decide that, despite the drawbacks, you do want to invest in commodities, putting your money in a commodity fund has advantages.

Tax

How any profits you make from investing in commodities will be taxed is far from certain.

Profits from buying and selling physical commodities are likely to be treated as trading profits, and so taxed as earned income. A loss might count as a trading loss and you could set it off against the total of your income from all sources, but not against capital gains.

Just one isolated venture into the commodity futures market is likely to be treated as giving rise to a capital gain (or loss). But if you make a profit from a series of transactions, or invest as a member of a syndicate run by brokers or by a professional manager, this is likely to be treated as investment income. In this case, a loss could be set off only against profits of the same kind, or against certain other income. For more on tax, see Chapter 7.

24

INVESTING ABROAD

If you have several thousand £££ to invest, investing some of it abroad is worth considering. Although you can't rely on getting a better return than in the UK, spreading your money among different countries could cut down the risk of your investments, as a whole, doing badly. Bear in mind that the outcome of your investment depends not just on how well it does in terms of local currency, but also on what happens to exchange rates. And what will happen to exchange rates over the next few years, in the light of relative inflation rates, and political and economic developments throughout the world, is anyone's guess.

Investing abroad involves more risk than investing in the UK, as more uncertainties are involved. It may be carried on at a number of diffcrent levels, from the occasional few pounds in overseas-based unit trusts or investment trusts through to perhaps the purchase of a holiday property or even daily participation in the foreign exchange or foreign stock markets, although a good deal of time, resources and skill would be needed to succeed at this most serious level.

You may decide to invest abroad for two main reasons:

- you reckon that you'll get a better return on your money than with UK investment, taking account of the return (both income and capital growth) in terms of local currency and the effect of changes in the exchange rate of the £
- you want to spread your money around different countries in the hope of cutting down the risk of your investments, as a whole, doing very badly.

Overleaf we look in more detail at these reasons. Bear in mind that investing overseas should form only part of your overall investment strategy. The first two chapters of this books give general advice on how to plan your investments, and can be applied not just to UK investments, but also to overseas investments.

Better return abroad?

Just as you might compare different investments in the UK to check which would give you the best return, so you should consider overseas investments as an alternative to UK ones. For example, you may have decided that a British Government stock paying a high income meets your investment needs. It could be worth checking whether a similar foreign investment might offer the prospect of a better return. The same goes, if, for example, you are looking for a capital gain from unit trusts, or want to put money in a bank savings account.

When comparing the returns, don't just look at the return in local currency (e.g. the rate of interest you'd get on your deposit account). You need to be aware that ups and downs in the exchange rate can affect your total return. Suppose, for example, you invest £100 in the US, at an exchange rate of $1.80 to the £, i.e. you invest $180. If you get interest of 15 per cent, at the end of the year you'll have $207 (ignoring, for the sake of simplicity, tax and the cost of buying and selling the investment). You discover that the £ has gone down a lot over the year compared with the $ and that the exchange rate is now $1.50 to the £. In this case, you'd get back £138 (i.e. $207 ÷ 1.5), giving you a total rate of return of 38 per cent – more than twice the 15 per cent you get in local currency.

Of course, things may not work out in your favour. For example, you may find at the end of the year that the £ has gone up in value and that the exchange rate is now $2.10 to the £. In this case, you'd get back about £98.57 (i.e. $207 ÷ 2.1), which is less than the £100 you originally invested, despite the 15 per cent your money has been earning.

In short, it's good for your overseas investment if the exchange rate of the £ goes down against the currency concerned. It's bad if the exchange rate of the £ goes up. But beware: a country offering high interest rates may well have a currency which is falling against the £.

Beware, also, of hidden and unexpected costs. At each stage of foreign transactions there will be fees: for exchanging your £££ for foreign currency and back again, and for briefing UK or foreign agents to act on your behalf in whatever capacity.

Check up as well on the tax situation and make sure you understand the range of local and other taxes to which your investment may be subject.

Spreading the risk

It's all very well to go for the best return on the money you invest, but few people are willing to face the risk of losing a lot of it in the process. One way of cutting down this risk is to spread your money around different types of investments, e.g. putting some in British Government stocks, some in shares and some in a building society. The chance of *all* these different investments doing extremely badly is lower than the chance of just one of them turning out to be a dud. Of course, reducing your risk of loss in this way also reduces your chance of winning the jackpot.

Spreading your investments around different countries is a way of cutting down another type of risk, e.g. the possibility of an economic setback in your home country. Although the economies of (and the health of investments in) some countries may, at times, move up and down more or less together, this is not true of all countries. For example, the problems faced by Japan are different from those faced by Germany, and different again from those faced by the USA.

So, by choosing investments in a cross section of countries you reduce the risk of all of them doing badly at once. However, it also exposes you to new risks, such as currency movements, unforeseen political developments and foreign regulations or costs.

A way of reducing the effect of short-term fluctuations in exchange rates is to take out a *forward-exchange contract*. This is a way of buying or selling foreign currency for delivery at a date in the future. There is a cost attached, but you may decide it is worth it for the certainty of a fixed exchange rate. Your bank should be able to give you more information.

Investing directly in foreign shares or government stocks is a particularly risky route to take, exposing you directly to the problems of obtaining up-to-date and accurate information on the economy, taxes, legal system and political developments in your chosen area, and to the full range of administrative problems and costs.

For most people, the best way of spreading the risk is to invest in a UK-based unit trust or investment trust, and take advantage of the expertise of the investment managers in their specialist areas. In addition, there are no currency transactions, and costs and information are available from the fund management group.

Diagram 1: Annual average exchange rate of the £

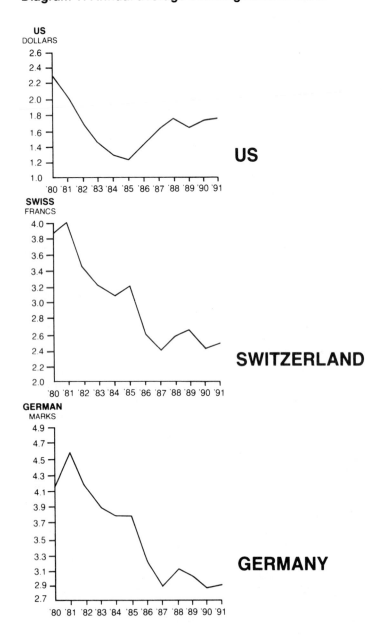

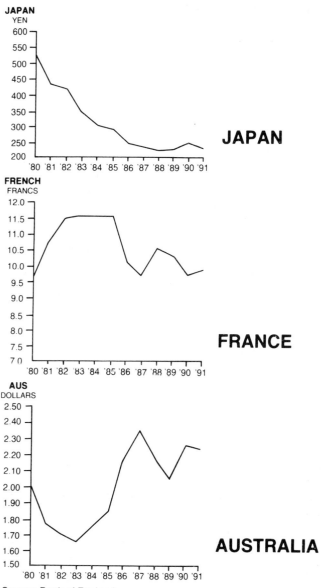

JAPAN
YEN

FRENCH
FRANCS

AUS
DOLLARS

JAPAN

FRANCE

AUSTRALIA

Source: Bank of England

Where to invest

Overseas, as in the UK, there is a wide range of possible investments (for a summary of the main types, see pp. 381 to 388) and since October 23, 1979, when UK exchange control restrictions were removed, you have been free to invest world-wide.

Exchange rate of the £

Changes in exchange rates can have a significant effect on your investment returns. Diagram 1 (see p. 374) shows how the exchange rate of the £ has changed against six other currencies during the 1980s, while Diagram 2 opposite shows how the effect of exchange rates alone could have led to a gain or loss over a similar period if you had bought £100 worth of each of the currencies in Diagram 1 at the end of 1982, and changed it back into £££ in July 1992.

In practice, currency speculation is an extremely risky form of investment requiring large resources and a strong nerve. You could make a lot of money, but you could lose even more – see *Warning* opposite. And, of course, small gains could be wiped out by the costs of buying and selling.

The changes in exchange rates shown in Diagram 1 reflect the changing economic and political situations in the UK and in the other countries shown. So, for example, at the start of the 1980s, the exchange rate of the £ was high against most currencies because of the measures being taken by the UK government against inflation, while the change in the French government from socialist to conservative in 1985 led to the franc rising against the £.

In October 1990 the £ entered the *Exchange Rate Mechanism (ERM)* of the *European Monetary System*. This aims to stabilise the values of the currencies within the system. The value of the individual currencies within the ERM can still fluctuate against other currencies, but only within certain limits. However, in September 1992, a wave of uncertainty hit the foreign exchange markets, due to factors such as doubts over the future of the Maastricht Treaty. The value of the £ fell spectacularly and the Government was forced to suspend membership of the ERM, effectively devaluing the £. As we went to press, it was unclear when Britain would rejoin the ERM.

Warning

Just because you could have made large gains over the period shown, it doesn't mean the same will apply in the future. A major problem in choosing where to invest is trying to predict what will happen to exchange rates. The £ could rise against other currencies, and your gains could be wiped out. It's important to be aware of significant economic events and trends in your chosen areas which can bring about changes in the exchange rate.

Diagram 2: Gains on foreign currency
1982 – July 1992 (ignoring buying and selling costs)

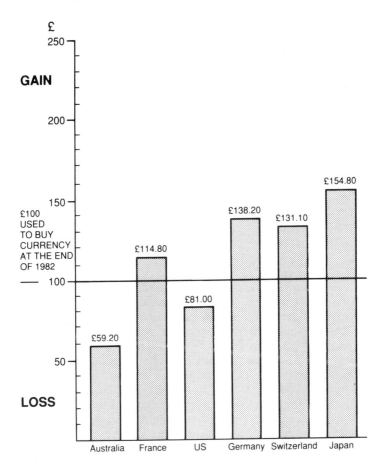

Inflation

In the long term, one of the key factors affecting exchange rates is inflation; if the rate of inflation in one country is considerably higher than in another, the first country's exchange rate is likely to fall relative to the second. You can see from Diagram 3 opposite that during the period when the exchange rate of the £ tended to be falling, the inflation rate in the UK was generally higher than in the other countries at which we looked.

The moral is, *don't* invest in a particular country just because you get a high interest rate. If the currency is going down relative to the £ (perhaps because inflation has been high) your extra interest could be wiped out by exchange rate losses.

The return in different countries

Diagram 4 on p. 380 shows how the returns on stocks issued by the governments of the different countries compared over the period of 1984 to 1992. You can see that in the UK returns were generally above average, but were outstripped consistently by Australia. The interest rate a country has to offer to attract foreign investors must reflect, to some extent, how people expect that country's exchange rate to move in future.

Diagram 5 on p. 380 shows how share prices have changed since 1984. You can see a pattern of steady rises, followed by sharp falls, then a return to rising prices. A skilled investor could have made a bomb, but timing was all important.

Cost of buying and selling foreign currency

Unless you're investing in UK-based foreign investments, e.g a unit trust, you're likely to have to exchange the £££ you want to invest for foreign currency. And when you cash your investment, you may have to turn your foreign currency back into £££ again. In both cases, you'll be charged for the transaction (the charge may be hidden in that different exchange rates will be used depending on whether you're buying or selling foreign currency). If you're changing a lot of money – several thousand £££, say – you should get a better deal than with smaller amounts. And if you're dealing through a stockbroker or other agent you may be able to benefit from the favourable exchange rates he or she can get.

Diagram 3: Inflation rates

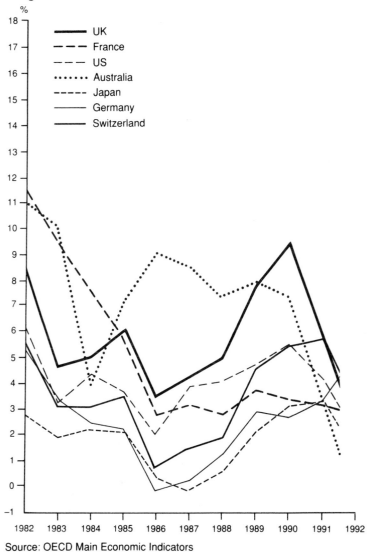

Source: OECD Main Economic Indicators

Diagram 4: Return on government stocks [1]

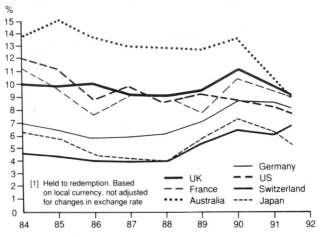

Source: OECD Main Economic Indicators

Diagram 5: How share prices have done [1]

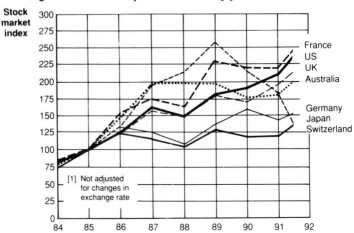

Source: OECD Main Economic Indicators

Administrative problems

If you have foreign investments, you have to make arrangements in the foreign country for the share certificate (or whatever) to be held by an agent, e.g. a bank or stockbroker, and passed on to the new owner when you sell, and for dividends, interest, and so on, to be collected and sent on to you. You could make these arrangements yourself or ask a UK agent, such as a stockbroker, to make them for you. Either way, there'll be a fee to pay and it could be high.

Ways of investing abroad

Foreign currency bank accounts

It is possible to make money simply by buying and selling currencies on the foreign exchange markets and taking advantage of differences in interest rates.

High street banks will open foreign currency accounts for UK residents. These can be either current accounts (i.e. you can draw cheques on them), or deposit accounts (where interest is paid). Some accounts may offer current account facilities and pay interest if a certain balance is maintained. You may, however, have to pay charges. You don't need to have a UK account with a bank to open a foreign account.

Interest rates vary substantially between currencies and can change from day to day. In general, the more you invest the higher the rate of interest you can get. If you have to give notice to withdraw your money, the rate of interest is normally fixed for this period. The interest rates and the minimum amount you have to invest vary from bank to bank, so shop around before opening an account.

You can now also get accounts denominated in *European Currency Units (ECUs)*. This is the (notional) currency of the European Community based on all the national currencies in the Community.

Points to watch

■ Current accounts don't normally pay interest, and you may pay charges for operating them. So it's not worth having one unless you travel a lot in a particular country, or plan to live there part of the time.
■ Some foreign banks with branches in this country will also open accounts for UK residents. These banks tend to

offer rates of interest similar to (or somewhat lower than) those given by UK high street banks. You could also open an account direct with a bank abroad, but beware of any local exchange control restrictions.

Points about tax
Interest on UK-based accounts is paid after deduction of tax. Interest will be paid without deduction of the tax generally only if the account is held *offshore* – in the Channel Islands, say.

Unit trusts

Many unit trusts invest overseas rather than in the UK. Some of these are based in the UK, some in places like the Channel Islands and Isle of Man (known as *offshore* funds). European companies can now sell unit trusts across EC borders. Many other countries have their own unit trusts. Some trusts spread their investments internationally, others specialise in particular areas, e.g. the USA, Far East or Australia. Most trusts invest in shares, but some invest in government stocks, Eurobonds or put money on deposit. A few specialise in investing in foreign currencies.

For the majority of people, unit trusts (or investment trusts – see opposite) are the most convenient and least risky ways of enjoying benefits from investing abroad. Investing through a unit trust means that you can get a stake in a spread of investments in an overseas country for a relatively low minimum investment, £500 say, and you don't have to get involved in the administrative problems associated with investing directly in overseas stocks and shares – see p. 385. For more details about unit trusts, see Chapter 15.

As there are now so many different funds investing overseas, specialist magazines such as *Money Management* and *What Investment* generally divide them into categories – standard categories include International Growth, International Income and specific regions such as North America, Europe or Japan. These journals provide tables comparing the performance of individual funds over different periods (though, of course, this is no guide to how they'll perform in the future).

Points to watch
■ Unit trusts are not a home for money you might need at short notice. They should be considered mainly as a long-term investment, though they can also be used for short-

term speculation if you're prepared to take a higher risk.
■ If you invest via UK-based unit trusts (but not offshore
funds), you get the protection of the Financial Services Act
– see Chapter 5.

Points about tax

Distributions from UK-based unit trusts are paid with only
UK tax deducted, while distributions from most offshore
funds are paid with little or no tax deducted, so there are no
problems with reclaiming tax held back by foreign governments. With foreign-based unit trusts, distributions are
normally paid with some tax withheld by the foreign
government. You'll have to arrange to get a credit for any
tax deducted – see p. 388.

Investment trusts

Investment trusts are companies which, in turn, hold the
shares of other companies – see Chapter 16 for more
details. Many UK investment trusts hold overseas shares
(perhaps specialising in particular areas of the world, such
as the USA, Far East and Australia). UK investment trust
shares can be bought and sold on the UK Stock Exchange.
Details of UK investment trusts, some of which specialise
in particular parts of the world, are published annually in a
directory available from the Association of Investment
Trust Companies – see p. 290 for address. Monthly
statistics on where the companies invest and how they've
performed are printed on the second Saturday of each
month in the *Daily Telegraph*.

   Investment trusts also exist in other countries, and a few
of the major foreign trusts are quoted on the London Stock
Exchange.

Points to watch

■ As with unit trusts, investing through a UK investment
trust spares you the administrative problems you would
face with overseas shareholdings. You'll also be protected
under the Financial Services Act.
■ Investment trusts are not a home for money you might
need at short notice. They should be considered, in the
main, as a long-term investment, though they can also be
used for short-term speculation.

Points about tax

The same points apply as do for unit trusts.

Foreign currency funds

These offer a means of investing in a range of currencies without opening individual bank accounts. You buy units in a fund (rather like buying unit trusts). The investment managers then shift the money in the fund around among a range of currencies, in the hope of taking advantage both of high interest rates and favourable exchange rate movements. So, in effect, you are staking your money on the skill and luck of the managers. Some of the funds are based in the Channel Islands (*offshore* funds), and operate like unit trusts. Others are UK-based and are linked to life insurance.

Points to watch
■ These funds give the opportunity of investing in currencies for a relatively low outlay – the minimum investment ranges from £1,000 to £10,000. But the funds all charge an annual management fee, often around 0.75 to 1 per cent.
■ Currency funds are *not* recommended as a home for money you can't afford to lose. You are taking on substantial currency risks.

Points about tax
UK-based funds pay interest after deduction of basic-rate tax, so higher-rate taxpayers may have to pay more tax. Offshore funds have the choice of taking either *accumulator* or *distributor* status. Funds with distributor status have to distribute at least 85 per cent of their income, and you are taxed on this at your top rate of income tax. When you sell units, you pay capital gains tax on any increase in their value, but you qualify for the annual tax-free slice – see p. 107. Accumulator funds accumulate income in the price of the unit, but any profits made are taxed at your top rate of income tax when you sell the units. So which type of fund is better for you will depend on your tax position.

Government stocks and company stocks

Just as the UK government raises money through issuing British Government stocks, so there is a wide range of fixed-interest stocks issued by foreign governments, and the return may be better than that available in the UK, even after allowing for currency differences. These are bought and sold on foreign stock exchanges and some are also traded on the UK Stock Exchange.

Many foreign companies issue fixed-interest securities which work in a similar way to government stocks. These normally pay higher interest, reflecting the fact that a company has more chance of going bust than most governments.

Points to watch
■ As with shares, extra costs and a certain amount of administrative hassle are involved in dealing in foreign stocks on foreign stock exchanges – see below. It may be simpler to invest through a unit trust that specialises in foreign fixed-interest stocks.
■ Remember that some governments may be offering high interest rates to offset a falling exchange rate.

Points about tax
Gains on foreign stocks are liable to capital gains tax, unlike gains on British Government stock, which are tax-free. Interest payments are generally made after deduction of some foreign tax, so you may have to arrange to get a credit for the tax deducted – see p. 389.

Shares

Direct investment in shares on foreign markets isn't a straightforward process. You'll find it difficult to get information on specific foreign companies or up-to-the minute information on prices on the foreign stock exchange. There are also practical problems in finding an agent to deal for you and get the currency with which to deal. You run the risk that, by the time you've set up the contacts and the currency for a particular deal, exchange rates or prices could have changed, and not in your favour. So, at present, direct investment abroad isn't recommended for non-professionals, although the increasingly international nature of securities trading and the effort to create a Single European Market mean that this may well change over the next few years.

A less problematic way to deal in foreign shares might be through the International Stock Exchange in London. Many major international companies are already quoted there; there are no currency deals to arrange and you face fewer administrative problems. Alternatively, stick to investing via unit trusts or, possibly, investment trusts.

Points to watch

■ To spread the risks adequately across countries and industrial sectors, substantial sums of money are required for direct investment in overseas stocks and shares – say at least £10,000 to £20,000.

■ Shares are not a home for money you might need at short notice. They should be considered, in the main, as a long-term investment, through they can also be used for short-term speculation.

■ Some countries' protection for shareholders is less extensive than is the case in the UK. It may be advisable, therefore, to stick to large, well-established stock markets, such as the US or Japan.

■ It's likely to be difficult for you (or your adviser) to have detailed knowledge about a lot of foreign companies, and the economic environment in which they function. Even those in the know may find it harder to keep up to date than those on the spot.

■ If you hold foreign investments abroad, you may have to make arrangements for the share certificate, or whatever, to be held by an agent, e.g. a bank or stockbroker, and passed on to the new owner when you sell. In the same way, dividends and interest have to be collected and sent on to you. You could make these arrangements yourself or ask a UK agent, such as a stockbroker, to make them for you. Either way, there'll be a fee to pay, and it could be high in relation to the value of the investment.

Points about tax

Dividends and stock interest are frequently paid with some tax withheld by the foreign government, so you may have to arrange to get a credit for the tax deducted – see p. 389.

Eurobonds

Eurobonds are a way in which international borrowers, e.g. governments, large companies and international institutions like the World Bank, raise money. The bonds, which pay interest, are generally issued in a particular currency, e.g. dollars or German marks, and are quoted on various stock exchanges. Eurobonds issued by companies (rather than governments, say) normally pay a slightly higher rate of interest, reflecting their slightly lower credit rating with the markets.

Points to watch
- Eurobonds come in fairly large units, e.g. $1,000. The minimum investment is around $50,000, and many dealers won't deal with members of the public. You may do better to go for a unit trust specialising in Eurobonds.
- The interest rate may be fixed, or may be changed at set intervals.
- Interest rates on Eurobonds generally reflect interest rates in the country of the currency they're issued in.

Points about tax
As with capital gains on foreign stocks, capital gains on Eurobonds are liable to capital gains tax. Interest is paid without any foreign tax being deducted, but the interest is liable for UK tax, and you must declare it on your tax return.

Property

Buying property abroad is full of pitfalls for the unwary. For example, the costs of buying and selling are usually considerably greater abroad than they are in the UK: perhaps 10 per cent on both buying and selling. If you need to borrow money to buy the property, you may find it difficult to get a loan from a UK institution. There may be severe restrictions on taking your money out of the foreign country again if you decide to sell. And there's always the chance that, at some time in the future, the political climate in the country might change and foreigners won't be welcome. You should certainly get professional advice before contemplating an investment in property abroad.

If you haven't the money to buy a property outright, you could buy a timeshare. This will give you a set number of weeks in your holiday home every year. Organisations exist for timeshare 'swaps' if you don't want to go back to the same place every year, and you can sometimes arrange to swap dates as well. But a timeshare may turn out to be a very poor investment as you may find it hard to sell and what you sell it for could be much less than you paid in the first place. There have been many reports of high-pressure selling of timeshares, so beware of being pushed into an unsuitable deal.

Points to watch
- Always visit a home before buying – don't rely on glossy brochures. Try to spend time in the area, and see the house at different times of the day, and even in different seasons.

- Check carefully on factors such as the reliability of local water, electricity supplies, sewerage, and on the structure and surroundings of the house you have in mind.
- Planning permission for new buildings is easier to get in many countries abroad than in the UK: your idyllic country retreat may become the centre of a concrete jungle.
- If you are planning to retire abroad, be particularly cautious. And check on medical facilities.

Points about tax

Gains you make on selling property abroad are liable to capital gains tax in the UK. Income you get from letting property is taxed as investment income, and you must declare it on your tax return. You can deduct any expenses incurred abroad in managing and collecting the income, e.g. paying an agent. If some foreign tax has been deducted you'll have to arrange to get a tax credit.

Unit-linked life insurance

Many life insurance companies run funds which invest abroad. These work a bit like unit trusts. For details of how single-premium and regular-premium policies work, see Chapter 20.

Tax on overseas investments

The tax treatment of investment held abroad (as opposed to UK-based foreign investments) can be extremely complicated. But even if you plan to hand over your tax affairs to advisers, a bit of background knowledge will help you to understand what they're up to.

Income tax

In general, if you're a UK resident all your income is liable to UK tax, whether or not it is brought into this country. So if, say, you have a bank deposit account in Switzerland, you have to declare the interest you get from it on your tax return, even if you kept the interest (or spent it) abroad. When converting foreign income into £££, use the exchange rate applying at the time it was due to be paid to you (not when you actually changed it into £££).

Income from overseas investments is often taxed in the

country in which it originates; so two lots of tax could be charged on one lot of income. The UK government has made agreements with a wide range of countries to limit the extent to which income may be taxed twice. Under one of these *double taxation agreements* the amount of tax which a foreign government deducts from income before it reaches you is reduced, and the tax actually deducted is allowed a tax credit against the UK tax charged on the same income.

Suppose, for example, that you're entitled to £1,000 in dividends from the USA. Tax at 30 per cent would normally be deducted in the USA before paying over the dividends to non-US residents.

However, because of our double taxation agreement with the USA, only 15 per cent is withheld, i.e. you get £850. If, say, you're liable for tax in the UK at 40 per cent on your £1,000 gross dividends, there'd be £400 tax to pay. But the £150 you've paid in tax to the USA would be allowed as a credit against the £400 of UK tax you're liable for, so you'd have a UK tax bill of £250, not £400.

If you are liable for no UK tax (or less than has been deducted under a double taxation agreement), there'll be no further UK tax to pay, but you can't claim back the extra foreign tax you've paid.

In general, double taxation agreements mean that tax on dividends is withheld at a rate of 15 per cent. With interest payments, the rate at which tax is withheld varies more between countries. For more details of how double taxation agreements work, see Inland Revenue leaflet *IR6* (available free from your tax office).

How to get your relief

If your foreign income is paid to you through an agent, e.g. a bank in the UK which passes it on to you after deducting basic-rate tax, the agent should allow for any double taxation agreement when doing the sums.

But if the income is paid direct to you from abroad, you have to apply for double taxation relief yourself – and until you do so, you may find the income arrives with substantial amounts of foreign tax withheld, and no credit against UK tax allowed for it. To get the foreign tax reduced, get an application form from the Inland Revenue, Inspector of Foreign Dividends, Lynwood Road, Thames Ditton, Surrey KT7 0DP. To get the withheld foreign tax allowed as a credit against your UK tax bill, apply to your tax inspector.

When UK tax is due

Your tax bill is normally based on the foreign income you get in the preceding tax year, i.e your tax bill for the 1992–3 tax year would be based on the foreign income you got in the 1991–2 tax year. Special rules apply in the first three and last two years in which you get foreign income of this type, in the same way as for UK income not taxed before you get it is treated – see p. 101.

Other tax deducted

In certain countries, foreign dividends are paid after deducting tax other than personal income tax. And non-residents may not be able to reclaim this tax. So before investing in a particular country, check that the return you hope to get allows for *all* the tax deducted.

Capital gains tax

Gains you make on overseas investments are liable for UK capital gains tax in the normal way – see p. 107. In general, you'll be taxed on gains whether or not you bring the sale proceeds into the UK. Your capital gain will be the difference between the value of the asset in sterling when you acquired it, and its value in sterling when you disposed of it, using the exchange rates that applied at the relevant times. Note that gains you make on foreign currency are liable for capital gains tax in the normal way (unless you get the currency for holidays or living expenses abroad).

There's normally no foreign capital gains tax to pay if you're a UK resident. However, gains on selling a foreign home may be taxed in the country where the home is situated. And if you have a permanent home in one of certain foreign countries, e.g. a country cottage in California, or spend substantial parts of the year there, you may find that you're treated as a resident of the country and are liable for local capital gains tax. Any foreign tax you pay is allowed as a credit against your UK capital gains tax liability.

Inheritance tax

UK inheritance tax is charged on foreign assets in the normal way – see p. 116. A similar tax is likely to be charged by the country in which the assets are situated. The foreign inheritance tax (or its equivalents) is normally allowed as a credit against UK inheritance tax.

Note that there are likely to be delays (perhaps lengthy ones) and complications in obtaining probate for assets held abroad in your name, on your death. It may be better to have them held in the name of a UK agent, such as a bank.

25

ALTERNATIVE
INVESTMENTS

If you are worried about the rate of inflation starting to rise again, you may want to look for less conventional investments. And it's certainly possible to show that, at certain periods during the last 20 years, an investor in certain alternative investments could have more than maintained the buying power of his or her savings. But other types have done very badly.

The diagram on p. 21 shows how gold sovereigns and antique furniture have performed over three different periods since 1972 compared with investing in shares, buying a home and so on. We've given returns over different periods of time because the success of your investment depends very much on when you buy and when you sell. You can see from the diagram that antique furniture overall has performed particularly well over 20 years, and most of the shorter periods we've illustrated too. The return from it more than kept pace with inflation, and produced higher rates of return than the conventional investments we've illustrated. But presenting the investment potential of alternative investments in this way can be misleading. If *you* had been investing in 1972, you might have chosen to buy things which didn't do nearly so well, such as the *wrong* piece of furniture.

Which alternative investment to go for?

Limited supply plus growing demand is what to look for in an alternative investment. Things like old stamps, Georgian silver and Roman coins are available in limited quantities; there is no way that more can be produced (forgeries apart). So if more people want to own them, or the existing number of collectors can afford to pay more (because of inflation, say), prices will increase.

But limited supply, on its own, is not sufficient to make a good investment. For example, limited editions (see p. 399) are produced in quantities of a few hundred or a few thousand, but they are unlikely to prove good investments unless people will want to buy them in the future.

Nor is a high level of demand enough to make a good investment. For example, many collectors will snap up new issues of British stamps (the Royal Wedding issue was widely bought when the Duke and Duchess of York got married in 1986, for example). But if several million are issued, it's unlikely they will become valuable. For the investor, only stamps in fairly short supply and popular with collectors are likely to gain significantly in value.

Should you put your money in alternative investments?

If you're thinking of alternative investments, you should consider investing only part of your savings in this way – no more than 10 per cent, say – and certainly not your emergency fund or money you can't afford to lose. And bear in mind that:

- because of the expenses of buying and selling, such as auctioneer's commission or dealer's mark-up, you may not make a profit unless you keep your money invested for a fairly long time – say, five years or more
- money invested in this way won't give you a regular income. And you may have to pay for storage, insurance and so on (see opposite)
- fashions in collecting change; what may have been a steadily appreciating asset 10 years ago, may no longer be so much in demand. You may even make a loss when you come to sell
- you may find it hard to decide on what price to ask when you sell, and, unless you sell at an auction, some haggling with buyers is likely to be involved. Going for a quick sale could mean you get a poor price.

Alternative investments have one advantage which most other types of investment lack: you can get pleasure out of finding and owning things in which you invest. Indeed, you're more likely to invest successfully if you do take an interest in them. And if your investments turn out to be unsuccessful, you at least have the consolation of owning a stamp collection, a set of prints or whatever.

On pp. 397 to 403 we look at a few of the wide range of alternative investments available. Bear in mind that these are included as examples only – we are not suggesting that these investments in particular are ones you should choose. But you should get hints on what to watch out for even if you decide to specialise in an areas we haven't mentioned.

How should you invest?

■ Do your homework before you invest. Read books and magazines on the subject, join societies for collectors of the things you are interested in, visit exhibitions, study auctioneers' catalogues and dealers' price lists, and talk to experts. See pp. 403 to 404 for a few details about societies, specialist magazines, useful addresses and so on.

■ Start small. Buy a few low-priced items in a narrow field, to get to know the things you are collecting. Develop your knowledge before spending more, and then stick to the field in which you are an expert.

■ Aim for items in a very good condition. You might have to settle for a poor quality item – to complete a set, say. But, in general, two or three items in good condition are likely to do better than several tatty ones.

■ Shop around. Prices are likely to vary considerably between dealers, so don't be afraid to haggle.

■ Be sceptical of 'guarantees' (to buy back the things you invest in at double what you paid for them after five years, say). These 'guarantees' are only as good as the dealer who gives them and are no good at all if he or she goes bust.

■ Invest in things which are collected world-wide, so that the price you get when you sell won't necessarily be reduced if UK demand slumps.

Ahead of the crowd?

You can make more money if you invest in things which other investors haven't cottoned on to which subsequently become popular with collectors. You can't expect to be right every time (or even most of the time) with this sort of speculation. If you're only in it for the money, and other speculators do catch on, you may need to be good at spotting when a craze is reaching its height so that you sell before prices start tumbling.

Storage and insurance

Careful storage may be important with things like stamps, wine or paintings. Damp, sudden changes in temperature, sunlight, insects and so on could reduce (or even wipe out) the value of the things you collect.

You'll also need to insure your valuables against events like theft or fire. Typically, this might cost around £4.50 to £7.50 a year for each £1,000 of cover as part of a normal house contents policy (more if you live in a high-risk area). Many house contents policies also offer cover against accidental damage as an optional extra. If you want all-risks cover (which includes accidental damage cover, for example), this might cost between £15 and £45 or so a year for each £1,000 of cover.

Before you decide on a policy, check the terms of the insurance carefully. There may be an unwelcome restriction, such as a low limit on the amount of cover for individual items. You might prefer to buy a special insurance policy for your collection. Consult the *Insurance Buyer's Guide* (available from Croner Publications Ltd, Croner House, London Road, Kingston-upon-Thames, Surrey KT2 6SR at £25.95, including postage and packing, or try your local library).

If your collection is worth a lot of money (more than a few thousand pounds, say), the insurance company is likely to insist on a safe, special locks and burglar alarms. The insurance company is also likely to ask for proof of your collection's value, so it's sensible to keep photographs of it, as well as a regularly updated professional valuation. A professional valuer (or a dealer) may charge perhaps one and a half per cent of the valuation figure given for your collection. Remember to review the level of your insurance regularly, whatever the value of your collection.

Alternatively, you could store your collection in a bank's strongroom; insurance may be less if you do this. The bank makes a charge for storage – from £5 to £20 a year for an envelope, say, up to £50 a year or more for a bulky item. You may also have to pay an inspection charge of around £5 each time you need to remove your collection from the strongroom. Bank storage costs are considerably higher if you want to rent a deposit box, but these can be difficult to get. Some dealers will also store and insure the things you buy from them; this may seem the simplest solution, but remember that you could have problems if the dealer you store with goes bust.

What about tax?

Because there's usually no income from investing in physical items, there's usually no income tax to pay (unless the Revenue decides you are carrying on a trade or business and taxes your profits as income).

You might be liable for capital gains tax if you make a gain when you sell or give away things in which you have invested. But the first £5,800 a year of gains are normally tax-free (in the 1992–3 tax year). So are gains on things like antiques, jewellery and other tangible moveable objects which you sell for £6,000 or less. You may even get some relief if the gain is over £6,000 and you'll only pay tax on the gain you've made since 31 March 1982. For more details on capital gains tax, see p. 107.

However, beware of tying money up in something just because of favourable tax treatment – the tax situation *could* change.

You will normally have to pay VAT on the things you invest in if you buy from dealers.

Some alternative investments

Wine

Laying down vintage wines and ports has been, in the past, a highly profitable investment. The return is free of tax unless the Revenue reckons you've gone into the wine trade and taxes the gain as your business profits. Note that private individuals without a licence are not allowed to advertise or sell any alcohol except via an auctioneer or wine merchant.

Vintage wines must be stored in carefully regulated conditions to maintain their quality and value. So unless you are in the enviable position of having your own suitable cellar, you will have to pay yearly storage and insurance costs to a wine merchant. For storage you can currently expect to pay from £4 to £6.50 per case per year, and this will normally include insurance cover at either the original purchase price or, if you're lucky, the current value.

Not all wine bought for investment can be expected to produce a high return. You have to be careful not to get in on the tail-end of a particular fashion, and must be prepared to tie up your money for at least five years and often ten or more. But a knowledge of what you're buying should help you enormously. Well-selected fine wines can best be relied upon to improve in value, though even these produced a disappointing return as recession hit the market from 1989 to 1992. But even if your investment doesn't produce a good cash return you can at least have the pleasure of drinking it.

Stamps

Apart from what they cost to use for postage, stamps are intrinsically worthless bits of paper. But they are avidly collected by very large numbers of people all over the world, some of whom are prepared at times to pay very large sums of money for stamps which are extremely rare, or of historical interest.

While there are many stamps and other items of postal history which would have given you a good return on your investment over most of the last 20 years, some stamps have increased in value much more than others. Values can fall as well as rise.

Stamps which, in the past, have shown some of the largest increases in value have included examples (in fine condition) of rare nineteenth-century issues, sometimes called *classics*. However, some investors have had their fingers burnt by innocently following the advice of a few unscrupulous dealers who have sold them 'investment' portfolios. The stamps turned out to be over-priced, not of the best quality and did not continue to appreciate at the rate that dealers claimed had applied in the past. The prices of some stamps fell dramatically between 1980 and 1983, making them difficult to resell, even back to the dealers from whom they were bought.

If you want to invest seriously in stamps, you will have to approach this as a hobby first, and get to know a lot about them, through studying catalogues and auction results, visiting dealers, joining a philatelic society and so on. Small variation in printing and watermarks, and even the sheet from which the stamp has been torn, can affect the price drastically. The condition of the stamp is also very important. Stamps with printing errors and, occasionally, forgeries can be worth much more than ordinary stamps.

Buying special issues of modern commemorative stamps is unlikely to be a good investment because they are generally issued in very large quantities. Don't take catalogue prices as fixed values of stamps, or proof of increases in value. Catalogues show the prices at which a dealer would hope to sell stamps in first-class condition. A dealer would normally pay much less to buy the stamps. The prices fetched at auctions are a more reliable guide.

Limited editions

Many things are sold as limited editions, e.g. plates, porcelain figures and prints. There are basically two ways to produce a limited edition:
■ the number to be sold is specified at the outset – 50 or 500 or 5,000, say
■ the number sold is the number ordered or bought by a certain date, e.g. 50 if only 50 are sold by that date, 50,000 if that is the number sold. With this method the total number to be sold (important in evaluating scarcity) is normally known only after you've agreed to buy.

There are variations on these themes. For example, with some limited editions, the limit mentioned in the advertisement may apply only to the UK, and more of the item may be sold in other countries.

Of course, the investment potential of limited editions depends not only on the number produced, but also on the demand for them from collectors. And with many limited editions, there's little hope of a big demand, so even if only a few dozen were issued, you'd be unlikely to make a lot of money by investing in them.

With some limited editions you may find that it's not the limited nature of the item which makes it profitable but the intrinsic value of the material from which they're made. A set of commemorative silver ingots, say, may be worth more for their silver content as scrap than as fully made up ingots, so they could make you money in times when silver prices are high.

Forestry

Clearing land and planting trees for the production of timber is one way you can watch your investment grow physically, as well as in terms of its value. But investing in forestry, or commercial woodlands, should be seen as a strictly long-term process. Timber takes, on average, about 25 years to produce any income, so it may be more likely that your children will get the benefit of the investment rather than you (from 1992–3, they will also benefit from some relief from inheritance tax on your death). The benefits of investing in timber last for a long time, however, as timber is felled and sold over a long period.

The government offers incentives to investors, in the form of grants to plant trees. Until March 1988 there were also substantial tax incentives, because the costs of planting and maintaining the trees could be used to reduce your tax bill on other income. This incentive now continues only for people who already owned or tenanted commercial woodland on 15 March 1988, and will stop altogether at the end of the 1992–3 tax year. However, the proceeds from the sale of timber are now tax-free.

Direct investment in forestry is pricey, and your minimum outlay would have to be at least £20,000. If you don't want to tie up so much for so long, you can invest a much lower figure in part-shares of a forest, available from forestry management companies.

There is increasing demand for timber, so the long-term prospects look good. However, in the past, a lot of the attraction of forestry investment came from the favourable tax treatment. Now that the tax rules have changed, make sure you can put up with the disadvantages before you invest. You have to be prepared to tie up quite a lot of money for a very long time, so someone looking for a quick return should look elsewhere. However, there may be other benefits to be had such as sporting rights which can prove quite lucrative.

Diamonds

Diamonds have always held a fascination for investors, but since the early 1980s, despite a few 'blips' in the market, they have proved to be a very poor investment. Prices for investment-quality stones reached their peak in 1980, but more recently the returns have been less than half of what you could have expected to get then.

There used to be three ways of investing in diamonds: buying them over the counter, buying from a diamond investment company, or putting money into a scheme which in turn invested on the diamond market. But with the losses made by investors in the 1980s, the second and third options have all but disappeared.

Buying diamonds over the counter
You can buy diamonds from a jeweller or a diamond merchant, or at an auction; they may be loose or mounted in jewellery. When you want to sell, you can hawk the stones around dealers, or put them in an auction. But, as *Which?* discovered the hard way, there are serious drawbacks to investing this way. In 1970, *Which?* bought some diamonds (both mounted in jewellery and loose). Since then, they've hawked them around jewellers and dealers several times, most recently in the summer of 1992. Each time, the prices they would have fetched were very

disappointing; a building society would have given a better return on the money involved.

Buying and selling loose diamonds over the counter seems to be a mug's game. Even if you get good value when you buy (and you've no way of being certain about that), the dealer's mark-up, which can be as high as several hundred per cent, is likely to make diamonds a poor investment, even over a 10-year period. And particularly if you're looking for a sale on the spot, offers from dealers are likely to be on the low side. Most can't accurately establish the value of a diamond on the spot, though having certificates from a specialist diamond-grading laboratory should help.

As for diamonds mounted in jewellery, you're unlikely to show a profit on *new* jewellery for a very long time. The investment market for *antique* jewellery is more like that for antique furniture or porcelain, say, than for loose diamonds. Putting antique diamond jewellery into an auction may be the best way to sell.

Gold

For thousands of years, gold has been looked on as a store of wealth, and many people the world over believe that gold is a good asset to hold in times of political upheaval. But if you are tempted to invest in gold, be prepared for a bumpy ride. Even daily fluctuations can be alarming, so gold isn't suitable for the faint-hearted.

For an indication of how gold has performed over longer periods, see the diagram on p. 21. Note that this shows rates of return for gold sovereigns rather than bullion. Nowadays, you can buy and sell gold in any form. Here we look at buying gold coins (not to be confused with the rare coins that collectors go for) and gold bars. Other ways of investing include buying gold shares (e.g. the shares of companies that mine gold), buying units in a unit trust that specialises in gold shares and dealing in gold futures. For how futures work, see p. 360.

The main ways of buying and selling coins and bullion are through banks, coin-dealers, jewellers and stockbrokers, or through the bullion-dealing companies that make up the London Gold Market (though bullion houses will not normally deal with transactions for small amounts). It's probably advisable to steer clear of jewellers because they tend to have high mark-ups on their prices. Note that if you invest via intermediaries such as stockbrokers, you will have to pay commission on buying and selling.

Bear in mind that the price at which a coin or bar is offered for sale will be higher than the current value of the gold in it. On top of the value of the gold content you'll have to pay a *premium* for the cost of manufacture and distribution of the coins. Premiums for particular coins fluctuate according to supply and demand, and it's possible for your investment to show a gain (or loss) without the price of gold changing. Note that bullion and foreign coins (but not post-1837 sovereigns and Britannias, the lastest British gold coins) are liable for capital gains tax – see p. 107.

Most of us couldn't possibly afford to invest in gold bars in the standard sizes in which they are traded (400 troy ounces, around 12½ kilograms), though it is possible to obtain much smaller sizes, from 1 kilogram down to a 1 gram 'wafer'. But the very small bars are not usually a sensible investment as the smaller the bar, the higher the

Buying and selling gold [1]

| | gold content | | prices | |
	troy ounces	grams	to buy [2] £	to sell back £
Coins Gold price as at 7 September 1992: £171.89				
Queen Elizabeth II				
Sovereign	0.24	7.32	41.50	40.00
Britannia 1oz	1.00	31.10	178.50	176.50
Britannia ½oz	0.50	15.55	91.00	89.00
Britannia ¼oz	0.25	7.77	47.00	45.00
Britannia ¹⁄₁₀oz	0.10	3.11	21.00	19.00
Bars				
1 kilogram	32.15	1,000	5,600	5,450
½ kilogram	16.07	500	2,800	2,700
100 grams	3.21	100	558	548
20 grams	0.64	20	114	108
5 grams	0.16	5	29	26

Source: Mocatta & Goldsmid

[1] Retail prices for single bars and coins. Selling prices do not include any assay fee
[2] Buying prices are subject to 17.5 per cent VAT

premium. Small bars are often sold to be made up into jewellery. You can do this with coins too, but if you want to sell your pendant, or whatever, you may get a very poor price.

In the table opposite we show the prices at which you could have bought and sold single sovereigns, Britannias and gold bars in 1992. Note that world trade in gold is transacted in US dollars, so the current exchange rate between the dollar and the pound will affect gold prices. When you sell, you may have to pay an assay fee, i.e. a fee for checking that your bar actually is gold and doesn't just look like it.

A few sources of information

Books
Diamonds by Eric Bruton (NAG Press, £22.95)
Miller's Antiques Price Guide 1993 (Miller's Publications Ltd, £19.99)
The Which? Wine Guide (£12.99 from Consumers' Association, Castlemead, Gascoyne Way, Hertford SG14 1LH)
The Antique Collectors' Club publish specialist books on art and antiques. Write to 5 Church Street, Woodbridge, Suffolk IP12 1DS for a list

Standard catalogues
Stamps of the World 1992 (Stanley Gibbons Publications, 3 volumes, £47.50)
Coins of England and the United Kingdom 28th Edition (Seaby Numismatic Publications, £12.95)

Societies
There are many societies, local and national. Here we give a very small selection. For societies near you, see the *Directory of British Associations* (ask at your local library) which lists national societies and federations that will be able to put you in touch with any local branch or group.
British Association of Numismatic Societies, Department of Coins and Medals, Manchester Museum, The University, Oxford Road, Manchester M13 9PL
The Antique Collectors' Club (for address see the entry under *Books*)
The British Philatelic Federation, 107 Charterhouse Street, London EC1M 6PT

WHICH? WAY TO SAVE AND INVEST

Magazines and journals
There are too many to name. Look in large newsagents, e.g.
John Menzies or W.H. Smith, for magazines about your
speciality, or see *Willings Press Guide* or *Benn's Media
Directory* at your local library.

Antique and Collectors' fairs
These are listed under 'Collecting' in the 'Leisure' sction of
Exchange & Mart (available at newsagents) and are often
advertised in local newspapers.

Auctions
Here we list the largest auction houses in London. For local
auction houses, see *Yellow Pages* under 'auctioneers',
specialist magazines and local newspapers.
Bonhams, Montpelier Galleries, Montpelier Street, London
SW7 1HH
Christie's, 8 King Street, St James' London, SW1Y 6QT
Phillips, 101 New Bond Street, London W1Y 0AS
Sotheby's, 34–35 New Bond Street, London W1A 2AA

Buying and selling gold
London Gold Market members who are prepared to deal
with the public:
Mocatta & Goldsmid Ltd (071-628 2825)
NM Rothschild & Sons Ltd (071-280 5000)
Also, try the high street banks for gold coins.

INDEX